Lesbian Polyfidelity

by Celeste West

By Celeste West

Revolting Librarians with Elizabeth Katz

The Passionate Perils of Publishing
with Valerie Wheat

*Words In Our Pockets: The Feminist Writers
Guild Handbook on How To Gain Power,
Get Published & Get Paid*

ELSA: I Come With My Songs with Elsa Gidlow

*A Lesbian Love Advisor: The Sweet & Savory Arts
of Lesbian Courtship*

Lesbian Polyfidelity

A Pleasure Guide for All Women Whose Hearts
Are Open to Multiple Sensualoves, or,
How To Keep Nonmonogamy
Safe, Sane, Honest & Laughing,
You Rogue!

by Celeste West

Booklegger Publishing   San Francisco   Montreal

Lesbian Polyfidelity © Celeste West 1996

Booklegger Publishing, Box 460654-B, San Francisco, CA 94146.
For sales inquires and bulk discounts, phone Booklegger (415) 642-7569.
Distributed to the trade by quality wholesalers including Bookpeople,
Alamo Square, Publishers Group West, Koen, Ingram,
Baker & Taylor, New Leaf, Airlift, Stilone, etc.

Cataloging In Publication: West, Celeste. *Lesbian Polyfidelity: A Pleasure Guide
for All Women Whose Hearts Are Open to Multiple Sensualoves, or, How to
Keep Nonmonogamy Safe, Sane, Laughing & Honest, You Rogue!*
Booklegger, San Francisco. 1996. Includes bibliography, index.
ISBN 0-912932-16-3 ($25) ISBN 0-912932-15-5 ($15)
1. Lesbians-Social Life & Customs
2. Lesbians-Sexual Behavior
3. Jealousy 4. Sexual Ethics
5. Sexuality Surveys
6. Polyfidelity-Women
7. Polyamory-Women
I. West, Celeste II. Title
LC Card 95-80606
306.7663-dc20
HQ75.5W47

A BOOKLEGGER PRODUCTION
Cover & illustrations by Nicole Ferentz
Design and typesetting by Olivia Destandau and SoftShoe Graphics
Conceptual editing by Irene Zahava
Copy editing by Dorothy Perkins and Erin Blackwell
Index by Top Girl

Printed in The United States of America.
Soy inks used which contain graphic olfactory messages.
Printed on acid- and chlorine-free paper which meets the Z39.48 standard,
resulting in the unmistakable feel of unvarnished truths.
✪ Save Forests—Legalize Hemp Paper!
↗ 9 8 7 6 5 4 3

Appreciation

A literary affair, like any other, is always more than one's own. This book belongs to the readers who have supported and challenged me over the years, especially with ongoing queries to *Lesbian Love Advisor*. *Lesbian Polyfidelity* is also a creation of its generous survey-takers and interviewees. The process was so much fun, I wave even to my earnest and worthy detractors, of whom I have grown increasingly fond. May I steal a kiss? Then, for their most penetrating insight, as well as countless acts of gallantry, I reserve life-long hugs for:

Deborah Anapol

Erin Blackwell

Joani Blank

Merijane Block

Melissa Hass
  Clairvaux

Jocelyn Cohen

Linda Ruth Cutts

Ginny Davies

Olivia Destandau

Nicole Ferentz

Judy Hadley

Silver Hall

Bert Herrman

Kathy Karr

Alice Molloy

Madeline Moore

Julia Penelope

Dorothy Perkins

Carol Rowan

The City of
  San Francisco

Venus Sardonica
  & the Mischievous
  XX Chromosome

Jeannine Toussaint-
  Caron

Irene Zahava

Julie Zolot

As always, I salute my muses in tails: Freyja, Minou, Tara, and Zenji, bemused the human species will never stop catting around.

This is dedicated to the ones I love,

with a benedictory

to the Faerie Queene,

one of whose forms in this millennium is surely

Jeannine Louise

Contents

Foreword: The Actualization of Desire   1

Lesbian Polyfidelity Survey:
Our Twenty Percent Queer Quintile   13

Triangles, Circles & Quads:
Polyfidelity's Designs & Definitions   21

Interviews: The Glorious Benefits of Polyfidelity   35

Evolutionary History Tells Us…Polyfidelity Was in Flower   57

Polyfidelity: Way of the Truth Teller   73

"I'll Cheat You Fair": A Closet Drama   95

Polyfidelity 101: Questions & Answers   108

Jealousy: Polyfidelity's Shadow—or Its Compost?   110

Jealousy as an Evolutionary Mechanism—Not!   118

Jealousy in the Jeweled Net of Indra   125

Villain in Your Own Jealousy Melodrama   132

Jealousy in the ACT-UP World of Behaviorism   135

So What's the Target of a Jealous Rampage to Do?   149

The Odd Woman: Pragmatic Romantic   161

Bridges and Boundaries: The River of Clarity   181

Hearts of Space: Territorial Boundaries   191

Mother Time: Polyfidelity in the Fourth Dimension   196

Leisure Rhymes with Pleasure   202

Schedules: To Love, Honor and Negotiate   210

Clitzzpah   219

Lust-Driven Lesberados?   224

Love Addiction?   233

Desire Discrepancy—Why Not?   244

Polyfidelity and Sexually Transmitted Diseases   248

Stud Muffins: Diet Desiderata   257

The Wealthy Philanderopist   261

The Kids & Polyfidelity   266

A Shrink to Fit: The Polyfidèle Meets the Psychotherapist   275

The Guilt and Shame Racket   282

polyfidelity:cyberspace   291

Community: A Harem of Friends   299

Chapter Notes   314

Lesbian Polyfidelity Survey, 1995   319

Bibliography   324

Index   330

Foreword:
The Actualization of Desire

I never felt doomed to sexual fidelity. I am not the adult child of an adulterer—as far as I know. My father is long dead, so I discussed the matter of my multiple relationships with my mother. Mother said cheerfully, "Polygamy is in your blood—and in your name..."

She was referring to my father's historic Mormon roots, although his immediate family had unceremoniously left the fold. If I can't get rid of a family skeleton, can I make it dance? The polygamous social order radiantly revealed to Mormon founder Joseph Smith in 1835 was termed by his inner light "celestial marriage." We know the earthbound realm of state and federal governments are horrified by celestial marriage. They criminalized polygamy with bitter, brutal violence, despite the First Amendment's freedom of religion guarantee and our constitutional right to privacy. The government neatly added its polygamy prohibition to a law written to abolish women's suffrage in Utah. Unlike women in other states, Utah's "harem women" had the privilege, well before the Nineteenth Amendment, to vote like a man.

Approximately forty thousand renegade, libertarian Mormons still pursue polygamy in Utah. One of these, Elizabeth Joseph, notes, "Polygamy is a feminist lifestyle. I can go off 400 miles to law school and the family keeps running... Government has claimed a compelling interest in confining the family to one structure. So far, this has not been demonstrated to our satisfaction."

At San Francisco's Gay Freedom Day Parade, the folks at the perennial Gay Mormon Booth, along with the half-a-million other free spirits in attendance, say the same thing. Let us celebrate diversity in love and relationship, celebrate intimacy and loyal community, however we create it. Lesbian feminism's most famous Mormon heretic, Sonia

Johnson, seemed to have escaped with polygamy intact. (Technically, this is "polygyny" for us Lesberados.) With typical fervor and wit, Johnson devotes her book, *The Ship That Sailed Into the Living Room: Sex & Intimacy Reconsidered*, to "the emotional and spiritual suicide" of Lesbian monogamy ("monogyny.")

We feminist polyfidèles naturally find the old forms of patriarchal polygamy repellent. One thing the Mormons did, however, like the more brilliantly utopian Oneida Community of New York, was acknowledge what virtually all naturalists and cultural anthropologists report today: life on this particular planet is overwhelmingly polygamous. This includes the past five million years of human life, including 99% of our current *Homo sapiens* era. So, a polyfidèle like me is really a traditionalist! The ancient blueprint I follow, however, is millions of years older than the family pseudo-values of this decade. In the hundreds of societies chronicled by anthropologists, the vast majority are openly polygamous. Very few cultures have ever valorized monogamy.

According to studies such as Van Der Bergh's *Human Family Systems: An Evolutionary View*, only 16% of human societies call themselves monogamous, in the manner of Western industrial nations. More than 80% allow or favor polygamy. The vast *Human Relations Area File*, an ethnographic data base recording information on more than 800 societies from Babylonia to the present, records a mere 5% of cultures disallowing polygamy. Monogamy is rare to the point of aberration. *HRAF* data led sex historian Moton Hunt to remark, "Faithful monogamy does not seem to be a natural pattern among human beings but a socially fabricated one. Some behavioral scientists therefore view fidelity as difficult, unnatural, and greatly overpriced, and insistence on it as producing hypocrisy, guilt, unhappiness, and broken marriages."

Anthropologists, such as Meredith Small in *What's Love Got To Do With It: The Evolution of Human Mating*, point out again and again that monogamy is a function of paternal insecurity, as well as the male desire for sexual servitude and indentured household laborers.

It was culturally constructed, then socially sanctified. Monogamy is no more the attribute of a female than a cage is of a cockatoo. Small declares, "When women have the opportunity and freedom, women are just as interested in several partners and frequent sex as men. . . In evolutionary history, women have been selected not for monogamy but to be promiscuous." Small notes that the sentence "Women want men who have power and resources" works just as well if you delete the words "men who have."

Not one society on Earth fully practices monogamy, despite torture and death penalties for adultery in several countries. U.S. marriages are now 50-70% adulterous, with the figures growing, according to typical studies like *Patterns of Infidelity* listed in the "Adultery" section of the bibliography. Monogamy is perhaps the inspiration for the phrase "honored in the breach"?

What I now call "polyfidelity" is really the cultivated version of women's free sensual nature. In this book, I'll be defining polyfidelity as the ongoing relationships of a Lesbian or bisexual woman who is romantically and/or sensually involved with more than one person concurrently, while being honest about it with all her lovers. These are the one in five Lesbians presently in or wishing to be back in honest multiple sensual partnerships. This "queer quintile" is a figure from my 1995 survey of 500 women, as well as one which emerged from another 1995 Lesbian sex survey of 8,000 women financed by *The Advocate* magazine. More on definitions, forms and surveys in subsequent chapters.

My own childhood history was one of polymorphous perversity in lush western Oregon. I was raised in a pentangle "all girl band," myself the youngest, with two amazing sisters, mother and fairy grandmother. I wonder if I was thereby freed to set sail in latitudes of love beyond the usual power perversions of a typical 1950s "nuclear" family? Each child is born a devotee of the senses, and my grandmother used to cry, "Dally forth," clapping her hands as we smelled sweet, warm lavender and touched like cats licking each other in the sunshine. I always felt a fierce personal loyalty to

3

later intimates as well, which has never wavered despite physical meanderings. Of course, all happiness is provisional. Our tiny ladies' marching band could not totally evade the prevalent social system all around us. We too played out many of its themes: suicide, shock treatment, illegal abortion, poverty, rape. The whole catastrophe. If it weren't for suffering on Earth, where would suffering go? Well, suffering is not enough. I learned one way to joy is living/loving with a pride of women. The Tantrikas say, "From pleasure proceeds the cosmos, it is sustained in joy and dissolves in ecstasy." Even in the Dark, everything is touching. . .

We catcher-in-the-rye teenagers of the fifties, among others, saw the social order's meanness of spirit. Witch hunts abounded. "Are you now or have you ever been yourself?" A militaristic and fiercely competitive economic system pushed an ideology of legalized, compulsory greed: personal, corporate and national. *Corpus capitalismo* lives and breathes one word: possessiveness. Rich, white, heterosexual men, their wannabes, and their media lied to us about everything. They said war addiction and toxicity provided peace and security. Their military broke in and has been stealing the silver ever since. The owning class swept the life experience of any race, class, gender, or age not in its image or interest out of normative reality. Rigid, traditional sex roles were glorified in the fifties' cult of pairs. Men pretended that lifetime monogamy was the norm. In real life, however, even Ozzie had a very visible mistress for years. We hope Harriet did too, in contrast to a tv portrayal where she had not one friend. The existential fact is that the majority of men philandered, fantasized adultery or lived in serial monogamy. "Serial monogamy" is an oxymoron. The sociologically correct term for hit-and-run marriages is "sequential" or "progressive polygamy." Sonia Johnson notes the "serial betrayal" of serial monogamy, suggesting "serial agony" is a more apt description.

The fifties were so uptight, all we could do was start the rollicking sixties, a seed-bed of altered, alternative, and cleansed realities. While it is clear that the unexamined life is not worth living, the sixties seemed to say the unlived life is not worth examining.

To the music of civil rights and civil disobedience, we awakened from a cultural thrall. Psychedelics opened new spiritual and political doors of perception. We looked at the banality of evil and longed for deliverance. It dawned upon a whole generation that the reigning plutocracy was by no means a meritocracy, despite the smugness of the "haves."

I became an anarchist free lover like my hero Victoria Woodhull and like Emma Goldman, who declared, "If I can't dance, I don't want to be part of your revolution." I saw George Bernard Shaw plays dramatize his thesis that, "The confusion of marriage with morality has done more to destroy the conscience of the human race than any other single error." I would not attend friends' weddings, embarrassed at their purchase of a license from the state to live together as sexual beings. I usually sent two dog licenses with my regrets. I began to realize, however, that marriage was, in fact, a business license. In the sixties, many women still labored as full-time homemakers so the husband could work outside, be propped up, and keep going back into the ring fully serviced. Corporate capitalism got two for the price of one in this sanitized knot of sexism. Middle class women's legendary household hyperactivity was nothing short of manic. As Gore Vidal observed, "Marriage is the central institution whereby the owners of the world control those who do the work." I also realized quickly that "free love" could be quite expensive for women, but with my tipped uterus and devoted diaphragm, I managed to keep my unique genetic imprint from replication and all its burdens. It seems that this lady's biological clock, like those of other *rarae aves,* was never set. Sex for me is creative, not procreative.

With my sexual experience and practicality, I wondered if I should go pro. I pondered the difference between legalistic rules and authentic honor. I became fascinated with, if not necessarily an adherent of, morality. With enough character, I decided, one did not need a "good" reputation. Once you lose a good reputation, you realize what a burden it is. It seemed to me neither reputable nor honorable that men did not care what a clitoris was, never mind how to find it. Fellatio was something girls got paid to do. (I didn't know then that gay men did it for free.) Sex was a two-minute seizure for guys, with two positions: "in" or "out." Afterwards, there was not much glow. Even for us easy women there could be an array of unreasonable expectations, recrimina-tions, violent jealousy, and emotional heartburn. My active sexuali-ty, however, gave me a feeling of power and self-worth. It made me ungovernable.

As destiny would have it, instead of dickering, I earned a scholar-ship to go East to graduate school in Library and Information Science. This was in the nick of time. I was now in bed with a 32-Beretta to protect me from crazed male jealousy. I spent after-noons sharp-shooting the red logo of a Safeway sack taped to a post. I was reading *Lord of the Rings*, "You must go quickly and you must go soon." I went. Life is a series of narrow escapes.

After grad school, I thought I was moving to San Francisco to be a librarian purveying the treasures of social change literature and to sample the fabled sex, dope and rock n' roll. Once here I quickly learned San Francisco's favorite sex toy is gender. Desire was every-where, like pollen. With variety as the mother of enjoyment, we had more than a two-gender, one-lover universe. We declared "National Coming Onto Day," before it was relegated to the cur-rent "National Coming Out Day." I fell in love with the girls, but I ran around like the boys. I became a femme faggot. This is where our story begins.

I didn't know back in 1969 exactly what to do when my Lesbian energy started moving. To marry one and leave the rest seemed to be our goal, but a terrible shame. Dam up the energy? Ride it like a surfer? "Women's Liberation" dances of the early seventies were bare breasted, and we didn't do the twelve step. The Goddess de-lighted in pleasure and we were divinely subsidized, each moon a new aphrodisiac. Lust was no vulture. To new Lesbians, she was a bird of paradise. We fed on flowers with wide open-mouths. I never again concerned myself with pregnancy, date rape, fast-food sex, nor being the sole emotions keeper. I finally got it: we can require more from a relationship than a man.

I did find women I wanted to marry, to harvest my heart with every day. Pair bonding! One problem with the pair bonding was that somehow monogamy was laced into it, like fluoride into water. Monogamy, though a cold belief, was supposed to be good for you. Heterosexuals, for whose acceptance we so longed, said it was. At first, I got monogamy resignation, like being in a dentist's chair. I was not in pain, nor out of it, but a little numbed in the traces. Usually I was content, in a lovely room with a soft robe and fleece-lined slippers. But what about when my body wanted to be outside—naked? Fluoride or no, I seemed to get truth decay. I cheated, then lied to my ladies. Herewith, I want to apologize to any of you to whom I lied in mock monogamy—except half of you are the ones I lied to see and later married.

We had an awfully good time playing house, until the next dalliance—mine or yours. Then, such moral indignation! Most of it was possessive jealousy and a denial of the wildness of Lesbian sexuality, itself totally new to most of us. So it was boom and bust for us in the seventies and eighties, with the famous rhythm of Lesbian serial polygamy: cling, clang, clung. Despite our sheen of monogamy, Lesbians became the most divorced group in society, outdistancing hets and gay men, according to both the eighties book, *American Couples*, and the *1995 Advocate Lesbian Sex Survey*. Is this why comedian Robin Tyler says she always thought monogamy was some kind of dark furniture that you polish? A wise old lover did tell me monogamy is really a board game: the Lesbian with the most hotels wins. I also like comedian Marga Gomez's story of joining a support group with her lover for Lesbians in monogamous relationships. "It was great for awhile, until she met somebody there."

In response to my comedy of manners, *A Lesbian Love Advisor: The Sweet and Savory Arts of Lesbian Courtship*, the greatest comments and wildest letters I receive are in regard to the sections

about Lesbian nonmonogamy and the chapter on break-ups.
Since the former so often leads to the latter, here is another *liber
amoris* loaded with hindsight, and perhaps insight, to see if we
can break the connection between roving and break-up. If I had
my life to live over, I'd make the same poly mistakes, only sooner. Some tasted so good; some were devastating. So I offer you
a highly complex passion play, the triangles within the Great
Round, in hopes our Lesbian postmodern polyrhythms will minimize social wounds. As poet Elsa Gidlow passionately asked,
"Why can't pleasure be kind?" She noted that only cats seem to
know how to secure commitment without confinement and love
without penalties.

Let me say that by the age of fifty, I am exhausted by the ancient
debate within Thealogica Lesbiana on nonmonogamy vs. monogamy. Do whatever you do and do it well. Wherever your place of
discovery is, go there. What counts is quality and honesty. A relationship is ideal to the degree lovers feel that they are trying to
live their highest ideals. I tip my hat to the few giant sequoias of
Lesbian monogamy, even if some of you wander in your cups and
in your dreams.

I actually committed monogamy myself for a three-year inter-
lude with a clever and beautiful woman. She said, "You call yourself a pluralist, but you've never tried monogamy. How can a
pluralist be so closed to a life experience?" Checkmate. I didn't
cheat. I obeyed the self-patrol of monogamy, a good thing
because there were so many other hair-raising issues to process.
I remember trying container gardening during these years too. I
committed sexual fidelity ten to thirty times a day, but survived
this excess. We broke up when I decided to experience celibacy,
"astro-sex," as we then called it in the spiritual supermarket. One
of the best things about celibacy is that you can do it with everyone at the same time, and I was by then due for variety. I cannot
valorize celibacy enough, perhaps another book, another life. As
silence is the basis for music, celibacy is a modality of sex. My

carefully honed cycle is now polyfidelity/celibacy and back again, perfect for this bipolar pansexual.

By the eighties, the Pagan Triple Goddess of Creation, Nourishment, and Clearing Away was directing me toward Mahayana Buddhism, away from all religions which nail sexuality to the cross. Non-puritan Mahayana Buddhism, such as Japanese Zen and the Buddhism of Tibet, finds harshly dualistic moral concepts, such as right/wrong, good/evil, us/them to be unproductive and fickle. In contrast, Buddhism is vitally concerned with each person building an ethical system by studying their own personal components of suffering and joy, while exploring skillful choices for joy. The Buddha Dharma eloquently, elegantly reveals how all suffering is born of possessive clinging.

Flowing through the Dharma is the "wisdom of uncertainty." This is the core acknowledgement of the utter fluidity of all phenomenal reality as well as culturally conditioned existence. See the nature of impermanence, the rising and falling of life's pursuits, and it becomes easier to live gracefully. One can expect, even accept, there is no final love resolution. There is no "bed and wed" ending, happy or otherwise. "No ending, no beginning." One may be comfortable in relationships like the triangle whose very structure embodies ambiguity. Ambiguity arouses us. Taking care of oneself and lovers in the present moment is deep awareness. The pure sense of the moment is vast. A Zen priest wrote, "In spring winds, peach blossoms begin to come apart. Doubts do not grow on branches and leaves."

There is Gertrude Stein's "I like it very well to change. When I change suddenly it is very nice. Because if I change very suddenly I do not have to change twice. Once suddenly is better than twice twice." It may be that two things never do seem to change, but co-exist for good reason: one, the will to change, and its twin, the fear of change.

Buddhism enumerates kind and skillful ways to avoid possessiveness in "Ten Cardinal Precepts." Precept Three concerns exploiting

no one sensually. Suffering is obviously created by any sexual relation imposed by terrorism or with the bondages of economic fear
and social censure. Suffering is also created in the deeply alienating notion that we exist as atomistic, separate selves to be hoarded. How do we understand the needy-greedy participation in
social scripts which have us corral a body's sensual desires as
unchanging? Suffering is created by treating any precious human
body, including our own, as a mere object to be owned and controlled. Precept Eight states, "A lover of the way is not possessive
of anything, but practices generosity and joy of sharing." For me,
living Precepts Three and Eight is to refrain from considering the
miracle of any other woman's sexual realms to be my private property. Indeed, for me, folly and suffering have ever been the result
of such delusion.

I hope not to be possessive even of the polyfidelitous concept—
just share it. Far be it from me to build a box around monogamy
and call it misguided, or label it a form of "fear addiction," as
some do. Certainly monogamy cannot be considered dysfunctional if it is unrelated to the elements of fear, control, isolation,
denial, or possessive jealousy. When monogamous behavior holds
singular self-fulfillment for its practitioner, it has no relation to
fear; its practice does not revolve around sexual self-denial, nor
the coercion and control of another, nor "forsaking all others."
The litmus test for positive monogamy vs. fear-driven, exploita-
tive monogamy is *self*-direction. Is monogamy rewarding to you
personally, in and of itself? Or does your monogamous identity
actually depend on your lover's monogamy: must you own her
body for monogamy to work for you? Rather than the practice
of monogamy itself, I am appalled by the *compulsion* toward
monogamy, its cultivated hypocrisy and its violently punitive
as well as subtle enforcements. I feel similarly that "voluntary"
monotheism is fine for those who freely choose it. Likewise,
I can find solace in tolerating consensual heterosexual acts
because they give me more Lesbians.

Anyone with a personally fulfilling lifestyle simply lives it with zest and self-focus. By example, one demonstrates such a life to anyone who wishes to emulate it. When one has a really good thing, she need force-feed it to no one. In polyfidelity, there is no attempt to compel another to poly, as is endemic with monogamous behavior. I have never sworn a lover to polyfidelity nor needed her to mirror my choice. My love's own body belongs to her. Whatever form, monogamy or polyfidelity, each requires an artfulness. Sex advice for the last hundred years has told us the world saving wonders of monogamy while suggesting how to jack up extremely prevalent monogamy dysphoria. Is monogamy false moral theory in the face of humanity's vast penchant for pluralistic sexual behavior through-out all ages? It is time for a feminist book on the suppleness of poly-fidelity, on expanding women's moral imagination. Why should we be bound by the limiting customs of a hetero-patriarchy we've out-grown? Why buy old style marriage off the rack, when the finan-cially independent woman can now customize her relationships?

Yes, het-patterned monogamy works fine for many Lesbians—until they get tired of it. It doesn't ultimately matter whether or not you champion monogamy. You will do whatever you want to anyway. If you don't, your lover may. Clits up and I wish you well. Besides, many notable figures have already deconstructed monog-amy: Isak Dinesen, Bertrand Russell, George Bernard Shaw, Natalie Barney, Friedrich Engels, H.G. Wells, John Humphrey Noyes, Emma Goldman, Edward Carpenter, Victoria Woodhull, Charles Fourier, D.H. Lawrence, and the Bloomsbury Group. Today, anthropologists are certainly proving that "mate guarding" is male, not female evolutionary sexual strategy.

I prefer to reconstruct passion, to compost adventure, and to plant the flower of polyfidelity for you. Forget the fig leaves. Come with me. Become the not-so-naive Utopian. As in other cultures, what if extra lovers were considered harmless fun, not framed as threat-ening? What if your lover having many lovers added to your pres-tige? Cultivating the presence of new worlds alongside this one means an enlargement of life. Look at today's gender revolution.

The world is changed by people living their visions here and now. Why not create the world you dream of with each choice you make? Why not raise your eyes to a vision, a love heroic whose time has come again to bring beauty into the world? As Gertrude Stein said, "If a thing can be done, why do it." Its very hardship is its possibility. Only we who risk going splendidly too far can possibly find out how far we can go. Polyfidelity is like Jacob's shimmering angel. She bestows her blessing only if you wrestle with her intimately. So, slide between these covers and roll around these ink-stained sheets, thigh-high in new research.

To you, three bows plus three blessings:

✸ Keep on loving boldly.

✸ Suffer not to mock yourself with conformism nor falsehood.

✸ May you be frequently married and seldom divorced.

With L & K,

Celeste West, San Francisco, Spring, 1996

P. S. Please check your pigeonholes at the door.

Lesbian Polyfidelity Survey: Our 20% "Queer Quintile"

$\mathcal{D}$ue to the shadow of society's self-appointed Pleasure Police, as well as biased protocols, sex surveys are often poopadoodle. Surveys and studies on adultery, the widespread, dishonest cousin of polyfidelity, abound. They focus mainly on a clinical entity, the disturbed and betrayed people who seek "treatment." This creates a distorting perspective on cheerful open arrangements, largely ignored in any systematic, objective research. If het sex life is a pseudo-poll, Lesbian sex is incognito. Virtually no one will fund Lesbian-anything but ourselves, and we don't seem to have the time, the cash, or the impetus for creating a Lesbian sex data base. Too busy being Lesbians? Too satisfied?

There are certainly no grants for a Lesbian Polyfidelity Survey. There is funding for elaborate research and lavish photos of the madcap adulteries of red-winged blackbirds and lovely creatures delightfully dubbed "fairy wrens." Meanwhile, the 1990 U.S. Census survey showed only twenty-eight human female "couples" living in the entire state of Wyoming—and two male couples. Gays, however, can't all have been overrun by fairy wrens. *The Janus Report of Sexual Behavior*, the most respected national compendium of sex statistics since the *Kinsey Report,* found 17% of all American women "admitted" at least one Lesbian experience. Just don't tie 'em down in Wyoming. Or in San Francisco for that matter. The same census found, of San Francisco same-sex couples under one roof, it was the boys doing the nesting: 64% male to 36% female. Are Lesbians the roaming fairy wrens?

Who can know? Are the women in a pathologized, criminalized minority who answer Lesbian surveys "representative"—or just brave? Until they call off the cops, any purported numbers count is a lie regarding a persecuted people, who stand to lose jobs, housing, kids, and status for revealing their sexual identities and practices.

Minorities know how numbers are used to beat us up, but there is little we can do without protection and our own survey funding.

Why do Lesbians tend to believe sex surveys by mainstream "experts"? Because we are all curious about others, and because we still worry about whether we are "normal." Will we be judged and found guilty by "all" the others who act differently? We also hope to find people like us, to discover that we are not alone. If "normal" is mis-defined as it often is: "statistically frequent," then promiscuity is "normal." Most of us will have concurrent sexual partners, and all of us will contemplate doing so. In my Lesbian Polyfidelity Survey, I interviewed women who mainly felt good about sex and their bodies, but more than a few, after detailing some rather colorful fantasy or practice, would ask, "Do you think that's *normal?*" My all-purpose answer: no one is normal. Even "The" Lesbian is an illusion. Each person is marvelously unique and therefore each abnormal. All human beings are queer. I remind normality-questers of Lesbian iconoclast Natalie Barney's observation, "Being other than normal is a perilous advantage."[1] I also remind them that to follow the myth of normality is not to discover yourself.

With the present anthropological revelations on multiculturalism, we can take comfort that everything we do or even imagine doing, despite how bizarre our own culture would judge it, is probably "normal" in some other society. In the eternally baffling, intense world of human sexuality, who is not just a little bit in hiding? Normality-anxiety is a profound form of social control. It gives one group the power to validate or invalidate, to reward or punish. But why should we hide any adult sexuality which is consensual, non-exploitative, and physically safe, as well as pleasurable and inducive of self-esteem? Why not tell the sex police to just get over it. Suggest they begin by working on their own abnormalities, like *anhedonia,* the deep fear of pleasure.

All surveys have a bias distortion. Fine, if their bias is upfront; ugly if hidden. The most smug and notorious example of hidden bias is the stupefying, arrogantly crowned *Sex in America: A Definitive Study*. University of Chicago's *Sex in America (SA)* does have the widespread distinction of being the most boring read in America. There are no anecdotes, flesh and blood case studies, no feelings, just numbers. How do you get big grants to make sex *boring*—and why? Antisex backlash is why. Moral "majorities" and guilt-ridden, jealous godniks need surveys to show they are not missing a life. You can always hire an academic to "prove" anything. Ask the tobacco lobby or the Pentagon antigay forces who pay for educated Ph.D. cant. How did the University of Chicago sex researchers skew the figures? First eliminate from a human sexuality study all human beings under eighteen and over sixty. In *SA,* teens and sea-soned lovers are neither American nor sexual! Then aggressively recruit other respondents; we are told how much badgering was done to get interviews. Why the badgering? Because the veils of anonymity were ripped asunder. Interviews were ninety-minute drills done face-to-face in the home. Oh, and be sure to violate all confidentiality, allowing partners to be present. *Voilà!* Nobody's doing "it," certainly not "abnormally."

With no anonymity or confidentiality, the scarlet "A" slips down to 10-25% in *Sex in America*. Never mind that all currently respected studies now peg adultery at 50-70% and rising, especially among women. *SA* says that American queers have faded away since the fifties, when we were 10% of the population, to only 1.5% Lesbian and bisexual women; 2.8% gay and bisexual men. A Christian supremacist's dream. By the way, it seems American women don't dream much anyway; only 19% of us think about sex every day. So 81% of us live in Carmelite cells sans media penetration? At least in *SA*'s bland world, men do not "force" women to have sex. The word "rape" is deliberately avoided. Certainly no one with name and address on file volunteered for the act. *SA* reports a full third of Americans never have sex at all, or maybe a couple of times a year for an average of fifteen minutes a pop. In short, most Americans are sex nerds. In short, the University of Chicago sex-ologists don't go to the same parties I do. "Those women," the survey's 3% hot mamas who have had sex with at least twenty-one partners, show up at every Lesbian potluck I attend. Since the median number of sexual partners for the *Sex in America* women is two per life, the latter must be watching tv at home alone—or responding to long surveys.

Luckily there are other entertaining sex surveys to be found. Exciting quotes:

- Lesbian and bisexual women are twice as orgasmic as het women. Moreover, only 5% of us report ever having a sexually transmitted disease. (*National Lesbian & Bi Women's Health Survey, 1994,* conducted by the Lesbian Health Clinic of Los Angeles.)

- Sex puts less strain on the heart than making the bed you did it in! Of the very few deaths associated with sexual activity, 78% involved adultery, people lying about a rendezvous. Researchers believe the guilt and anxiety increased risk of heart-attack. (Harvard Medical School's *Harvard Heart Letter,* 3/93.)

- Elaborate sexology lab tests on "women who love sex" reveal 64% of this sample easily orgasm by imagination alone, with-out physical touch. The "big bang theory" of orgasm is also debunked as penile, along with the ubiquitous male and hetero-sexual protocols of sex therapy and research. (*Women Who Love Sex* by Gina Ogden, Pocket Books, 1994.)

- Americans over the age of sixty-five have sex more often than eighteen to twenty-six year olds. (*Janus Report,* Wiley, 1994).

- Europeans note American lack of sexual sophistication, but a survey found we are downright ignorant. Fifty-five percent of adult respondents resoundingly failed the most elementary sex quiz. (*The Erotic Silence of the American Wife* by Dalma Heyn, Signet, 1993.)

- Fifty percent of het women queried said their cats are better looking than their partners. Sixty-four percent said they'd rather cuddle with their cats than said partner. (British survey reported in *S.F. Chronicle,* 10/15/94:20.)

Survey takers with such leading pussy questions usually find what they are looking for. I did. Then again, some don't. One Lesbian sex researcher and therapist wrote an exhausting book to disprove the results of extensive, expensive research she herself had conducted on Lesbians! *The Lesbian Erotic Dance* by JoAnn Loulan deduces that since the large majority of Lesbians who responded to its survey simply refuse to identify in her essentialist, binary model as butch *or* as femme, they are "in denial." Neat. Within each of you that inner child struggling to be born must be a baby butch *or* a fem-mette. Rumor has it that this intrepid analyst is intensively interviewing—especially babe butches—for her next survey which will prove "the reality" that all Lesbians prefer to be either receptive *or* active in the sex act. The therapist is correct in one regard. There really are just two kinds of Lesbians: ones who believe there are two kinds of Lesbians and ones who believe there are many.

Who am I to mock self-funded, self-serving surveys? They are better than the personals for meeting women because they are, so, well, personal. I did a survey mainly to find a variety of wise and colorful talkers to interview for *Lesbian Polyfidelity*. I chose to interview especially the women who wrote outside the survey lines and boxes. Some drew pictures and diagrams, sent poetry. This shows the accuracy gap of the one procrustean bed offered in limited choice, menu-type answers. Statistically "firm" answers often hide complexity, conflict and doubt. Statisticians also noted in refining three drafts of my survey how question wording and order make mischief with the results. Sex survey projections are about as accurate as picking petals off a daisy.

The statistician who helped process my questionnaire despaired of ever tabulating our open-ended questions and eccentric responses. So why even try to wrestle qualitative data into quantitative? Because we are always trying to control chaos. I am glad we attained a cosmetically pretty quota sample, with proportional representation of age, ethnicity, class, etc. After all this exhausting "representative" sample work, however, we lumped together the oranges, apples, and wild berries—each one deserving a focus on its own complexity. Deep down, I believe whoever showed up on the form was meant to be there for her reasons if not for mine. Respondents were self-selected, with referrals from daisy chains of acquaintances. Do we care if the sources are eccentric as long as the results are fascinating? If I can't purport this survey to be "definitive," it was fun. I found great interviewees, whom I thank with all my heart. I do like the social part of social science.

What pleased me the most was finding what I dub a *queer quintile* of Lesbian polyfidelity. Our 500-woman survey showed that at present approximately one in five (21%) is or was practicing polyfidelity *and* has thereby found "much happiness" (88%). Make that one in three if we include the Lesbians who strongly believe that honest, responsible polyfidelity is an ideal relationship form, but "cannot find polyfidelitous partners" (81%) and/or "fear a partner's jealousy" (88%). If the queer quintile is indicative, we polyfidèles get to be a generous sexual minority within a sexual minority. This means twice the transgressions, twice the fun, and maybe twice the hassle —until we learn to finesse our way around.

Another Lesbian sex survey completed after my specifically poly one reveals an identical poly quintile. As reported in the August 22, 1995 *Advocate,* the *1995 Advocate Survey of Sexuality and Relationships: The Women* gathered 8,000 responses. Most of these women report a variety of partners; the average number of lovers is ten. "The bias of the sample is toward more, not less, sex." Unfortunately, the *Advocate* questions were pitched as monad or dyad. Survey women protested "the lack of answer options that would express their dedication to remaining nonmonogamous." Despite the deterministic questions, twenty percent refused to label themselves as monogamous. Those steered into responding "monogamy," often noted "trying" and "lapses." Contrary to women's image as better nesters, more gay men have been with partners longer than ten years (men 26%; women 12%).

From my own participatory field research, I believe at least a third of American women have Lesbian /bisexual proclivities. No doubt the proportions are increasing, thanks to the results of experimentation among youth and the media's licking up to Lesbian chic. This would heat up to around nine million possible Lesbian polyfidèles in the gay nineties. The new physics reveals it is not a finite universe, so why not? Just pull up your socks and don't be disappointed when you have to search for these quint-essential women.

Search? You see, the trouble is, folks, that according to our survey, 71% of Lesbian polyfidèles do not reveal their multi-relationships to their larger community, no matter how honest they are among themselves. You, in fact, do know many successful feminist polyfidèles, at least by name via the media, but believe me, they don't seek publicity in this regard. Such hidden lives are also true of most het swingers, nudists, s/m-er's and sexual heretics who maintain a reproachless facade. *It's dangerous out there for sexual minorities.* "Everyone assumes we're all 'just friends,' so I don't reveal things," says the third-party Lesbian in a long-term triangle with a so-called couple. "When I confided a few times in my friends, they seemed to think I was pretty sinister or just a victim." In various other arrangements, despite open consensuality, poly women tend to be criticized as "temptress," "philanderer," "romance addict," etc. "To come out polyfidèle would be a disaster professionally," says one doctor, echoed by three therapists. "People would say I'm bragging," states a bike messenger simply.

Polyfidèle Profile

If polyfidelity is not always outwardly revealed, is there a tip-off profile of a woman who dares to be polyfidèle or a likely candidate for one? According to major peaks in our survey, she is either young, not beyond her early twenties, or she is forty plus. Late twenties to forty-five, we tend to drape ourselves in the weeds of monogamy. Could the midlife drop in estrogen, the "nesting hormone," have anything to do with a poly rise? Or our typical midlife rejection of old conformities for a mature cycle of personal values? The polyfidèle tends to be coastal, urban and well-educated. She is often self-employed and/or an artist, especially a musician. Like everything else, polyfidelity is easier with money. Poly women used great terms for present economic class: "prole," "1040 EZ," "bohemian," "owning class," "gentlewoman farmer." Via interviews, I found that one reason for polyfidelity is to raise lifestyle quality across the board.

Polytheists seem to run to polyfidelity, while monotheists believe in only one goddess at a time. Patrifocal monotheists and closet Lesbians are the most voluble monogamists. Political activists prefer poly almost as much as artists; both types worry about time commitments. Virtually no one worries about woman-to-woman transmission of diseases via poly, especially healthcare workers *not* employed by AIDS organizations. It is true what they say about Sagittarian independence and Gemini love of variety, also Enneagram #7, "the adventurer." Our typical polyfidèle does not usually self-describe herself as highly sexed or a "renegade," but she has a history of many lovers. She has virtually always tried relationship deception, but grows away from adultery-type dishonesty. Only 3% of polyfidèles are "jealousy proof." One of the leading reasons for polyfidelity is (gasp!) "intellectual stimulation." We are surprised that monogamists—and monotheists—seem to do more dope than polys, but this survey showed a proportionately larger percentage of moms taking Ecstasy, so go figure. Maybe moms want to be on the same trip as their babes?

Most women (80%) judge monogamy banns can be violated with *no* physical touching but via any romantic environment like a heart-fluttering candlelight dinner. We seem to have gone the Pope one better: Life begins at foreplay. So you may as well steal a kiss. But partners will know! A whopping 91% said they usually discovered an affair by "instinct." A copy of our Lesbian Polyfidelity Survey may be found in the appendix, as perhaps a useless appendage, but don't miss the Poly Preparedness Quotient.

Surveys are like polyfidelity: easy to do, but challenging to do well, usually worth a try and a wink. ⭒

Triangles, Circles & Quads: Polyfidelity's Designs and Definitions

I will now proceed to define polyfidelity several more times, a good thing to do with any six-syllable neologism. A primary need of a free people is to define their own terms. Women would still be in a coma had we not brought up "sexism." The whole concept of polyfidelity is as fluidly evolving as feminism or Lesbianism, since it too is a social movement. There is no crisp social science definition yet. There may indeed never be, since polyfidelity is, by its very nature, a process hard to bolt to the floor. It is also a mixed model. Even the word "continuum" is too linear for polyfidelity, although I may simplify it this way for discussion. Polyfidelity is most like the sphere. You may view a sphere via cross sections, slicing vertically or horizontally or diagonally, or maybe in a curling twist. You discover something different every which way.

Still, like any behavior, a few guidelines, some structure, and real support are useful for a polyfidèle's felicity. To be polyfidelitious in our society without provoking any disturbance is obviously impossible.

I dutifully did a "survey of the literature" for glimpses of nascent Lesbian polyfidelity. A lit search is like doing a body search of Ph.D. ambitions and emissions. I entered rarefied "extra dyadic," "multilateral," and "paramarriage" realms. Here Lesbians don't cavort much. We exhibit an "etiology," a cause or nature, usually theoretical, but things are looking way up since literature searches used to turn up Lesbian=Zero. For some reason, whenever I see the word "etiology," I slide into glowing patterns of sunlit leaf veining, of unfurling fiddleheads and tree fern fans. I stare into mid-space like a cat and thank the Goddess these academic articles are preceded by abstracts. Not that fiery leaves of Lesbian polyfidelity abound. No single-focus articles on "multilaterals," in fact.

Only one green frond waved. I found an entire Ph.D. thesis on *The Diverse Nature of Nonmonogamy for Lesbians: A Phenomenological Investigation* written ten years ago by Elizabeth Holly Kassoff in San Francisco. It is quite a romp as well as careful, positive and kind.

I am cheerfully indebted to Ryam Nearing, who first introduced me to the word "polyfidelity" in her 1989 book *The New Faithful: A Polyfidelity Primer.*[2] (Perhaps the Kerista commune of the San Francisco seventies was the very first to coin "polyfidelity.") Nearing's orientation is largely hetero/bisexual. Her definition of polyfidelity tends to emphasize that all participants live under the same roof, in a closed sexual circuit. Such communal marriage is definitely not the focus of my study of Lesbian multiple relationships, for which I adopt the term "polyfidelity" anyway. Lesbian co-housing, however, with its private living space and its variety of sensual and familial relationships is beginning to receive much attention, especially by midlife Lesbians. See the last chapter on community. "Polyamory," rather than "polyfidelity," may emerge as the term for multiple relationships, since, by the summer of 1995, even *Newsweek* was bandying about "polyamory." Neo-pagans favor "panfidelity." Many women practitioners savor a "fidelity" ring to poly relationships, so we'll see. My mother says polyfidelity sounds "beyond stereo."

The other leading pioneer of the het/bi polyfidelitous movement is Dr. Deborah Anapol, whose book on responsible non-monogamy, *Love Without Limits: The Quest for Sustainable Intimate Relationships* is a marvel of inspiration and practicality.[3] I thank her for the portmanteau word "sexualove." Anapol, an indefatigable resource gatherer, founded the IntiNet Resource Center and organizes many workshops and conferences. In 1995, she began publishing a quarterly with Ryam Nearing, called *Loving More Magazine*. *Loving More* celebrates the shift from enforced monogamy and nuclear families to "polyamory" and intentional families, in the larger context of a shift toward a more balanced, peaceful and sustainable way of life. Nearing and Anapol are the *salonnières*, the Woodhull sisters of het/bi poly circles in this country. Graceful poly, after all, requires a woman's touch. Sensitive, dynamic and adventurous, much of Anapol and Nearing's work is transferable to Lesbian polyfidelity.

The concept of "polyfidelity" and "polyamory" resurfaced in the 1990's, after a 5,000-year hiatus. You may want to review some of the more common terms for sizing up relationships.

Relationship Forms

Polygamy	*Poly* is multiple; the suffix *gamy* simply means marriage. Therefore, in the broad term polygamy, we have more than one partnership running concurrently, with females and/or males, plus all the genders in between.
Monogamy	Marry one at a time. Our culture's prevalent "serial monogamy" is more correctly termed "sequential polygamy." Monogamy defined in older dictionaries was one partner for life. Now we live too long—or grow too broad—so this definition is obsolete in current dictionaries.
Bigamy	Marry two at a time. For a charming bigamy tale, see Miou-Miou in the French film, "My Two Husbands."
Digamy	Marry one, then end it to marry one other at a later time. Lesbians by their sixties are usually up to at least "sex(6)gamy."
❤ *Polygyny*	Marry more than one woman at a time. *Gyne* is from the Greek meaning "woman." Thus *polygyny* is closest in literal meaning to Lesbian polyfidelity. We may be called *polygynes* or *polyfidèles*.
Polyandry	Marry more than one male at a time. This takes place only in societies where women are wealthy

23

and propertied and men can share. The least prevalent form of human relationships.

Polygyandry Female/male group marriage, as the "complex marriage" of the Christian Communist Oneida Community and certain communes of our own time like Kerista. Rare due to cross-gender volatility.

Hypergamy To marry a surrogate self, i.e., someone of one's own age, race, class, politics, etc.

Open Marriage Popularized in the swinging seventies when a het couple would consensually take intimate friends and lovers. Often undermined by male jealousy.

Swinging Sport sex usually by het/bi couples, often in a party setting. Now popular in Lesbian sex clubs. Note most of the bi swingers' personal ads are for an added female. Women tend to be more numerous than men in swinging both ways, probably due to women's higher sexual desirability and superior relational talents.

Misogamist One who hates marriage, like Ambrose Bierce.

Marriage "A community consisting of a master, a mistress, and two slaves, making in all, two."

— *Ambrose Bierce*

Polyfidelity may be involved in these forms, but the "fidelity" or loyalty component contrasts it with swinging, brief encounters, and random sex. These latter forms are transient and low maintenance, which is much of their allure. Sex is for sex in one-night stands; in polyfidelity, sex is also for emotional feeling. For kiss-and-runs, suffice it to say: develop the style to make a fast connection (see the "Clitzzpah" chapter). Keep it honest, responsible and consensual, of course, and don't forget to pamper your immune system. You don't need this nonfiction book to cover one-night stopovers because in a few hours, it's ova and out. Great novel stuff, though.

24

I define polyfidelity as the state of being in ongoing *erotic intimacy* with more than one woman concurrently, while being *honest* about such involvements with each lover. The three operative words here merit further discussion. You certainly know what erotically intimate is since you have it forever written on your body. "Sensuality" is erotic intimacy's middle name. With Lesbians, it usually includes, and runs lotus rings around, orgasmic genital sex. It includes flirting, clitzzpah, conversational foreplay, body language, seduction dinners, heart connection, etc.

In the initial High Romance state, the infatuation component of erotic intimacy involves a ravishing play of the senses. The senses are virtually stripped, freed of daily sludge to become highly receptive and sensitive. Music can move you to tears; lyrics have layers of meaning. Food is divine, wine jeweled. Flowers become wands of sensuality. Sex is sheer abandonment, the body quicksilver and honey. One may fluster a bit drunkenly, with a blushing heart. The experience is sometimes likened to taking the purest acid or potent hashish. You are open, on, at last empowered to drench yourself in beauty and meaning. Petty problems and chores don't exist or can be shortcut. Barriers are down as you are called into the Great Union. Disarmed, you are vulnerable, suggestible. You avoid any conflict around "should be," because everything is "could be." For many of us romance is not permanent, but our love for it is eternal.

Lesbian erotic intimacy may be subtle as finger to finger whorles. It may also be what they call "raw sex." I am not sure what "raw sex" means in contrast to, say, *al dente* or well-done. Is it sex with no past or future, sex with no face or name? Is it vulva flooding with juices, with the deep liquid energy of ripe, glistening fruit or floral tissue, of dream or poem? Is it the shaft of tongue and clit rising, plunging together through tide pools into crimson grottos of grace? Is it leather and lace, silk neckties and satin panties, the hot waterfall sting of whip, the fivefold kiss of S&S (spirituality and sex)? Is it sublime surrender, the glad-fuck of double, triple, quadruple entry? I'll tell you this: it is stunt lovers and makeout artists, sacred sluts and spiritual consorts. Well, you get the drift.

Intimacy means you can be yourself. Just say that the entire world of Lesbian erotic intimacy is art meeting life. Let it go at that. Except for this: even in polyfidelity, if you want a perfectly tuned woman with zero erotic intimacy problems, hire a bedroom professional because that is her job: to be honestly dishonest.

Since erotic intimacy descriptions could go on forever, let's roll along to the other bold word in our poly definition: *honesty.* This word separates polyfidelity from grimy old adultery. Truth telling is *the* central issue in multiple relationships. Open or secret? I will never understand why hot, sensible Lesbians imagine *de facto* adultery is less dangerous than *de jure* polygamy. The honesty aspect of multiple relationships is so hotly debated, it takes up two entire chapters in *Lesbian Polyfidelity.* Actually it takes a lifetime. These chapters may be summed up as: Learn to say what is true and kind and colorful. Truth telling takes great practice and awareness in this smoke and mirrors society, but when you begin to think of truth as a great flirt, you are halfway there.

Let me outline how lovers may choose what I call a Fear Zone or Open Zone relationship model, first beginning with the issue of honesty. Note the pleasure/power contrast between Zone F and Zone O.

FEAR ZONE RELATIONSHIP	OPEN ZONE RELATIONSHIP
Secrecy	Truth Telling
Highly Judgmental Love	Easy Loving
Control & Manipulation	Allowance
Fear Driven	Joy Bound

Things descend into various grades of misery in Zone F after the first, inevitable power struggle. If one woman is in Zone F and the other is in Zone O, the Zone O catches much Zone F pain. No Zone O polyfidèle knows peace with a Zone F woman, so let her go, PRONTO.

Polyfidelity Style & Design

Let's look at the variety of poly sexualove styles, since polyfidelity is a sexualove continuum just like Lesbianism, bisexuality, s/m, etc.

Crypto-Poly

First we must include in our spectrum the vast majority of Lesbians in so-called monogamous partnerships who are emotionally unfaithful. Who alive isn't? We fantasize about other lovers; use sex magazines; sex videos; surf cyberspace and cruise personals; are voyeurses/exhibitionists at the clubs; titillate and frighten each other by distant crushes on celebs. (For some reason, few Lesbians get "hooked" on anonymous phone sex.) We all know devoted "monogamous" couples who regularly invite all the above extra dykes into their erotic intimacy. Whether it's a need or an enhancement, who cares? Theirs is not really a closed system. Someone else's sexual energy is triangled in, or the monotony could suffocate. Here we have poly in its quietest, most diluted and sanitized form, "crypto-poly."

I suspect the main reason Lesbian polyfidelity is not prevalent is that Lesbian monogamists won't stay married long enough.

The Freelance Polyfidèle

Let's move on to the mutually subjective forms of poly, to the more complex love juices. Begin with the type of polyfidèle I term the "freelance." She has a circle of sexual friends. Here is the woman who has more than one lover but lives with none of them. She considers herself to be in a primary relationship with herself. This girl probably loves to date, to go out on the town, and usually has a passion for something besides: art, profession, studies. The freelance clearly prioritizes her own needs. She is usually quite socially adept, while not always socially inclined. She loves her own privacy, acres of personal space, her own love nest. Here she need not modify personal habits and preferences or deal with

27

in-your-face jealousy on a daily basis. One reason why the libertine women in feminist utopias like *The Wanderground* and *Woman on the Edge of Time* enjoy multiple relationships is that, while sharing communal space, everyone lives in *private* dwellings. It is often said that polyvalence is less a relationship question than a housing issue.

To be a single-poly in today's dystopia takes quite a bit of selfhood. Look at the Lesbian characters Daria in the merry hit film "Go Fish" and Lois in Alison Bechtel's brilliant strip "Dykes to Watch Out For." As a single polyfidèle told me, "Players bow out fast if you won't take vows." But she rolls with it. "Why should I limit the variety of my sexual practice because of fear of being alone? Things done only because of anxiety create more anxiety. I won't let fear limit my experience and puritanize my natural patterns of love." Another: "My heart is reserved for questers. I cannot be faithful to others, only to myself."

You probably recognize that the single-poly pattern is somewhat uncommon. Why? Women, all women, especially Lesbians (women to the nth power) tend to sexually bond. Perhaps not for long, but bond we do. There is a neat hormone theory to this, the prevalence in the female of oxytocin, the "cuddle chemical." There is more certainly the influence of intense cultural conditioning. Lesbian surveys come up with fewer than three years for the average sexual bonding of Lesbians.[4] Other studies show an average of four years for straight women.[5] Evolutionary biology theorizes this three-to-four-year sex bond emerges from our previous five million years of female sexual strategy. Three to four years is the approximate time a human female with a helpless child needs resources and protection from another non-pregnant adult. After this time, for most of human history, the child could be weaned, could walk, play with others, and meld into the child care of the extended tribal family. The female was then free to sexually bond again, usually with a new mate for genetic variation. More on our female heritage of a polygamous sexual strategy in the chapter, "Evolutionary History Tells Us..." The prevalent goal and pattern of a Lesbian polyfidèle is also for a woman to bond sexually in some kind of couple, live-in or apart. She then opens the relationship circle erotically. This is in contrast to the agony of breaking up the old relationship for a new one, as Lesbian sequential polygynists (monogamists) do.

The Odd Woman

The figure whom I call "the odd woman," in contrast to the freelance, closely bonds with one member of a couple. A whole chapter on her later because she often plays a tantalizing role in an emotional drama set largely by the couple, if she's not experienced. The adept odd woman has part-time involvement, but deep-time enjoyment. Some form of couple bonding or linking is intrinsic to all but five of the twenty-five polyfidelitous women I interviewed in depth.

The couple bond may be limited to the famous triangle, or expand into my favorite, the "queer quadrangle," where four women are each in a couple while each play an odd woman somewhere else as well. Whether triangle or quadrangle, each form is in turn part of an entire emotional circle which includes the actors, the circles of extended family, the immediate social network, possibly a therapist or two, plus the predominant social system. If you like systems theory, poly is really fun to watch in motion. Sometimes it is like a hot billiards game. "A" may not touch "B" directly, but with "C" alters the directions everyone takes. The billiards effect is indeed a favorite novelistic aspect of poly. You come to see that events themselves may not be as important as their ripple effect. A single emotional collision can cause a four-woman pile-up—or epiphany.

The Triad

Look at the triad, or at the "trinity" as the spiritually inclined say. The triangle, besides being the core of structural engineering with its tripod of stability, is gloriously associated with the magic delta of woman power and mystic yantras. A "Grand Trine" in the zodiac is astronomically auspicious. The triad is often presented as the basic emotional molecule of all relationships, since the pioneering work of Murray Bowen in *Family Therapy & Clinical Practice*. A solely two-person connection is inherently too volatile or too confining.

One of the more coherent schools of psychotherapy, transactional analysis (TA), popularized the paradigm of the self-contained triad. Remember trying to figure yourself out in terms of your Adult/Parent/Child motivations? TA's neurotic power dynamics also come in a triad: Victim/Rescuer/Perpetrator. Most emotional systems can be understood in terms of interlocking triangles. As the fundamental unit of an emotional system, the triangle is the mechanism which dissipates tension or stabilizes volatility within the couple. When the tension between two people heats up, we diffuse it by triangling in a third person or object to absorb the surplus emotional energy. In families, the child completes the triangle between adults, sometimes an in-law or friend does. Solar collecting cats are also proficient at soaking up human emotional currents. Gossip is another universal form of triangulation. In many organizations, especially workplaces, triangulation as an avoidance strategy is a safety valve. It keeps people from quitting or being fired. It occurs when we complain to a third party about the actions of someone else to receive some kind of feedback without ever confronting the nuisance. This kind of triangulation is usually ineffective in resolving serious conflict, but may help to keep an okay system afloat. Useful as safety valve triangles may be, no one funds studies on the sheer pleasure, variety and motion of non-clinical triangles.

The Eternal Triangle

One triad not to be missed is one which could truly be called the "eternal triangle." This is the well-worn, wise trinity of "A," "B," and "S." "S" is a spiritual mistress, a tripod formed by a couple's co-creation, a third energy of connection. "S" is a flow-through which opens the hearts and helps keep them unblocked. "S" can be a committed spiritual activity like meditation; some form of community work practice; a core of values mutually aspired to; any of the arts or political service. The "S" point creates a spatial figure, an entity beyond two mere parallel lines, which may get sidetracked. When "A" and "B" cannot

THE ETERNAL TRIANGLE

find the way to each other, they often remember, reconnect, rekindle in the vigor of the eternal "S" point they share.

When I met my now live-in love, my co-vivante, she said, "My eternal mistress is painting; the others come and go." I said, "Great, I'll look after her too. Will you support a new booklove in my life every few years?" So the eternal odd woman in our life is art. She is obsessive, jealous, beggaring, infuriating. She is endlessly fascinating, a faerie godmother of hopes and ecstasies. She keeps us apart and she keeps us together in her eternal triangle.

Dynamics

A major goal of Lesbian polyfidelity is to help protect you from what is called the "competition triangle," also known as the "perverse" or "inferno" sexualove triangle. Here lovers get caught in a battle of winners and losers. Not much can be done, however, when this triangle is set up to run what is called "a transitional," an out-the-door affair. Here, there is no goal of parallel or poly relationship. In the transitional triangle, the involved partner uses another woman to bury a relationship already dead.

Contrast this with the stabilizing third lover who holds a tipping twosome together by diluting their emotional intensity or supplementing their lack thereof. Because of this third party, the couples' issues may not matter so desperately. Example: incest survivor A takes time out from sex for two years. Her partner B openly finds an understanding romancer, C. All sexual pressure is removed from A with B's presence and support, but B is not merged in A's celibacy.

Here is another example of how a triad can be fine for resolving and reconnecting a divergence. One Lesbian, the ebullient Bea, wants romance and a musical companion. Her partner, the brilliant Jay, a lawyer, has few romance receptors in her psycho/chemical makeup, cares little for music. Bea and Jay love one another for scores of things they do share and fascinate one another by their very differences. Enter Kay, a professional musician and sweet romancer, but far too involved in her career to set up housekeeping with anyone. Kay buffers the divergence between Bea and Jay while being artistically and erotically in the buff for Bea and likewise.

No human triangle is static. Poly women represent a triangle in motion, more the dynamic shape ▼ than ▲. Satellite involvement may become primary and vice versa. Note: there is all the difference in the world between a person and a position. Each human being is primary and precious. We rarely "rank" our very best friends into primary, secondary, tertiary, etc., because it's irrelevant and because everyone has a unique place in our lives. Degrees of commitment and involvement simply vary over time. The same three women can shift shape depending on what issue is active, roles being played, or degree of energy involved. For example, I once became more emotionally linked with a woman's husband than with her because it turned out he and I had more interests in common, plus she fussed so much at us, we teamed up in defense. Here are two triangles indicating style and involvement.

In Triangle #1, we can indicate that Bea and Jay live closely together (entwined) and are committed in many areas, whereas

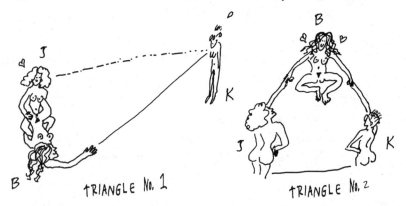

TRIANGLE No. 1   TRIANGLE No. 2

Bea sees Kay when they can make time. Jay and Kay have little continuity. In Triangle #2, the participants become more equally linked over time. Kay buys a seaside get-away with both Bea and Jay. Bea now manages Kay's bookings and they spend much time together on the road.

The Quadrangle

Let's slide into home with the stable diamond of the quadrangle, which is really two triangles: ◆. This form does not represent double trouble because of the symmetry of the square, the four directions, the four elements. In the queer quadrangle BJKV, let's return to our ongoing poly plot. To recap: lawyer Jay does not radiate the aroma of romance with its idealizations, playfulness and flowery props. But Jay likes regular s-e-x and good conversation. When Bea is on the road with Kay, Jay successfully defends Madame Vee, owner of a New Orleans bordello, on a mega-morals charge. Savvy Madame Vee wants to "retain" a sharp lawyer, is enamored of Jay's energy, and has a nice vertical smile. Welcome to the quad ◆.

The quadrangle may last longer, with fewer emotional flare-ups than a single triangle. This is because there are fewer lonely nights for anyone. These can be grueling, if only at first, for the odd woman and the uninvolved partner. In a quad, when your lover is with her lover, you can often be with yours. Since a quad is composed of a pair of couples, no one feels left out of a nest. The power balance is also easier to equalize two-to-two than in a one-to-two dynamic.

It is highly unusual for couples in a quad to all be erotically involved with one another. A foursome who tries this usually finds that the emotional attachment equation comes out $2+2 = 3$. Two women, A, of couple AB and C are in love with one other, D of couple CD. Period. It is hard to splice B into their romance circuit. The bonds of CDA arose by spontaneous combustion and can run on this organic energy. To "logically" shoehorn in the fourth partner rarely works.

You cannot negotiate romance or ever cajole it into service. Besides, there could be close-quarter resentments or instant aversions arising between B and D. This typical foursome dynamic may be diagrammed as two, wide-open V's.

The drama of the diagram may have its ups, downs and tight angles. May your lines not be so rigid as to break rather than bend. At the hearth of love, luckily, most lines become like spaghetti that twirls when heated. So, in reality, think circles. Here are notes from a renowned Lesbian poly-matician, who was bothered by this chapter's linear angles.

- Straight lines are rigid and predictable. Arrange a round table of friendly circles and curves.

- Be careful of individuals who are squares. When they touch, border disputes often arise.

- Honor the cloverleaves of love's freeways. These are what provide the opportunity to get where you are going, or at least another chance.

- Notice that circles have no sides. Circles' lines meet to say hello, touching only at special points to respect each other's space.

I'd like to close "forms" with gay, utopian philosopher Edward Carpenter's wondrous image of polyfidelity one hundred years ago:

So free, so spontaneous, that would allow of wide excursions of the pair from each other, in common or even in separate objects of work and interest, and yet would hold them all the time in the bond of absolute sympathy, would by its very freedom be all the more poignantly attractive, and by its very scope and breadth all the richer and more vital—would be in a sense indestructible, like the relation of two suns which, revolving in fluent and rebounding curves, only to recede from each other in order to return again with renewed swiftness into close proximity—and which together blend their rays in the glory of one double star.

Interviews:
The Glorious Benefits of Polyfidelity

When Lesbians initially hear of polyfidelity, they are apt to visualize a Jacobean drama of mayhem and intrigue, with bodies piled high on the stage. This may indeed be the scenario of old-time het adultery, but not of the emerging Lesbian polyfidelity. First and foremost, with the removal of deception, the searing pain of betrayal fades. Betrayal is an even deeper wound than jealousy. Trust which takes years to build can be blown to bits by one quick lie.

The drama of polyfidelity tends to be more drawing-room sophisticate than Jacobean. Consensus, communication, self-revelation, and humor are its suit. This is not to imply that poly is no-conflict, but it may be as workable as any form of relationship, including that bed of roses, serial monogamy/serial betrayal. A large part of this book, in fact, deals with the challenges of polyfidelity, since it is still a pioneering philosophy. But let's bring on the positive testimonials first. Here Lesbian/bisexual polyfidelity practitioners discuss some of polyfidelity's benefits and tantalizing possibilities.

Sara: Shapeshifter

I'm a pluralist in everything: work, politics, religion, women. I think I graduated from the School of Adversity into the School of Diversity. I can't imagine being a sexual macrobiotic, discouraging my appetite, distancing people, shutting down. With only a short-term lease among the stars, why be afraid to browse? Is there only one star, *my* star, on whom I can and must depend for light? To me, monogamy is a little cardboard house with holes punched in for light, air and regular food. It's an emotional Berlin Wall.

But my complaint is not really with monogamy's suffocating closeness or even its hypocrisy. My question is: where is monogamy's purpose and meaning for Lesbians? What good does it do? I notice Western culture's social purpose for monogamy is becoming increasingly murky. Monogamy is only a fig leaf to me with its lack of ideals. Here we have a venerable cultural phallacy whose contents have wasted away. Only its shell is intact, much like the

church, the "two" party system, the "defense" establishment.
I need meaning, not vestige. Why not admit the ideology of
monogamy is based on one major factor: deficiency. The historic
deficiency is patrilineal anxiety: who is *his* true heir? A birth mother feels no lurking deficiency in her gene replication. Or, the deficiency monogamy excuses can be a person's lack of time, energy
or talent. Just ask a financially independent woman monogamy's
benefits. It usually comes down to, "Monogamy gives me more
time not to make romance." Wow, what an adventure.

Here's what I dub the "Significant Udder Theory of Monogamy."
Monogamy is for people stuck in a mother/baby dynamic. Look at
the exclusiveness, the attachment. Woman as emotional protector,
as soother, not the explorer. Should this be the ideal for an adult
relationship? Monogamy is for infant emotions.

I am an utterly loyal and devoted friend to my lovers, yet if I find
someone new available and amenable, I follow the energy, emotionally or physically. Sexual positivism has been a wonderful road
of discovery for me, usually self-discovery. I live more *consciously* in
polyfidelity. I must really look at my motivations, use my imagination in clever and endearing ways while recognizing sex is not a
superficial game and that people are not toys. I can really practice
combining passion with compassion for myself and others. I must
examine current social values in regard to what is wise for me.

For example, one night I was privileged to share love with an
eighty-year-old very "married" woman when she visited my city;
I was her "escort." Late, at her hotel, she kissed me and said, "Come
and join me in the springtide of my death." I have never been so
shocked. What if she had a heart attack? Then I thought—what if
I do? What a great way to go! How we laughed and wandered that
night. A gathering of the sweetest *chi*. From her, I viscerally learned
that age is mainly a matter of experience and some of us are more
experienced than others. Women like my generous guest have big
chi to share. If this is what happens when you are presented with

the one opportunity to come together with someone, why block it? Like nature, I play for seasons, not eternities.

Promiscuity means mobility and mobility is a mark of civilization. There are so many things I like "mobilizing" with different lovers. I love taking hot showers in different bathrooms. I like different love styles: athletic, intellectual, sacred, transgressive. One of the best aspects of poly is that I can try on the different personalities who live within me. Somehow, to split up my ego structure gives me a greater sense of security. I do not believe I have one true identity to discover, anyway. I am stimulated by different women to be a different woman, to explore the range of my being. I even dress in different styles; sometimes I change everything but the kids. Remember Vita Sackville-West: femme with Harold, butch with Violet? I grew up with the elegant and ironic novels of pluralistic sex like Durrell's *Alexandria Quartet*. Here the bewitching Justine says, "I realize that each person can only claim one aspect of our character as part of their knowledge. To each one we turn a different face of the prism."

I can step from one present into another with each lover.

A multiple who enjoys herself, that's me.

Caroline: A Sweet, Strong Support System

Everyone knows that lovers usually come through for you better than anyone else does. What we all need is a really strong, stable support network in this world. This is one reason why women are often in such a panic to couple-up. I am with three local, long-term lovers, and we've had more love and sex to give and receive than I ever imagined. I call them my "seed circle." Two of my lovers are each in their own separate couple, and the other lover is a single mom with a small child. We don't do very many things together, except child care. Both of the lover-couples adore the other's child and often take turns keeping her for the entire weekend. For both me and that little girl, it seems like one lover still has some love and sympathy to spare when the others are running down and need a rest. When I share my deepest experiences, it is wonderful to see what each lover thinks is significant or the variety of details each one is individually curious about.

With three local love bonds, my social ties are extended, not to mention ideas, information, world views. To me, monogamy is a crowded waiting room where the windows are closed. With the openness of polyfidelity, I enjoy a marvelous pool of talent, customs, experience—even tools get shared. I can round-up so many caring viewpoints on a problem, who needs a therapist? I guess we're all somewhat dependent, and what I like in polyfidelity is that this dependency is diffused, spread among several responsible, consenting adults. In an emergency, there is no major burden to any one woman, less burn-out.

I am presently very ill, and I am not alone. Whatever happens, I like knowing my lovers will not be alone either.

Molly: Holidays and Homecomings

How come all these Lesbians want to have sex with a lot of women who don't have sex with a lot of women?

Poly is the way I can have my cake and eat her too. A multi-flavored cake of stability and excitement, of security and liberation, intimacy and novelty. My lover Alice and I live together, while supporting each other being on the stroll for sexual entertainment. Some of my sexy girl pals are also best friends, some are one-night stands. Alice is a bicycle (bisexual), and we're into the leather scene, mostly me. Alice does a lot of professional downtown drag in the clothing trade. I'm the one who's really a lamb in wolf's clothing. After hanging an all-nighter, with stud-ladies and pussy galore, I love to be a cuddly little homemaker for most of the week. Alice and I have these beautiful little garden brunches I fix, and we talk about everything in the world. We hold hands through everything. She paid my way for three months when I couldn't get work.

Alice knows I'll never leave her for another woman. Why should I?
I can see 'em all. Study on that old saying about grass being green-
er—the crucial part is the fence. I know Alice can kiss on boys and
girls and still want me to make a real place for her in my bed, my
heart, our life's ride together.

This is what I like: dangerous women out there in the night and a
relaxing love at home.

Seneca : Human Rights

For me, the great value of polyfidelity is that polyfidelity shouts
out for civil liberties, for basic human rights. *Vida es corta, pero ancha.*
Although life is all too short, it could be ever so wide. As a professional organizer now, one who watched my pregnant mother beaten
for drinking from a "restricted" water fountain, I support no system
of organized violence, of which enforced monogamy is one. Monogamy often sets the stage for murderous criminal jealousies against
lovers. The monogamous mentality has led to ongoing domestic
violence toward wives and daughters even suspected of off-site sex.
Meanwhile, "crimes against monogamy" are punished by statute
and via monogamous judges and juries. The government boot comes
down to jail and persecute any alternative forms of polygamous marriage. Even today, most of the states in the union can prosecute a
spouse merely accused of common adultery! Adultery is grounds for
divorce; it used to be the only one.

"Special interest" monogamists also receive economic favoritism,
including better tax and estate benefits. Often, pensions, housing
and subsidized health care are available only to legally wedded
spouses, no matter your personal definition of "family." Hospitals
can sever dying patients from their lovers and chosen family unless
an unmarried patient happens to be in a jurisdiction of "liberal"
Domestic Partnership laws and can conform to a DP's residential
monogamist rules. Such social abuses created by relationship biotry
must be challenged, rather than aped by sexual positivists. Let's
believe in justice along with our pleasure.

Only a slave-holder mentality believes one person's bodily functions should be *owned* by another. Hell, no person is good enough to be another person's master. Even taking care of my infants or paying an employee, I don't presume that I can *own* their bodily functions. So called "natural" monogamous behavior in women is the highly unnatural result of living in a heteromasculinist culture that wounds and punishes women into adopting "owned" behavior. After all, adultery was originally a capital offense in the colonial U.S. Then the theocrats made the penalty public whipping and lifelong wearing of a scarlet "A" by women.

We still have the Teutonic and Catholic tradition where a man is handed god-like dominion over "his" wife. Monogamy warriors stop at nothing, including the destruction of peaceful societies, to protect "their" women from outsiders. The lynching of many Afro-Americans on false rape charges is an example of this. Hypocritically, married monogamists sexually colonize women of other cultures to claim territoriality and inflict humiliation and fear. To compel monogamy as the supreme code and to persecute sexual self-determination just ain't pretty and never has been.

Debating all the niceties of polyfidelity shouldn't detract from its primary civil and human rights core—and the most important question of all: *Can we freely express the sexual energy that naturally exists between people and maintain the historic hierarchy of relationship/ ownership?* Obviously, not! This is why what I say about politicized polyfidelity will probably be edited out. 🍎 Polyfidelitous power upsets the feudal apple cart—of which media gatekeepers are near the top of the heap. I tell you, Euro-Americans think they're being moral about sexuality when they just feel uncomfortable about it.

So, I'm glad to say my polyfidelity declares sexuality to be my own personal possession, my own personal experience, a creation and function of me, not the property of some absentee landlord. If pantric Lady Love smiles on you and me, babe, what you've got is blessed access, not ownership. Lovers have power over my heart, yes, my body and spirit, no.

Lee: Independence

One reason I became an ardent feminist is that I enormously value personal autonomy. How dare we use the possessive with any living being? I'm a freelancer; I can't stand people breathing on me about work, and I don't like giving orders either. Typical, willful Sag. I grew up in a large, cramped-for-room family, and feel like I'll never tire of wide-open spaces. This is not to say I don't value interdependence—spiced with open self-interest. Among my self-interests are sex and travel. I realized, though living with my beautiful lover Judith, I wanted an open system for sex, to be free to enjoy women on my many work-related travels. Judith agreed that I should be free as long as we both share power about *how* it is done and continue to cherish one another. Sexual exploration/variety is not an arena Judith particularly cares about, though she is quite the Renaissance woman. She never had a home before and loves any chance to settle in. With a bit of work, we've both learned to protect one another's ways. We are discreet between ourselves and totally private about polyfidelity to anyone not in the loop. Our relationship is stronger now, and we're both happier. Polyfidelity has been one of our gateways to finding out who we really are, what we appreciate about one another, what we do and do not need.

I think of our home as a beloved harbor, my affairs as lovely ports of call.

Judith has time in the house alone so she can do her projects. Then she loves to socialize and entertain house guests and large parties. I can fade out to *tête-à-tête* somewhere else because I dislike groups. I'd rather go traveling, so my other lovers meet me on junkets. With them, I like having special hideaways, a unique love nest for each woman. I own this inner space, tumbling intimacies of memory. I don't talk about it much. It is my own secret honeycomb.

Melinda: The Odd Woman

CW: You are one of several women I've talked with who whole-heartedly not only enjoy, but prefer, being the third turn in a love triangle, the odd woman.

Melinda: I use the term "odd woman" too, rather than the sinister "other woman," the existential alien. We're flesh and blood too. I *am* an odd woman, queer in lots of ways. I've always pretty much flourished being a third. I don't expect a committed relationship to go out the window when I arrive.

CW: You probably know one of the most witty, philosophical novels in the great genre of adultery, Gail Godwin's *The Odd Woman?*

Melinda: I love it, but how so humorous, self-aware and independent a woman could get in such a stew perplexes me.

CW: Maybe because her relationship is het-powered. The woman professor has to deal with the gaping gender gap in sensibility, in status and power, in negotiation.

Melinda: Well, I have a het in my happy triad now, but it is true I interact with Joan and not him. Although Michael is nice enough: placid, fatherly, discreet.

CW: How long have you been, ah, "interacting"?

Melinda: Oh, it's quite an act. Let's see, over seven years; we're not exactly on the cutting edge of nonmonogamy anymore. Joan and I try to get together a full day each week, a couple nights. This is more an ideal, but Joan has her own room, her own bath, even her own tropical fish here. Most of all, she has her very own closet. She's a well-known political figure, so you know what this means...

CW: You are her secret rendezvous with destiny.

Melinda: *(laughing)* Well, everyone who matters in her life knows, except the voters. I myself feel that intimate sex acts should be private, of course, but not a lifestyle. How silly. My profession, however, does not depend on a lifestyle. I work in a hospital emergency room weekend nights. No one cares what the hell I do with my hands elsewhere as long as they move fast enough here to bring 'em back alive. I get paid big bucks, the hours run like minutes, my co-workers are real, with shocking senses of humor. We accept each other's lives and laugh at most of the details.

CW: And you come home to these dazzling fish.

Melinda: Yes, we meditate on one another. Then I hit the street with my camera. I've done several photo-essay books on issues I'm concerned with, and just for fun. I could blackmail Joan; she's such an exhibitionist for my camera. I also donate time to cancer activism.

CW: You said you try to see one another a few times a week. Is it lonely otherwise?

Melinda: We do pretty well. I don't fight for time in competition with Joan's husband. She's really married to her career. Politics is voracious. They say politicians should be orphans and bachelors. I used to worry that Joan came over just to get patched up. That's okay, I said, but I don't do only rehab. Focus on us, sunlight on a moving fin, listen to the incense. It takes us a few hours, but we're getting pretty good at tasting the moment. Plus I finally came to terms with the fact that I'd rather have a third share in a first-rate woman than exclusive possession of a so-so one.

CW: Do you see other lovers?

Melinda: I've been known to keep my bed open. I don't get lost there after all. Passion is a safe enough pastime once you learn her ways. I want to hear my heart pounding before it stops.

CW: Do you find sensual passions, especially new ones, to be quite consuming?

Melinda: I believe people who get lost in pleasure are extremely conflicted about their enjoyments. They may associate passion with fears, shames, loss of control—strong negative feelings that jam your way home.

CW: Home?

Melinda: Home is our body, our private wilderness. There is a tantric song something like, "Here in the body are the sacred rivers: here are the sun and moon, as well as all pilgrimage places. I have not encountered another temple as blissful as my own body."

CW: Is fear of passionate lovers (plural) fear of the body's intensity?

Melinda: Give the body some credit. I like the assurance, "Mindfulness of the body is the body's mindfulness."

CW: So do you think it's true that the odd woman has to overcome mega-conditioning and accept she is, shall we say, a supplement—not the main show?

Melinda: Well, what's the main show? *(angry)* If politics is the main show, I don't want to endure the banquets and bozos; Michael does. More to the point, you see I am the main show here! I love my patch-ups, my art, my friends. Not just all my busyness, I love being with me at night. Being an odd woman works if you have a big primary relationship with yourself. So many Lesbians seem in the grip of "relational fever." They just exchange women for men as relational objects.

CW: Do you think the odd woman is usually presented with too much a "take it or leave it" ultimatum?

Melinda: Everything is negotiable up to a point, even sudden death, or I'd be out of business. But there ultimately comes a time in any relationship where you accept the package with grace, or you take the goods but resent them, or you get out. May no woman have to settle for anything not worthy of her. We certainly once had to. All we could be was nanny, concu-

bine, or whore. True, I don't get to be with Joan as often as
I want her, but this keeps things very hot and exciting too.
I make sure I have good friends to get me through times until
she can be here. Moreover, I truly prefer to live with fish rather
than lovers. I love separate environments, order, things stripped
down, uncluttered. I need to be mobile to work on my projects
with magnificent obsession.

CW: What about the future?

Melinda: It never comes. Ask many of my patients.

CW: As a stable odd woman—I guess no one is secure—what
advice would you give the odd woman in a triad?

Melinda: Advice to the love worn? *(laughing)* Well, you'll really get
lonely if you fuck with both partners of a couple in bed at the
same time. They can work out their feelings together, revise your
character and performance, forge a united front. At least get the
right to a private time with each one. Otherwise, you're essentially being used as the sex toy in a three-way.

Do not necessarily believe what your lover says about her other
partner or their relationship. She'll often say what you want to
hear, be making momentary judgments, or be stone-blind. I
think the odd woman is often deceived as much as the uninvolved partner, especially if the triad isn't honest and upfront
among themselves.

It goes without saying that you lose essential, precious dignity
and meaning if your lover lies to her intimates regarding your
existence. You are probably being used to keep her in the old
relationship. You are a marital aid.

Don't invest much hope that your lover will leave her earlier
lover for you. She well may, but give her a definite deadline if
that is what you want. If she does breakup, it's because she really
needs you as the boost out. She is unable to make it alone. Be
clear about this dynamic; it's endemic in Lesbian relationships.
We prefer to see ourselves swept up in a tide of passion we can

scarcely control. We don't want to confront ourselves and our partner and admit, "These are the areas where we now fail." So when your lover merely makes a divorcée of her wife and a wife of you, her same issues will come up again. I stay a mile away from complaining, decaying relationships that would use me as a "fixer." This is a grisly drama, and you usually make out with a poor third billing. Wait for her to get out alone.

Maybe it's just that I don't like blood on my hands.

Diana: The Way Seeking Heart

I was a priest in a Buddhist monastery for nine years. We had lots of sex—oh, not the scandalous, open kind—but out-of-body sex with others and lots of self-intimacy. Most sex takes place in the mind, and that's what the monastery gave us time for: minding the mind. The monastery was good for me, but now I am no longer priest nor laywoman. I love, let go, wear life's robes as loosely as I can. I won't marry again or pledge troth because now I live in old hotels in the Tenderloin where I practice, and I like to change towns every year or so.

I see polyfidelity as my practice too, not a virtue, just a practice. I use polyfidelity as a medium of self-discovery. It is not a panacea. I don't idealize it. But it is an error to ever devalue it. Polyfidelity is just one way I participate in life and in women's and men's lives. One of my current lovers is so "working poor" he donates blood for a living and the other is so rich, she spends almost full-time donating money to the stream. Their sexual vitalities put a halo around my existence. It enhances the way I can touch those whose vitality has ebbed.

I was surprised that the first person I had sex with after I left the monastery was a sex worker who lived in my hotel. She took one look at me and said, "When you see a sacred cow, milk her for all she's worth." I said, "To the pure, all things are pure." We found each other irresistible. I couldn't own her sexually. I guess no one worth possessing can quite be possessed. She chose her vehicle and worked it, robes over her head. I chose mine, robes in the closet. In our separate vehicles, we each had good and bad days. Now she's gone, but she left me much of her affectionate detachment.

There was a courtesan in Buddha's time named Pass-a-Million. She became Buddha's devoted supporter and student. Interesting both Buddha and Christ hung around with loose women. Pass-a-Million continued her trade even after she became enlightened. It is said her energy enveloped her lovers in a wondrous net of lovingkindness and compassion. I suppose Pass-a-Million knew rapture is one of Buddhism's "Seven Factors of Enlightenment." Rapture in Buddhism is perceived as delight, as deep appreciation. It is what we can feel in the presence of music, great vistas, sunsets, beautiful love-making. Rapture is not possessive the way desire is. You can't really control desire or rapture. They just pop up if you are human. All you can do is dance with them.

I wish I could list all the many gifts of breath, touch and tease lovers give me—not that I am a "better" person for them. I don't have a permanent self to improve. I laugh when I hear that relationships are supposed to make you "evolve," like some sort of tandem spiritual fitness training. Will we never love our own selfhood and stop trying to improve our shining, original face? We're all just fine—with affectionate detachment from the ego-shell and its narratives of an idealized self-image. In love, I think personal fulfillment, growth and development are futile. All that matters is kindness.

When I touch, I touch the way I learned to meditate. No finger prints. Pluck the Goddess' eye and sit in the hollow. Orgasmic ecstasy helps to empty the notion of a separate self. Why do we see love as solid, instead of liquid or gas or space? This is what I do, touch and go, flow with several lovers. I try to pay close attention to each lover in our own present moment. "Paying attention" does cost a bit. You "pay" in constant realizations. Some pleasant, some not so pleasant. But if I don't stay completely present, I can be haunted by ghost lovers and all the suffering I see, trailing behind me like the wake of a ship. I have to remember that the ship causes the wake, not *vice versa.* The past is only what the present did before. By staying in the holy present, I see my ghost marauders are but a wake, that planning, planning ahead is a spook too.

I want to be like a tree, self-possessed, neither owning nor being owned. Independent, yet interdependent, on the whole web of life and greening in it. This doesn't save me from meeting situational tyrants and my own emotional despots. I can feel clinging and possessive and want to be taken care of and appreciated more. We are all desire machines. With lovers, I really have to confront this, then try to work out solutions. Lovers give me immediate responses, hot feedback, unlike my out-of-body sex in the monastery or cooler friendships. A lover's mirror may reflect me back—or just my false images. It takes awareness and practice to know. I like to find out how I make myself suffer, where I'm still stuck. Polyfidelitous bonds provide me with a really large palette to paint my predicament. Bright, various colors too.

I gradually expand my comfort zone as I learn to let go of how I think my lovers "should" be. In poly, I don't necessarily know when I'm enlightened, but I sure know when I'm not. Lovers polish my relations. The skills are transferable on the street. Surely, a spiritual journey is to learn how to express love. With each new lover, I experience a world of not knowing, then all the pleasure, mystery, conflict and joy fill me in. It will empty out, too, I've no mania for resolution.

I guess I can't provide much of a poly tour guide on what is "really" happening, or how things could or should be. Here's one favorite observation from thirteenth century Dogen Zenji, "To be intimate with all things is enlightened action."

A Boston Marriage in Southern Comfort

This interview with a remarkable Lesbian couple took place in their getaway cabin on the outskirts of a lush Southern town. Kate and Jeffrey Anne said they take subversive joy in their "radical intimacy." They rarely have genital sex with one another. ("Maybe once a year when the moon is mauve.") *Instead, each has a circle of sexual companions, locally and else-where. Kate teaches science and Jeffrey Anne manages a gallery in town. They also take subversive joy in grass-roots organizing and in being avid botanists, developing an herbal cottage industry they call "The Bud-Head Sisters."*

CW: You seem as courtly and excited together as new lovers, yet you say sex is entirely incidental to your "companionate love."

Kate: We pretty much ceased having genital sex with one another when we moved in together and started the farm out here. That was a little over a year after we met; now it's been seven years together. We both get aroused by new sex and undomesticated "honeymoon sex," free from the kitchen sink, bills to pay, termites gnawing. I think Jeffrey Anne likes uncomplicated sex almost outside the boundaries of reality.

Jeffrey Anne: Take off those ankle weights and get sky-clad! Every time one Lesbian kisses another, an angel gets her wings, darlin'.

Kate: Jeffrey Anne is still the most exciting woman I've ever met; she's a gentle pirate, a story teller, a cat dancer (stroking a giant tabby in her lap). And we're totally different; unlike "sisterly love," ours seems to come from two different planets. I'm a techie, she's a mystic.

Jeffrey Anne: Our poor sex therapists couldn't figure us out in the famous "Lesbian Bed Death" syndrome. We don't fit the dead bed: we have little unresolved anger, no resentment—just natural conflicts and conversational jousting. Neither of us is locked into mother/daughter roles. There's scant "merging," due to our independent careers and different interests, friends, lovers. We appear a classic butch/fem couple, which is supposed to be a turn-on. We lack shame and are out. We really like to spend more time together, so we even schedule special times to connect.

CW: Why did you ever go to therapists?

Kate: Well, we fell for the current party line on Lesbian "deviance": If you're not having electric purple sex with your live-in Lesbian beloved, then you are dysfunctional and you need to be fixed. Get a make-over, a libidinal lube-job.

Jeffrey Anne: Yet, just two decades ago, therapists mangled Lesbians with electric shock and lobotomies when we *did* have homegrown Lesbian desires. They wrote us up as "perverted" in their manual for craziness, *The Diagnostic & Statistical Manual of Mental Disorders, (DSM.)*[6] After great gay activism, shrinks' official organizations voted that queer is not crazy [American Psychiatric Association and American Psychological Association.] Can you imagine putting to majority vote whether or not someone is crazy? Suppose the vote were 49% to 51%. Who's crazy?

CW: They're still at it. Morbidity means money, keeps the trade going. The psychiatric establishment wanted to vote PMS as a crazy in the *DSM,* to marginalize as mentals all women with estrogen ebb and flow! This means not only expensive time and drug dickering, but with a PMS psycho label a woman may face the loss of civil liberties, opportunity for advancement, etc. By the way girls, the *DSM* still says that if you use marijuana or acquaint yourself with magic mushrooms, you are mentally ill. This brushes drug testing with a "medical" imprimatur, so the government can ignore your constitutional rights.

Kate: Well, somehow we got suckered into the therapy machine, its confessional technicians and patrifocal standards of passion. The first therapist, who seemed on prozac herself, wanted us to time travel to the past to see if our childhood histories explained our lack of sexualized passion for one another. I kept saying, "I am not what I was." Besides, there is no particular "reality" in the past. It's just what your thoughts tell you it was. Then Jeffrey Anne got all tripped out in her "Everything-is-happening-all-at-the-same-time" dimension, which the therapist considered dementia. Dr. Prozac also discovered that both of us are pretty sexual; each inner child seemed to be doing something illicit and fun. She finally dropped the prozac mode and herself started to date. In the meantime, I found out that there is "reality therapy," for here and now types, so we tried a version of this for me.

Jeffrey Anne: It was almost worse. This therapist had us do all kinds of inane exercises like erotizing our elbows, playacting passion, a bundle of gimmicks that made me feel like a trained seal in a sex arcade. Plus, it was suggested we invest in commodities like fur gloves, studded leather tit for tats, dancing dildoes. Instead, we longed to once more direct our own intimate time, like play with our new kittens rather than pretend to be in lust. Like talk about cosmic, colorful questions and exchange news and views without sex toys barging in.

Kate: I finally said, "So, what's wrong with a massage just being a massage?" We realized that we could never solve our sexual "problem" because we didn't have one. Between us, there was no alienation, confusion, or oppression. Our relationship is pretty much one of openness, passion, action, and contact. Our goal is to deviate from the world's madness with as much awareness and verve as we can. As far as possible, we now play "no-contact" with anything in the boy's status quo, which therapy-for-hire usually upholds.

CW: So you consider yourselves a free and happy Lesbian couple without "conventional" Lesbian sex together—whatever that may be?

Kate: Yup, we both admitted we wanted to have "sex-sex" with other women, to build a home and hearth together, create a loving, companionate type of open Boston marriage. Wed community and desire, and not be in denial or defensive about how we choose to do it. Stop overanalyzing. Jeffrey Anne meets a lot of artists and people passing through the gallery who are looking for a good time. I tend to be more bonding. Right now I see someone here regularly. I have another lover in the southwest, and we get together about three times a year. Now that Jeffrey Anne and I are succeeding in this magic herb business, we both meet women who are pleasure-oriented and innovative. We are meeting health care workers looking for r & r themselves, while dispensing our organic pain suppressant/ appetite stimulant.

Jeffrey Anne: Our model is one with love moving in two directions, with inner and outer spirals. We don't have to cut off the parts of our hearts that like to touch others. We have a bond that is not disposable, like serial monogamy usually is. What do they say about monogamy? "It works—'til it doesn't." In polyfidelity, we have the undeniable benefits of companionship, emotional support, economic advantages, and we are friends to one another's passions, including "extramural" sex.

Kate: Why destroy a good marriage and a good affair at the same time, like lots of our friends do? They play house and vow to hang up their shoes—until someone comes along. Adultery is what adults do naturally, why pretend otherwise?

Jeffrey Anne: I like Oscar Wilde's "The chains of marriage are heavy and it takes two to carry them—sometimes three." Three or more—what we're doing is not anti-couple, but pro-spectrum.

CW: Do you have any conditions?

Kate: We had a raft of rules for seeing other women at first, which I think was a good thing because it was new to us and nobody is born knowing how. We luckily agreed everything is an experiment, and we'd just keep experimenting to success. Some of our old conditions were no involvements unless both of us liked the woman; no "falling in love"; our right to veto a date if one of us was in crisis at home; even the right to veto an outside relationship if it felt unmanageable. The vetoes turned out to be forms of suffocation.

Jeffrey Anne: Laying down conditions was as hateful as it would be for me to grouse about a lover's clothes or harass her about weight.

Kate: We've pretty much dropped all the particulars now and hold to the important general vows of loyalty and honesty. We each agree to work on any polyfidelitous problems to our utmost capacity, and, whatever happens, neither of us is leaving by the back door. Everything else is pretty much details. We

Great Les"bi"an Adulterers
Hall of Fame

Tallulah Bankhead

Natalie Barney

Simone de Beauvoir

Gladys Bentley

Jane Bowles

Rachel Carson

Charlotte Cushman

Emily Dickinson

Janet Flanner

Elsa Gidlow

Lorena Hickock

Alberta Hunter

Mabel Dodge Luhan

Margaret Mead

Mary Meigs

Edna St. Vincent Millay

Anaïs Nin

Ma Rainey

Eleanor Roosevelt

Vita Sackville-West

George Sand

Sappho

Bessie Smith

Violet Trefusis

ALelia Walker

Mary Wollstonecraft

Virginia Woolf

You??? Me!!!!!!

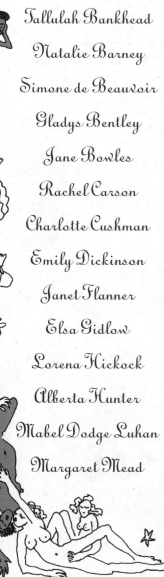

53

deal with these as they come up, not by fiat. We do have positive goals and hopes which we wrote up. These are a much stronger bond than "Don'ts."

CW: Do you ever feel pangs of sexual jealousy, knowing someone is sharing your partner's pleasure and attention?

Jeffrey Anne: *(laughing)* I keep repeating, "All in one, one in all, all in All."

Kate: Oh, I don't think my jealousy ever completely goes, I've just learned to work with it. I still get what I call "polyfidelity panic." Will this be the woman she runs off with? We talk about it. I'm a nicer person for the competition. It may be hypocritical, but I don't want to come across as a selfish bitch just when Jeffrey Anne has found a dashing, courtly soul showing unconditional love—at least for the moment.

CW: How do your other women feel about this arrangement?

Jeffrey Anne: Some like it for a while, then drift off if they want a primary partner. Kate stays with lovers for years. We try to be very clear about our "Sister Double Happiness" routine, but some lovers think we'll do a trade-in with 'em, and they are disappointed. We all live with a degree of ambiguity, and those uncomfortable with ambiguity and shifting roles select out. We've both been hurt. When you open yourself to intimacy, you are vulnerable in many ways. But I'd rather be open than live in a bunker.

Kate: And breakups are a thousand times easier with our system! I have someone to come home to who cares and who does want me. I have no enormous disruption of my home base.

Jeffrey Anne: In many other eras and societies, romantic love and sexual impulse are not necessarily related. All this varies over a continuum, I'm sure, but many troubadours entertained all-consuming emotional and spiritual relationships with the beloved sans physical sex. No one considered this a medical problem. "Troubadour bed death." Platonic and Renaissance idealism found perfect friendship superior to sexual love. The wonderful depth of feeling and romance of a "plighted friendship" was not suppressed, perhaps reaching its height in the eighteenth century. Today society denies plighted friendship except for a prospective or current sex partner.

CW: Lesbians frequently do have something like a plighted friendship with quality former lovers. *Après deux* is one of Lesbianism's most highly evolved and prized states. Some say this is what courtship flames aspire to: the *après deux* cult of *grandes amitiés*.

Jeffrey Anne: As the candle melts, so too our struggles melt.

Kate: We've studied the character of famous Boston marriages: the Ladies of Llangollen; Sarah Orne Jewett and Annie Fields; Rosa Bonheur with Nathalie Micas and after Nathalie's death, Anna Klumpke; Willa Cather and Edith Lewis. I would even say Susan B.Anthony and Elizabeth Cady Stanton; Madame de Staël and Madame Recamier. Let me read you what Henry James wrote about Katherine Loring's love for his sister Alice James: "A devotion so perfect and generous was a gift of providence so rare and so little-to-be-looked-for in this hard world that to brush it aside would almost be an act of impiety."

Jeffrey Anne: If any of these Boston marriages were sexless— some no doubt were—are they abnormal, or remarkable models of kinship and flexibility? Why force a genital construction as normative on any profound intimacy?

My sex drive, much as I like it, is not my foremost instinct. It is not necessarily entwined with "real" love. Plus there is nothing "natural" about sexuality. It is constantly being reinvented in a kaleidoscope of fashions: Greek paedophilia, Christian celibacy and Eastern sacred sex, forced sex, loving sex, Madonna genderfuck sex, virtual reality sex. . .

Kate: Women practice Lesbianism for far more complex reasons than their sex drive: for the quality of the interactions, aesthetic to political and beyond. . .

CW: But don't you think women's sexual exchange can be like signing a pact of mutual trust?

Kate: Ha! It can fizzle out in the first spring rain. What we need to exchange is conviviality, common purpose, daily support, respect—surrounded by the warmth, even fervor, of passionate caring. Plighted friendship helps guarantee happy, generous lives. People live horrid lives just full of sex.

CW: So you would say that passionate *friendship* is a primary element of much Lesbian love?

Jeffrey Anne: Colette did. "What woman would not blush to seek out her *amie* only for sensual pleasure? In no way is it sex that fosters the devotion of two women, but a feeling of kinship."

Kate: Look at the personal ads—women's generally compared to the guys'. We write overwhelmingly about whole-person modes of relating, about communion and sensibility.

Jeffrey Anne: It is not lack of sex, but lack of exciting partnership/fellowship and creative community, that's what's sad.

CW: It seems like you both cultivate a romance that doesn't fade, but keeps changing color.

Jeffrey Anne: For me, our alliance is a realm of enfoldment. It is okay for my parents to have sex and hate each other, so I figure it's okay for us to not have sex and love each other.

Kate: In an alarmingly loveless world, why scorn women who wish to commit ourselves to a relationship based on devotion? We should be applauded.

Jeffrey Anne: Hey, the moon is applauding and it looks mauve…

Evolutionary History Tells Us...
Polyfidelity Was in Flower

History tells us...whatever we want to believe. The story of evolution was once cast by men: a saga of aggression, big-game hunting, killer apes, male domination and male superiority. There was "natural" female subordination for grueling household and child care duties. As usual, sciences such as archaeology and paleoanthropology have been servants to the prevailing social system. But today, the lifetime pair-bonding hypothesis of monogamous sex, such as popularized in Desmond Morris' 1967 *Naked Ape,* is considered a laughing stock. Morris' mode, like others, was to get rid of unsightly, inconvenient, albeit prevalent, data by declaring such data "aberrant." Now, prestigious women archaeologists, anthropologists, and biologists are revealing a more balanced and harmonious view of prehistory. New narratives of sex and gender roles present the view that virtually all species' master switch is tuned to the female sexual strategy. In the mating game, the selective female is on top—unless her position is usurped by force or subverted by deceit (including her own self-deception?). As Harvard anthropologist Irven DeVore notes, "males are a vast breeding experiment run by females." Behavior leaves few fossils, but for a fascinating post-sexist look at dem bones, see page 328 in the bibliography, "History of Polygamy & Monogamy."

Many anthropologists acknowledge female polygamy, polyfidelity's ancestor, as women's sexual strategy throughout ninety-nine percent of primate, hominid and human existence. Current "cultural" monogamy is bucking the biological tide, likely designed for oblivion. Anthropologists Lionel Tiger and Robin Fox sum up: "All cultures may not be monogamous, but they are certainly adulterous." People who trumpet female monogamy as "natural" cite only the last 5,000 androcratic (*Homo sapiens* male-ruling) years, a mere blip in our five-billion-year-old earth and five-million-year human history. Earth's cosmic birth would not, in fact, have occurred but for the saving grace that one in each billion paired protons and antiprotons was free to roam.[7] Today, we even classify chemical elements according to the vast number and variety of bonds they can form. Earth is far from a pair bonded planet.

Nature Ablush in Pantric Sex

Primates nearly human, "hominids," descended from the trees around five million years ago. Much research has been recently popularized about the merry libertine sex life of our immediate human predecessor, little Ms. *Homo erectus*. But let's go back beyond her for a moment to look at other animals. Life long pair bonding among any species is extremely rare. According to anthropologist Helen Fisher of the American Museum of Natural History, there is simply no biological, evolutionary reason for any creature to mate for life with only one other creature. She notes barely three percent of all mammals ever form long-term relationships with a single mate. When pair-bonding does occur, it is usually a sweet marriage of convenience, as brief as a breeding season or merely as long as infancy. Even during this "marriage," both mates usually philander: males randomly, while the female's roving eye is strategically set on a higher-ranking male than the one at home. Biologists who once believed that many species were monogamous, especially birds, had to revise their views in the light of more accurate tracking, such as DNA prints. Only a dozen or so creatures among millions of species remain on the monogamy trail.[8] Are they happier and more successful than the rest of us philanderers?

Termites lead biologists to speculate that monogamy arose from "mate guarding," a male, not a female invention. The competition among termite males is so fierce that once a male finds a female, the pair stay together for life, sometimes sealing themselves inside the nest. Among the minority 18% of primates who are rather monogamous, most are endangered species. The most monoga-mous, least intelligent and least social of the primates, the gibbon, is sexually quite inactive—in contrast to the chimpanzee, our very closest relative, with whom we share 99% of our genetic material. Whereas female chimps may have sex sixty times a day with a dozen different partners, including other females, monogamous female gibbons come into estrus every two or three years, and then breed only a few months.

Human primates are classified by biologists as a "mildly polygamous species," mild I guess in comparison to chimps. Approximately 84% of contemporary human societies are polygamous, with the 20% industrialized ones classed as "culturally" monogamous.[9] That's monogamy with a wink. Blood tests show that in some urban areas, more than a quarter of the children are sired by another man than the father of record.[10] In liberal Scandanavia, marriage is already a minority preoccupation. Women choose to bear the majority of infants outside wedlock.

Promiscuous Ms. Homo Erectus

Let us go back to *Homo erectus, Homo sapiens'* easy-living, free-loving predecessor. *Homo erectus* evolved around two million years ago in the African savannas and spread around the globe. Our ancestors are now portrayed as lolling about non-violently in non-possessive love, a golden Buddha Land until Earth began to chill and our lotus-eating days were over. *Homo erectus* may have been less ambitious than *Homo sapiens*, precisely because they were less possessive, more sensual creatures. *Homo erectus* was a communal species who used fire and tools, gathered edible plants, scavenged, and captured small game which abounded. Then, *Homo erectus'* brain/head grew too large for the mother's pelvic canal, a canal growing smaller itself due to erect posture. Nature's startling solution? An event considered a revolution in the course of human female destiny. Bear the young undersized, at a very early stage of development, really an embryo. Thus, we are all born too young; human infant and child dependence is hopeless compared to other species. The burdens of human motherhood stretch for years. The human mother usually needs help during the difficult, narrow canal birthing process too. Hence, the oldest profession, midwifery, was born, an opportunity for women to bond with one another and with each other's young.

Such premature birth shaped the female human sexual strategy. A mother needed another non-bearing adult who would share resources while she was vulnerable and eating for two during pregnancy and long lactation, up to two years and more. She needed resources she could not gather while employed in holding and carrying her infant to make sure it did not end up as a carnivora's dinner, and while she performed the myriad tasks of child welfare and maintenance. I emphasize here that a woman caregiver is not dependent, she became a person who cares for dependent humans.

As the *Homo erectus* brain ballooned, so did male testes and penis, as well as female breasts. Anatomically, this always indicates polygamy in a species. Penis and testes, large relative to body size, invariably means keen "sperm competition," *i.e.*, lack of a monogamous partner. Males must compete inside a promiscuous female's reproductive channel. Copious sperm and a long penis give swimming sperm the advantage of being deposited nearest to the cervical canal and uterus. Men have a penis larger than a gorilla's two-incher, despite the gorilla's body being three times a man's size. Gorillas do not have to compete for partners; they live in stable harems arbitrated by females. Human concealment of ovulation, with no visible or scented estrus, leads a male into continual attention toward the female. He demonstrates his attractiveness to her as a regular provider via gifts, comforts, and service. Full breasts in all other mammals round out only in lactation, signaling a period when the female is infertile, already supporting offspring. Here again, the male human is left guessing, hoping—and providing. Promiscuous females receive the most offerings as they and their dependents reap favors from a number of consorts. A species also benefits as its evolutionary options are increased by the genetic variations of different partnering.

The Sacred Mother

Ultimately, from a *Homo erectus* womb in Africa, about 600,000 years ago, came our mutant, *Homo sapiens*. Its number and society advanced by about 30,000 B.C.E. into the Paleolithic, the Stone Age of the Old Goddess Culture. We were tool-using gatherers, small game hunters, scavengers, and crafts people. Where Earth began to warm again, women invented farming, and the so-called Neolithic cultures arose, in some areas by 13,000 B.C.E. This was a time of amazing civilization and creativity, only literacy was lacking. Thus the era's "bad press" by later writers with their own agendas of historical reality. The cycles of the fertile Goddess were revered; the arts of living were refined and flourished in gender harmony and matrilineal descent. Tombs reveal that there was relative peace and no extreme disparity of wealth. War had not yet become institutionalized, so we find few weapons, no fortifications. Workable metals like copper and gold were used for tools, magnificent art and decoration. We find no hallowed conqueror monuments. Practically all the material and social technology essential to civilization was developed, even indoor plumbing in Crete![11] Writing, once thought to have been invented for commerce around 3,500 B.C.E., has now been discovered in Neolithic sacred inscriptions associated with Goddess worship.[12] In the East, the first writing is always acknowledged to be sacred script.

For most of the Paleolithic and Neolithic era and certainly before, it is highly unlikely that anyone had the slightest interest in monogamy—simply because the male did not know he could beget children. As late as the 1960s, anthropologists found fathering ignorance among peoples in remote areas. Scholars speculate that for most of evolutionary history, mother and siblings were "clan companions," along with children of the females and nieces and nephews of the men. It was a kind of group marriage where every child's maternity was certain, its paternity irrelevant. As Margaret Mead remarked, "Mothers are a biological necessity; fathers are a social institution." Today's aberrant closed-couple nuclear family is probably moving in self-destruct fission because of its wild capacity to concentrate neurosis and become a model of structural violence. Statistically, the most dangerous place for an American woman is the home—one with a he-man in it. No non-human female primate is subject to the kind of male abuse inflicted on human females.[13]

The Punitive Sky God of Monogamy

Such male violence arose in the colder northern steppes and the harsh deserts where life was meaner and leaner for *Homo sapiens*. As a quick fix, males used their non-childbearing freedom and muscular prowess to seize scarce goods and dominate the weaker. Thus began violent possession, the war that never ends. Battling Mother Earth for survival, males ceased to worship her and invented an abstract Sky God in male dominator mode. What might does not make right, religiosity can. Religious ideology set up a "Patriarch," the male who chooses himself not only to give woman orders, to focus her desires, but to compel her worship. Patriarchal might did not, of course, make for security or creative, lasting solutions to problems of scarcity. Instead, males had to continually turn up the violence. Trauma became institutionalized. Sky God religions glorify suffering, stimulating the need for "heroics" because of system-engendered harshness. War power became magnified with harder metals and horses. The new Bronze Age ran red.

The loving, primordial mother/child bond, however, could not be subverted by violence, or *Homo sapiens* would self-destruct. Female blood empathy for her helpless infant survived, only to be exploited during our last five millennia. A female now needed male protection from male violence, as well as goods and services while she performed labor intensive child care and heavy household work. The male, in turn, wanted exclusive sexual conduits (monogamous or harem) to breed his own clone-sons, the relationally impaired who would "fight for peace."

Homo sapiens became *Homo economicus*. Male power, ironically, increased with the invention of farming by women. Resources could now be sequestered. As males fought for goods to hoard, those of superior strength and cunning reproduced and entrenched themselves. Males grew larger, stronger and more aggressive. Man could make woman his indentured slave, controlled by violence and superior wealth. This was stoutly rationalized by the myth of a brutal, omnipotent Sky God. The He-Man projection, now in full state regalia, defended gender inequality as ethical, eternal law. A Lord of male projection ordered transcendence of nature and the lure and mystery of female flesh. Appetite came to be renamed "lust." Earthiness was circumcised. Eternity was disembodied.

The Sky God's harshest penalties were often reserved for female adulterers, not murderers. With the invention of writing, men created gender specific taboos which could be carved into seemingly unalterable codes. In early code law, a man's promiscuity was usually ignored, but a woman's could be punished by death—or worse. The earliest gender code is in the Code of Urukagina (2,400 B.C.E.). If a woman violates monogamy, her teeth are to be bashed out with bricks. The Code of Hammurabi (1,900 B.C.E) quietly sentences an adulteress to death by drowning.

No culture has likewise regarded adultery by a married man to be a violation of his wife's property. A male owns his sexuality and is not expected to renounce or disown it. Adultery is always defined in the *Old Testament* and in Roman Law as sex with a married woman, another man's *property*. Legal scholarship in this country declared in 1935, regarding adultery, "It is not immorality which is punished, but theft." The brand of monogamy on female flesh is scorched into the phrase "man and wife." "Husband and woman" is as unheard of as a "husband swapping party." With monogamy's possessive double standard, women are the property to parlay.

In Islamic societies and elsewhere, female husband swappers are still punished by death or amputated hands as well as branding, banishment and public shame. Adultery "prevention" is currently achieved by the torture of infibulation in the Mideast and Africa, where a woman's vulva is sewn shut in her husband's absence. That female adultery has persisted in the face of such unspeakable torment, speaks volumes on the power of the emotional drive for sexual freedom. It also shouts the profound male fear of woman's unleashed sexual power. The violence of the U.S. antiabortion forces is another version of organized "sperm protection," totalitarian biological control. Perhaps all male despots of woman's body will be reborn as the little fly *Johanseniella nitida*. In reproductive kamikaze, after depositing sperm, Johann wedges himself in the female genital opening using his body as a copulation plug, blocking further sex games. While Johann is in this position, the female eats him, using the protein to nourish her eggs.

Male terrorist bashing of women reached fever pitch in the Judeo-Christian religion during "The Burning Times" in Europe when nine million women were murdered for being "unfaithful" in some way. Sky God dogma, whether Judeo-Christian, Islamic, or other—control-ridden, violence prone, pleasure fearing, evil obsessed—is anything but sane. Yet it stands as the primary bastion for sexually possessive monogamy. Feminists have consistently asked why any woman would freely adopt a relationship form born in the violent desperation of a Bronze Age nomad. By Roman times, adultery was so commonly accepted, officials taxed it. Adultery brought in the revenue to build great temples, like the one to Venus. Monogamy would probably have remained pretty much a joke. Then it became resanctified and reconstructed by the state-perverted teachings of a charismatic faith healer and zealous social reformer.

This was Jesus of Nazareth. Supernatural mythology paints Jesus as an out-of-wedlock son of an unmarried Sky God who adulterously stole into a virgin Mary's uterus. "If I was the Virgin Mary, I would have said, 'No,' " remarks Stevie Smith. Whatever her wish, the Virgin Mary's spontaneous generation remains as embarrassingly inexplicable as the identity of Adam's and Noah's sons' wives. The Virgin Cult was created to brainwash women to renounce our own bodies' sensual power. While men crave, even sanctify "despoiling" a virgin, women exhibit scant interest that their partners be virgins.

Ironically, the defiant yet kindly Jesus, himself did not choose monogamy. He was, in fact, an exponent of the revolt against marriage. With discovery of the early Christian gospels, like the *Dead Sea Scrolls* and *Gnostic Gospels*, censored from the canonical *Bible*, Jesus' lifestyle is conflictingly presented as being one of celibacy or homosexuality—or, my favorite: that Jesus may well have been one of the consort disciples of Mary Magdalene, temple priestess of the Old Goddess religion.[14] After all, Jesus was a pretty fem guy. Even the male-edited *New Testament*, unrecorded and unrevised until hundreds of years after Jesus' death, reveals that when the Pharisees brought Jesus a woman to be stoned to death for adultery, he defended her saying, "He that is without sin among you, let him cast the first stone." After they retreated, he said, "Neither do I condemn thee." Another great quote is Jesus' why-split-hairs: "You have heard that it was said, 'Thou shalt not commit adultery.' But I say unto you that everyone who looks at a woman lustfully has already committed adultery with her in their heart." So go for it, heart throbbers.

Bible babble regarding the patchwork *Bible's* conflicting edicts is, in any case, moot except to fundamentalist print fetishists. Have they not heard of the priceless 1805 *Adulterer's Bible*? This strategically abridged edition was perhaps created by a printer "error," rather than the usual scholarly manipulation. The "not" was dropped from the Fourth Commandment to read: "Thou Shalt Commit Adultery." As verily, verily, most of us do.

Today we can understand how *most* men are better off in a het monogamous system and most women are worse off. Via monogamy, men have access to regular sex, gene replication and amazingly valuable, comforting PRODUCTIVE LABOR passed off as "women's work." In the absence of polygamy laws, het women would flock to the resources of cultivated rich men, signing on as legal second or third wife as long as there were generous resources to go around. With wealthy men attracting as many desirable women as they could support, many poorer men would have no wife at all, especially with Lesbianism on the rise. Few women, if able to choose, want to live in relative poverty servicing a domineering ne'er-do-well. Single males, however, are a terrifying proposition in terms of safety. In all cultures, womenless men wreak the most havoc, with the most ferocity. Married men adopt a lower risk, less destructive lifestyle.

Why don't we call real "family values" what they are—"women's values"?

The Three-Year Itch

Back to evolutionary history, the major point regarding our female ancestry for five million years, until the female suppression of the last 5,000, is that the unfettered female is promiscuous. Our female promiscuity is not bred to be random or mindless—given the high price of eggs. Even today, many men will have sex with a person whose name they do not know, whose face they may never see. Women rarely do—except for money. The number of our precious eggs is finite, set at birth, usually limited to one egg per moon, for a few decades of life. We cannot afford to squander our eggs as males do their kadzillions of sperm. Sperm are a glut on the market; one male ejaculation yields two hundred million of the critters. Thus, Bay Area fertility centers offer $40 for a sperm shot of millions, whereas one egg fetches $2,500.

Until our present era of frightening overpopulation, for millions of years the sex strategy of humans, like all other living creatures, was: replicate your own specific gene pool. Male sexual strategy was to impregnate as many fertile females as often as possible. Female sexual strategy was to select the fittest, best provider. This is a person who has the power, resources and emotional ties to help care for an occupied mother and her helpless infant, until the child can be weaned, play with others and be absorbed into the extended family network. Such a bond lasts around three to four years.

Meanwhile, promiscuity within this companionate bonding is advantageous to both sexes. More sperm swim; more offerings are made to the survival of the female and her offspring. After the child runs off to the group, the cycle can begin anew. So it does to this day. As statistically noted before, the average marriage worldwide lasts three to four years, then we move on. It is around the same period for Lesbian relationships. Evolution has so far programmed us not for lifetime relationships, but for sequential sexual bonding with outside cavorting. Listen to an anthropologist asked why her marriages failed. Margaret Mead replied, "I have been married three times and not one of them was a failure."

Polyvalent Neurochemistry

Besides demographics, experiments in human brain chemistry reflect this on/off pattern of the "three-year itch." Most couples, especially Lesbians, experience what relationship mavens call the "attraction phase" and the "attachment phase." During attraction passion, couples glisten in sensuality and energy as natural brain stimulants and sensitizers, like the amphetamine PEA (phenylethylamine), kick in for a couple of years, or longer, if meetings are infrequent or full of exciting obstacles and uncertainty. All romantic highs seem to require the components of unpredictability, insecurity, barriers, or limits. This adrenaline-like rush, with its hypnotic intensity and visionary quality, is easily mistaken for intimacy or love. It is more like a really nice manic episode to blast you out of a rut.

Ultimately the brain develops a tolerance for its own stimulants, unable to sustain this revved-up state of romantic bliss. Nerve endings become habituated, or the stimulant supply somehow drops. Breakup or the attachment phase occurs. In attachment, the brain now alchemizes endorphins, the opiates which dull the fires, but bring peace, a feeling of security and comfort. Endorphins cause a lack of sexual tension, and perhaps a little too much stability. Endorphins ease pain and seem to disperse stress and urgency. Finally, our brain receptors build up a tolerance for the endorphins too. The stimulants begin to stir once more, and it's off to Romance

Land with someone or something new. Thus do the brain baths of nerve endings spell planned obsolescence for infatuation. Pair obsolescence rules unless, of course, a couple depend on each other to flourish psychologically or to survive economically, or if one person does not have the power to run free.

Women Brainstorm Polyfidelity

A certain configuration in the female brain, our highly developed *corpus callosum*, probably makes us more adept at polyfidelity than men. This remarkably rich sward of nerve tissue connects the right and left brain lobes. In women, our denser, thicker *corpus callosum* gives us high interplay between language (left brain) and emotions (right brain). The *corpus callosum's* electric dance is one reason why women are "in touch" communicating our emotions so eloquently. Woman's corpus circuitry is a superhighway; man's, a country road. (One study shows gay men's corpus callosum is bigger than het men's.)[15] Everyone knows that good relationships, especially multiple ones, require quick volted, quality communication. Recent research by scholars Nancy Chodorow, Carol Gilligan, Deborah Tannen and others shows that very young girls seem to be immediately relational, little boys competitive and autonomous.* Girls tend to "process" an action; boys to battle it out, reverting to a power hierarchy to enforce the "winning" view. Most women become highly adept at the crucial process of negotiation which comfortable relationships require, actually savoring the practice of diplomacy. Each one of my sisters personally feels she could have been our Grandmother's favorite, although Grandmother in no way ranked us and was appalled at the idea, when asked. Thus, there was no constant jockeying for position in our multilateral system. Woman's gentle style of social linking,

---

* Beware "the relational woman/autonomous man" stereotypes gleefully appropriated from Chodorow and Gilligan's "difference feminism" by those who hate "equality feminism." Research also shows that while girls desire independence too, they have to fight harder for it. Woman as "sharer and carer" is not only developmental, but a direct result of second-rate economic and social power. Colonized peoples necessarily fall back on "sharing and caring." Gender "separate sphere" ideology steers women into nurturing guess who? Men.

rather than ranking, leads to stability and ease in relationships, especially parallel, multiple ones.

It is also undisputed that women are the most profound artists in eroticizing the full plumage of romance, sensuality and intimacy. Lesbians, surely the most romantic creatures on Earth, are perhaps super-synthesizers of the brain romance fuels like PEA. Or, perhaps it is the other way around—copious PEA nudges women into Lesbianism, where a girl can treat herself to other world-class players. Studies also show that subtle chemical perfumes called "pheromones," found in all body secretions (perspiration, sex juices, urine), are likely to arouse women romantically more than men. Moreover, women have keener senses of smell than men, especially at ovulation. How can we not be polyfidelitous with such an array of natural talents and all these subliminal sirens at work? The entire world is a swirling laboratory of love for a woman in her natural glory. The post-domesticated woman is polyfidelitous.

Nature AND Nurture

Don't worry, beautiful feminists, I am not arguing that biology is destiny, though biology so neatly supports a female polyfidelity thesis. It is not for me to be a biologically-fated essentialist when we truly live in the "both/and" world of nature and nurture. The artificial, if sometimes useful, "either/or" is merely imposed by our language and binary logic scheme. Yes, the DNA helix of the female double-x chromosome can be a powerful influence, especially if it has been selected for success over five million years. So do let us use any and all sociobiology tenets for self-acceptance. Never let anyone box you as "deviant" when the three-year itch is arisin' and the romance lights seem to inconveniently flick on or off, or you are tempted to stray—or to stay—despite social dictates or Lesbian therapy fashions. For example, a "Lesbian bed death syndrome" of long-term couples was discovered as "unnatural" behavior you can "fix" for $85 an hour. Evolutionary psychology suggests any couple, like interviewees Kate and Jeffrey Anne above, could each use the money saved to happily date around, meanwhile keeping their carefully selected, now cozy, love base.

But let's say you never believed in fated biological destiny. You feel it is the 5,000 years of socially controlled, institutionalized monogamy that really holds sway over women. But couldn't we just say that evolution proceeds by choice as well as by chance? I, for example, "chose" to become a Lesbian partially because the 1969 political climate was ripe; because I was somehow alerted, right and left brain, to trust spirit and variety over common monoliths; because on acid I experienced the glorious synesthesia of a woman named Sue dancing in the Sierras, her long hair flowing. It occurred to me at that moment I had overlooked the sensuality of half the human race. All these events were chance, yet women in similar situations made different choices. In every lifetime, there is an evolution, an adaptation of awareness, within our given social and genetic makeup. Our personal role is one of *becoming,* an ongoing dance. We are no more a tightly rolled, involuntary, inescapable loop of DNA, than we are the sum total of our conditioning and beliefs. Though both genetic coding and socialization affect behavior, the biological and/or socially fixated life is tragically unaware, unrealized. I think of a Lesbian as a brilliant hybrid in a landscape of het ho-hum. Why should our opinions and decisions not be as stunningly hybrid?

According to Nobel prize winner Gerald Edelson's theory of "Neural Darwinism," strong reactions in the brain to certain stimuli result in the individual nerve cells reforming into brand new sheets of "maps" which interact with one another. This means brain circuits actually regroup, indicating a structural plasticity in the nervous system. We also reform in cyclical spirals depending on endocrinological variables such as estrogen and the moon, the seasons, our age. Don't tie me down—least of all in nature/nurture dualism.

Autocratic Genes?

It is noteworthy that seekers of gene dots for static behavioral/character traits—gay genes, crazy genes, jealous genes, dirty genes—are the ones most to benefit from the status quo (designer genes?). Why not do as painstaking social and environmental research on say, hoarding behavior, to yield information far more valuable than funding deterministic, simplistic molecular biology? It is obvious, for example, that homosexuality is always a variant sexual behavior. Do we search *why* there is not only rose sexual display, but also sunflower? It is people *opposed* to something, a disease like diabetes, who want to discover a biological cause. Some Lesbians hope discovery of a gay gene will somehow absolve us from het persecution. ("Poor dears, they can't help it. Let's give them a guaranteed annual income.") No way. The genes for skin pigmentation and for ethnicity were identified long ago, and there has not been a moment's surcease in racism and nationalism. Find that gay gene, with its little pink triangle, and the "master sex" will try to cut it out. Gay genes are the enemy's pursuit, not ours. The whole nature/nurture debate is hopelessly reductionistic. We are vastly more than body or mind. We are also spirit. Spirit is where infinite question/answers lie. I like Jane Rule's discovery: the cause of Lesbianism (and polyfidelity) is love. We are attracted to each other in delight and love. An extensive, objective reading in psychobiological and neurophysiological research sees what looks more like a mess than any real answers to human sexual behavior. Studies contradict studies. Methodology is suspect. Questions multiply. What determines the sexual tastes of each furless, bipedal primate with a giant brain is a vast personal mystery.

This is not to say that I am displeased that evolutionary history seems to imprint women as the polygamous, promiscuous, yet highly selective sex. So, perhaps by imprint, most women will become ardent polyfidelitous Lesbians, but it obviously takes a blending of other factors as well. Today, ecology and the environment itself certainly favor gay relationships, which mean population control by Lesbians' extraordinarily mindful and rare decision to inseminate. I am sure other species would declare humans extra-terrestrials. Lesbians who do inseminate are likely to be natural caregivers, whose art form is child development and, therefore, our future. Lesbian moms could do with a bevy of attentive lovers to help out.

Nature selects for quality and diversity over quantity. A two-gender, two-parent world has proved alarmingly dangerous. Since Lesbians today are murdered less often—albeit still legally stoned-to-death by Islamic states and killed by U. S. anti-human rights fanatics—we can be fruitful and multiply. Most essentially, it is now possible to have jobs, careers or inheritance which provide us the economic autonomy to survive and prosper without sexually servicing men. Two women cannot live quite as cheaply as one, but multiple loving friends add immeasurably to one's standard of living. There are psychological influences too. By experience, as well as from twenty-five years of Lesbian visibility and current Lesbian chic in the media, more women are recognizing that women tend to be the more cre-ative, loving friends. Who needs an emotional flat tire on board? Why limit emotive, loving friends? The more the merrier. The more various our lovescape, the less possibility of holding on to unwise roles. The dyad is often a "lock-in" of neurosis, if not violence.

Finally, awe shucks, there may be spiritual energies that coalesce with any or all of the above to make it congruent for a Lesbian to seek the feminine Beloved in Her *many* guises. Each of one's lovers can fuse in sacred passion to form an aspect of the Mother of Evolution, the Mother of Change. Through Her hands, the galaxies, the planets, especially the double helix of infinity pass like gay beads. Such a flowing Creatrix did not invent the fierce dichotomy of cultural determinism *or* biological fate, polyfidelity or monogamy, Lesbian or anti-Lesbian. People did. Nature does not fixate as we do. She dances on feet of chance with wings of choice to a vast rhythm, beyond the great divide.

Polyfidelity: Way of the Truth Teller

The word "polyfidelity" is used to express multiple lover relation-ships *openly* enjoyed in candor and good faith. Thus, polyfidelity is honest politics of the heart. "Faithful to many" distinguishes polyfidelity from the cheating, betrayal, and hypocrisy of common household adultery. Adultery as a form of sexual dishonesty is the eternal corollary of monogamy. The vow of monogamy appears to be sexual dishonesty itself. One who takes it pretends to forsee her future needs and guarantee her behavior over an entire lifetime, even while recognizing monogamy is largely a myth.

Since most people obviously do not practice lifetime monogamy in our society, the clearest and kindest book on the adultery self-help circuit is entitled *The Monogamy Myth* by Peggy Vaughan. Statistics on the underground world of adultery are necessarily an estimate, as are all figures on proscribed behaviors. Most sex researchers and sex workers, however, speak of adultery now hitting in the 50% to 80% range, with married women now matching their husbands in affairs due to their outside jobs and economic freedoms. The myth of monogamy thus encourages self-deception, denial, isolation and exaggerated feelings of duty and shame. While an affair is not the symptom of something wrong with the relationship, lying certain-ly is. The liar has lost faith in her own truths, mistrusting their validity or fearing punishment.

One of the most valuable aspects of polyfidelity, besides its joys, is that polyfidelity asks us to look very consciously at core value judgments, to develop an ethical system based on positive self-dis-closure and integrity. This is not, I hope, a chapter of puritanical moralizing, but on ethics in the sense defined by Epicurus: dealing with things to be sought and things to be avoided, and with the *telos* (chief good, aim or end of life.)* In polyfidelity, one is invited to wake up and exercise the self-examined life of personal choice and responsibility. No one ever said this is as easy as it is valuable, least of all me. Women in our survey compared abstinence from the covert and overt lies associated with multiple lover relationships to the rigors of snapping a connection to valium or coke. Rough! Some multiple lovers become virtually addicted to a lie's rush of rebellion and danger, lured by its temporary sense of mastery, its fleeting impression of protection. We are drugged on danger—where to meet, when to speak, how to survive public scrutiny. Ah, intrigue… Oh, the stolen moment…

Most of us in this mode do not give up lying because we suffer from scruples. I indeed salute those noble souls naturally at home on the moral high ground, but those of us who insist on testing the wild waters quit lying for one good reason: lying does not work. Sure, a cover-up may possibly last for years if you live alone (see "I'll Cheat You Fair," next chapter), or for some months if you share housing with lovers. But NEVER underestimate the fabled Lesbian radar, *laydar*.™ Lesbians seem born with a deeply-set crystal for sensing any foreign body vibration. With high decoding powers, laydar™ ultimately hits target. Or, there will be a slip by the lover, her paramour, or an acquaintance. Even the most punctilious double agent cannot totally control every circumstantial variable and dangling detail, especially in the intricate emotional mine field of Lesbian love. Further, the creation of new lies to shore up old ones is exhausting maintenance, with increasing slip-up potential. It may be easy to tell one shenanigan's lie, but it is hard to tell only one as the affair progresses. The first lie must be thatched with yet another or the rain will come through.

When the deceived woman fatefully discovers the affair, she is usually more devastated by the act of betrayal and its erosion of a

---

* Two elegant works, philosopher Sissela Bok's *Lying: Moral Choice in Public & Private Life* (Viking, 1978) and psychologist Harriet Lerner's *Dance of Deception: Pretending & Truth Tellng in Women's Lives* (Harper, 1993), are marvelous revelations on the meandering path of truth and her detours. Another classic is Adrienne Rich's essay, "Women & Honor: Some Notes on Lying," in *On Lies, Secrets & Silence* (Norton, 1979).

social trust than by the extracurricular sex act itself. A betrayal feels so threatening because a pledge of security has been eroded, dreams have been shattered. Usually, a betrayed person feels profoundly disoriented. She is, moreover, fundamentally insulted that one has played with her heart. Her respect for you is thereby lost. It is not the truth which is brutal here, but the lie.

For the sake of argument, let us say however, that your deception is never fully discovered. Have you harmed no one? The liar often overlooks an honest examination of herself. How good for anyone is the corrosive worry and "damage control" duty which go along with systematic lying? Constant lying may also foster the paranoia of no longer being able to believe in others' honesty. Then there is the matter of self-esteem. The false persona is often the shamed self, one who fears her authentic, core self would be rejected. We often lie out of fear of projected disapproval. Lies attempt to deny this fear by maintaining a facade of controlling the situation. It is a circle game: we lie because we are fearful, then fear because we lie. The liar can become an isolated partner, as a barrier of guilt emotionally distances her from the beloved.

We also lie to avoid pain and complexity, as in, "We are the perfect Lesbian assimilationist couple living happily ever after." We will not face up to the plain, harrowing truth that we do not perfectly meet all of one another's intimate needs. We thereby deny the dazzling possibilities of exploring radical Lesbian intimacy. We lie because we are lazy and want to stay comfortable for the moment, keeping emotions at bay, muzzling the difficulties—and creativity—of conflict. All in all, lies actually carry a negative value for the liar herself. If the false life dies, with relief, we lose the need to cover up, shut down, close up, spin off. This is what happened to Virginia Woolf's dashing Orlando in her vast experience of several lifetimes. "To tell lies bored her. It seemed a roundabout way of going to work."

Our lies are understandable, of course, since as children or women in a violently monogamous system, we may have had to use lies to survive, not only emotionally, but bodily. In an adult Lesbian love system, however, this once adaptive strategy is demented. Do we want the kind of power that lies purchase? Men are expected to lie about and conceal feelings. Women are expected to lie with our very bodies: to dye, to diet, to distort – as long as we are physically faithful to a man. Deception in love is yet another outmoded patriarchal standard of passion. Adultery is, well, so common, the typical melodrama of bleak heterosexual coupling. "Plausible denial" is the emblem of an ugly, cold war world. Are not lies the common cohort of an ethic of force? Machiavelli advised his warrior prince to use the force of a lion and the deceptive cunning of a fox. Let me suggest to the Lesbian love warrior that lying forces you into a side-saddle position on the carousel of love. In this mode, you can rise only to the perfection of awkwardness, spine twisted, legs cramped. Full-bodied communication with your boon companion can never be more than second-rate. As June Jordan said, "To tell the truth is to give birth to yourself in the world."

There are also matters to consider quite beyond one's immediate circle of deceit. Most women, especially spiritual and political Lesbians, hold a relational world view, the feeling that when we pluck a rose we disturb a star. Aware observers are understanding more and more how actions have a ripple effect, cumulative power and long-range consequences. We can apply ecological principles and general systems theory to the deep, yet delicate balance we call "the social trust." Even petty deceits litter and pollute the climate of integrity which upholds faith in the social contract. Lying is the opposite of communication, a form of counter-communication. If it is to survive in health, a living system simply must keep open to feedback, positive and negative. As you destroy feedback loops, you gradually disable the system.

In our Lesbian community who wants to feel like Alice playing croquet with the flamingo mallets? In Wonderland, everyone cheats, but why should Lesbians mimic this madness? Why should our own community, like irrational government and corporate plutocracy, also punish the honest? Juvenal could speak for those now ruling the U.S.A., "Honesty is praised and left to shiver." This, after all, is the land where national policies *require* deception. Look at the military's phobic "Don't ask, don't tell," and corporate "paper loss" tax evasion. U.S. codes of professional "ethics" function largely as shields to protect incompetent colleagues. The media glorify betrayal and feed off taffy-pulling doublespeak. Political success equals contempt for the truth in the lies of Ollie North *et al.* In Wonderland, U.S.A., to tell the truth is certainly revolutionary, so let's get on with it. The hundred nuanced varieties of the lying game—to cover up, camouflage, evade, withhold, mislead—what do these have to do with the Lesbian revolution?

When I came out as a Lesbian, I did so because finally it was more comfortable to be who I am in San Francisco than to hang up in a closet with lots of work 'n' worry outfits. Neither did I want to add my power to the legacy of false valuations with which the persecuted Lesbian has to deal. I came to feel the same about polyfidelity. We are disempowered by any Lesbian lover's cowardice to admit all her relationships. We are empowered by one lover's courage to proudly declare her body is free, her heart open and receiving.

I imagine many of you may agree with the above, "but..." But, one of the most fascinating characteristics of the human mind is our infinite capacity for rationalizing lies. A clever woman can manufacture a convenient mental reservation for any falsehood. You may have met or used one of the following five major rationalizations for lying about multiple relationships. I have (gasp) used them all myself. They may be handily grouped as 1) The Truth Does Not Exist School, 2) the Cynics Anonymous "inherent duplicity of the human species" view, 3) the Noble Lie, 4) the Mutual Deception Game, and, of course, 5) the purportedly inconsequential White Lie.

The Truth Does Not Exist School

Let us begin with The Truth Does Not Exist School, a great favorite with academics, if not with authentic intellectuals. The

School is enjoying renewed popularity since "No Truth" is the spoiled pet of the postmodern deconstructivists. It is also the ancient mode in which Pontius Pilate jested Jesus, without waiting for an answer, "Truth? What is that?" What would the world be had intelligent Pilate not believed the question of truth to be quite relative, even when it comes to torture by crucifixion? Along with the extreme deconstructivists, Pilate would likely agree that truth is merely a social production. "Truths" are held to be artificial constructions slapped together by the vagaries of the arbitrary, imprecise and shifting language of human discourse. Indeed, each religious cultist, conservative Pharisee, or imperial Roman, forms a different, limited word frame around events. Each has a differing conceptualized belief system using unique thought labels for emotional and sensory perceptions. Thus, no sophisticated person can dispute that truth is pluralistic, that truth is subjective and relational. But many deconstructivists miss other vital points in their own "no-truth" dogmatism.

One point is that truth is vastly *inter*-subjective, an interspecies production of every Earth creature, including the Earth and Universe themselves as "subjects." Hubristic humans are not the only subject bespeaking the cosmos, nor is our socially produced discourse its supreme engine. The grand subject may be universal radiance. There are eternal patterns and cycles in which we can discern a harmony, truths that exist despite us. Listen to the sound of sea, the language of season, the call of wild creature and green realm. With a larger context than deconstructivists envision, general systems theory suggests that there are certain "universal" values, requirements and movements toward satisfaction, a Tao of living systems, if you will. You need not study Taoism nor general systems theory; if you open your eyes you can see that vital, sustainable ecologies balance themselves by operating via accurate communication. Even nature's most elaborate displays of camouflage, like deceptive coloration, scent, or size are overwhelmingly used to enhance a pansexual mating game and physical prowess, not to *deny* them.

Deconstructivists also seem to confuse the vital distinction between truth and truthfulness. Perhaps for the word "truth," they could use "human perception" or "human point of view," for such an errant creature. Cyril Connolly painted point of view as a river continuously splitting into tributaries that reunite. "Islanded between the arms, the inhabitants argue for lifetimes as to which is the main river." Truthfulness, in contrast, is a regard for illumination, for verisimilitude. Ask your deconstructivist love if she values, indeed actively pursues, truthfulness from her realtor, bookkeeper, health worker, bus driver, or lover with an STD. The Pilate-old, now postmodern notion that truth telling is impossible, that there is no distinction between what is true and what is false, takes its fallacious nosedive.

"If You Don't Cheat, Your Lover Will"

Moving right along to a quick rebuttal is easy for the Cynics Anonymous' ploy that you may as well lie because everyone lies in love and war. Lesbians are a certain aristocracy in that we most emphatically do not "do what everyone does" in love, a strikingly heroic response in a phallocratic empire. Lesbians are not lemmings compelled to rush headlong into the great Mississippi of falsehood and its monogamous mud of concealment. Besides, I am not sure that "everyone" else does take this low ground. The dogmatic assertion of the fundamental duplicity of the human species is simply one metaphysical belief regarding the human condition, among many others. As such, it contains vast self-contempt and excuses untold destructiveness. It is not a statement of fact about how each unique individual always acts or should be treated, based on empirical truth.

At least one third of the world, Buddhists, take the opposite belief, that humankind is, at core, essentially unsullied, with perceptions originally able to relay what is going on, undistorted by socialized ego. Buddhists posit that we can and do learn habitual thought patterns and behaviors which may fog our mirror of light. The mirror may also be wiped clear whenever we care to notice and make the effort. No one is saying that every manner of lying can everywhere be eliminated, but each person can certainly try to reduce disguise and misdirection in her own realm. Human history is illuminated with people who continue to present their "shining original face" even in the darkest of times: natural healers, pioneer scientists, conscientious objectors, religious martyrs, racial, sexual and gender liberationists. Lying is not immutable, certainly in regard to polyfidelity, or the women of this book would not exist.

The Paternalistic Noble Lie

Leaving metaphysics, the hands-down, warmest rationalization for a love relationship cover-up is a variation on The Noble Lie. This is not quite the noble lie associated with a conflict of duty, as when one lies in a crisis to avert the injury, for example, of a persecuted innocent. Nor is it quite the "lie of conscience," sometimes based on spiritual conviction, and told for perceived public good; for example, lying to prevent panic or hoarding, or lying about one's share of the rent to enable a welfare mother to get food stamps for her children. Is honesty a duty in any system where justice and decency are irrelevant? The lover relationship noble lie, like the above, however, also relies on moral justification. We rationalize that we lie about lovers to avoid harming yet other one(s). We lie to nurture such desirables as peace, comfort, serenity and simplicity. We claim both concern and benevolence toward the deceived. What is amiss in this fictive brace of beneficence?

Let's say you are still a gambler. Do you believe that your noble lie will somehow outflank laydar™ more easily than a selfish lie? Do you believe that betrayal discovery will somehow be even less insidious because your grateful victim will wake up to forgive your lying on her behalf? Do you believe that anxiety-producing stress on yourself is of little consequence, that lying may not disagreeably affect mutual friends as unwilling co-conspirators?

Above all, can you overlook the effect of betrayal on your relationship itself? The noble lie is usually trotted out in a relationship of
extreme mutual dependence, of "significant udders," as my inter-
viewee Sara dubbed them. Here any confrontation is deeply feared,
a vision of creative conflict's growth rings seems inconceivable.
Problems are thus left unexplored. False hopes are maintained,
along with a superficial, if rigid, relational power balance. Yet,
facts do not cease to exist because they are ignored. In power
dynamics, the withholding of liaison information by the ostensibly
weaker partner can serve to make her feel "one up." Or, it can
make the seemingly stronger one feel even more powerful as a
"free agent." Any such double standard is also strategic protection
from pesky turn-about competition. How different this relationship dynamic is from the statement one poly couple made to me,
"We share a life where we try to listen and understand each other
and all the reality that flows in." Some say a fidelity lie is like a
worm destroying the blossom of love, day after day deepening
in pretense, finally to kill the tree.

There is also the matter of how dishonest sex affects the core sensuality of a relationship. Lesbians are often practitioners of sacred,
tantric sex. Sex as a sacrament must be practiced within a temple
of integrity or create a split between the sexual and the heart
chakras. Women attuned to their energy pools also understand
how much energy it takes to keep a secret. This is why secrets
often make passions go awry. To be unable to express a love energy
which nourishes us deeply is ultimately not possible. As Jeannette
Winterson's adulterer says in *Written on the Body*, "Love demands
expression. It will not stay still, stay silent, be good, be modest, be
seen and not heard, no. It will break out in tongues of praise, the
high note that smashes the glass and spills the liquid."

Despite all the foregoing ignoble spin-offs surrounding the noble
lie, the liar still declares that the real effect of her lie on the deceived is "protective." Most healthy adult lovers, however, feel such
protection is more like suffocation. Feminists would certainly call
this noble lie by its true name, "the paternalistic lie." Paternalistic

behavior, always exuding great whiffs of arrogance, is usually levied upon certain classes of people: children, the incapacitated, anyone perceived as lacking the ability to act reasonably. The coercive lies of most governments, all fascistic ones, are soaked with paternalistic justifications. They rationalize that "someday" a grateful populace will retroactively consent to all manner of manipulation and outrageous means to a mythical end. The censor is another raving paternalist. These self-appointed folk, somehow superior and incorruptible, feel they have the ability to interact with dangerous material and remain unscathed—in order to pro-scribe it for us weaker sisters. Whose goal, whether citizen or lover, is actually considered by the paternalist? How many paternalists are not actually servicing their own agenda? Paternalism is rife with the risk of exploitation of every kind. The paternalist is far, far too uncritical of her own motives and self-bias. Usually the effect of lying to "protect" someone else is amazingly self-serving and full of ongoing control mechanisms. Meanwhile the paternalis-tic lover is free to behave as she wishes, but to take no direct responsibility for the immediate or far-ranging consequences of her actions.

The deceived is deprived of the information and opportunity to take stock of her own situation and thus act in informed self-inter-est. Ignorance is not bliss. It is oblivion. The intimate of a cheater is apt to become disoriented. She correctly intuits an existing reali-ty, then is deliberately misled that her perceptions are crazed. The continually gaslighted person is likely to become more dependent, anxious, delicate and over-reactive. Then, who wants to find out later that she is perceived as an incompetent inferior, not respected enough to be able to handle the real world around her?

If your lover is some kind of child-bride, too delicate or too explo-sive to understand your preferred mode of sexuality, she needs help, not the negative, confusing fog of lies. Even if you feel she gives "implied" consent to your fraudulent monogamy and to her enforced chastity, then you do not have a comforted lover in your bed, you have a broken spirit. This ignoble paternalistic lie is merely strategic, told to advance one agenda at others' expense. May any such manipulated lover jump your fence to run with the wolves.

Mutual Deception

A more equitable and sophisticated justification for lovers' lies moves us into the complex scenario of mutually agreed upon deception. This is deception almost as theater. Because it is so common among worldlings, I've included a whole interview on it; see the next chapter, "I'll Cheat You Fair." It is mutual deception which caps Shakespeare's famous sonnet, "Therefore I lie with her, and she with me/And in our faults by lies we flattered be." How about an eye for an eye, force to counter force, and *a lie to meet the lie*, especially if both partners have agreed to each lie about seeing other people? This arrangement is a rather poignant response to the human craving for variety, yet one without "too much reality." Mutual deception combines a delicate measure of bitter tonic in a colorful *frappé*. Mutual deception mingles trust and distrust in game-like bargaining and gambling. The players prefer to play the game of deception than to confront what deception masks: pain, anger, jealousy, imperfection, insecurity.

If you are going to play the game of *mutual* deception, carefully, openly explore the pact so as not to create more pain than you are trying to assuage. Consider these

Rules of the Game for Mutual Deception

- What is the payoff? What are the mutual benefits each gains? Often, only one partner actively pushes for the pact because she is in a better position to take advantage of it with more free time, contacts, power, social skills, etc.

- How do you cut your losses? Can either partner terminate at will, speak or ask for the truth, and begin afresh? Players say mutual deception is a game very hard to call quits. How about a safe word like s/m folk use to end this war of nerves?

- What is the spillover? Must other lovers and friends act out the ruse or is their participation voluntary? Do you forfeit the right to be treated honestly in associated areas? Beware of manipulation becoming habitual.

- How *much* deceit do the rules allow? One woman believed her deceiving lover had a full-scenario, part-time job with a close "fellow worker." The "working gals" owned no business, but had stationery, phone, business card, and car—with lots of fringe benefits to go with the "overtime." Or, a woman characterized the couple living down the block as her "former lover with present lover." The "former lover" was actually her continuing lover, living with a roommate. In San Francisco, you can legally have one domestic partner, but they don't cross-reference things at City Hall, and I met one woman with three! They all know she is undomesticated, agree to part-time "deceptions," but each believes she is the trigamist's one DP.

Mutual deception can begin as a supportive lark, but often becomes rather grueling. It can become a bond painfully upheld, inconvenient and hard to terminate with grace. It usually works best for certain personalities: the theatrical, the lover of intrigue, the "adrenal personality," and the extremely private non-processor. Mutual deception requires an excellent memory and boundaries that easily recompartmentalize; one must sometimes move with alarming swiftness from lover to lover in a close call. Above all, mutual deception casts a wide net, while it usually benefits only the two principals. Other friends, acquaintances, and especially other lovers, can become compromised in embarrassing social slips, which ultimately leads to their offense or contempt.

When I tried mutual deception, I was continually struck by the question: How does this lying to sustain lovers' illusions feel different from the lying between real enemies? People who lie to me feel more like adversaries than friends. It began to get really bizarre when I wondered if telling an occasional truth was cheating in our system? I finally gave up living in this novel to write one, which I wholeheartedly recommend as more manageably and safely schizophrenic.

A less jarring course than mutual deception is mutual discretion—with right to limited, but relevant facts — which brings us to....

The White Lie

The final type of cover most rationalized in the rondelet of love is the sweet song of the little "white lie." It is billed as too trivial and harmless to be of any moral import. Less poetic polyfidèles may take the absolutist position which prohibits all lies, period. I am reminded, however, of Agatha Christie's comment, "If one sticks rigidly to one's principles, one would see hardly anybody." Truly, I have not yet met any of this purist set. I imagine most of us have told enough white lies to ice a cake. I am afraid I will still be licking my fingers on Judgment Day.

The socially pleasant, small lie seems almost necessary to stay afloat and navigate in this world, among lovers, anyway. A feather of inaccuracy may save a deadweight of explanation and justification.

If one defines the white lie as one which benefits its hearer more than its teller, which never diminishes its recipient's power, dignity or integrity, then social lies do seem fairly harmless, if not benevolent. In polyfidelity, the truth is clearly told that one indeed has or may want to take, other lovers. Then all information *useful* to the relationship is shared. Here, our social lie may "soften" information without misrepresenting it, as in the query: "Do you ever use the same pet names with XX?" Answer, "Oh yes, and if you keep inspiring me, I'm going to start writing them down to sell to the phone sex people." The flip, the sugar coating, the embellishment, the polite evasion, the careful euphemism, the calculated minimization or exaggeration... These truth stretches are not meant to injure anyone, to gain unfair advantage by violating the rights and powers of their hearer.

It is the motive which gives character to the lie. Is the social lie's motive altruistic or self-serving or harmful? Again, be careful of self-bias if you play with the thousand and one shadings of the white, pearl, gray, and silvered lie. We tend to be extraordinarily self-flattering and simplistic in ascribing what are often mixed motives to white lies we tell. Watch that the lie of convenience does not actually become the lie of self-protection. By and large, however, the labyrinth of social intercourse, with its intricacies of integrity, leads me personally to accept those social lies by which I "may be beguiled, but not betrayed," as Lucretius put it, and to offer the same.

Private: Do Not Enter

In interviewing polyfidelitous women, a useful, even essential, concept often comes up as an excellent alternative to white lies: our splendid right to privacy. Privacy is patrician while shame is bourgeois. Privacy is the realm of the "special." Poor shame is acrawl with anxieties and excuses. Shame is a bruise on the victim by some disapproving "authority." Shame is usually darkened with secrecy, a powerful component in dishonest adultery. Secrecy binds errant lovers to one another in exciting roles of intrigue, while the noninvolved spouse is distanced from their daring, secret club. Privacy is easily distinguished from secrecy in that a secret is evidence concealed from a person whose life is being directly affected by it. Secrets can disempower and destroy when they censor useful information from a person with valid interests in a matter. It takes deliberate intent and action in order to conceal a secret. A secret path is camouflaged, whereas a private path posts but a discreet sign.

Privacy is the spacious, quiet, restful area of our own which is the business only of the principal(s) involved. It is of no "social concern." For example, since I am writing a sex book, you may legitimately inquire about my orientations, standards or qualifications.

But what I literally do in bed and with whom is privileged, private information available only to intimates involved. Privacy is precious and special, a balm to the soul, independent, free, safe, uncluttered by outsiders' baggage. Publicity, with its tariff of insincerity, is one of the most exhausting things in life. The truly rich and powerful pay enormously, without quibble, for privacy. Inaccessibility is a hallmark of power. In final irony, privacy becomes the most sought after luxury of the celebrity.

In polyfidelity, the invocation of privacy is probably the best alternative to any form of white lie. Lady Privacy gently replies to a doomed sexual query: "No comment." Among polyfidèles, the question regularly comes up, "Does one reserve the rigors of truth telling only for serious affairs and ongoing relationships, but keep the no fallout, one-night stand in the realm of privacy?" My counter question would again take a utilitarian focus. What could possibly be the *purpose* of recounting the fact of a casual dalliance? There could, of course, be many motives to tell, ranging from delight and pride to shame and revenge, but are they congruent with useful speech? One should explore the factor of honor here too. Are you betraying a private intimacy, or do you have your casual lover's explicit permission to become grist in the gossip machine? Compassion is as much a part of integrity as honesty. Compassion asks you to consider how much others' feelings are billed for your total, raw honesty. Clear process does not mean that you always tell everyone every little bedtime story—unless you are sworn monogamous and need—what? Absolution? Especially if never questioned about a fling, why in the world subject anyone to compulsive disclosure? Admit to yourself that sexual encounters are often sheer, trifling frivolity. Frivolity has its own value, but swollen with meaning it is not. Perhaps the greatest truthfulness is admitting to your own soul that you are riddled with all kinds of folly. Frivolity can be the froth of life. I hope it sparkles with affection. Drink or blow it from the cup, but why belabor it? Just praise the Goddess you've come out polyfidèle and are not soiling any short, monogamous tether.

The easiest questions to dispense with, of course, are from mere acquaintances prospecting for gossip about your Sapphic traffic. Acquaintances, unlike devoted friends and intimates, do not have your interests at heart. They have little claim on your truths. The Japanese have no word for "hypocrisy." They cannot imagine why one's private and public world should jibe. My rule of thumb is the old Erasmus adage, "It is safe to admit nothing that may embarrass one if repeated." So my stock reply to the inquisitive acquaintance is "Ah…only poets kiss and tell, and I am but a freelance journalist." Overt or veiled poly insults can also be a hook for gossip. In response, I compose my facial muscles into the "knowing smile," one which suggests I know all the exquisite details my baiter never will, and say, "How kind of you to mention that." Another nice generic judo line is the open-ended, "Is it so?" repeated often with "ahs" and nods. Let those who reap the so-called rewards of celebrity endure exposure probes, prying, and personal questions. Let them call defensive press conferences regarding intimate acts performed in private by consenting adults. Meanwhile, in aristocratic privacy, gaily carry on as you please.

When it comes to heart friends and especially love intimates, the old Erasmus rule still holds when you are asked to satisfy one lover's anxious curiosity without betraying the privacy of another. Unfortunately, in this country, we are under the bizarre notion that personal information should be distributed as a reward or withheld as punishment. I myself am one of the most curious women alive. My first-grade teacher once said to me in exasperation, "How can you be so inquisitive?" I immediately asked, "What's inquisitive?" I have since learned that social curiosity can be a dangerous game, one that requires good sportsmanship and discipline. When tempted to ask for privileged information, I now try to ask myself first, "Is there any *useful* reason knowing this?" One of my loves has helped me a great deal. When I ask the unspeakable, she simply "fails" to hear it. If I don't catch on and repeat the invasive query, she is apt to remark, "Oh, dear, what can I say?" Her query usually provokes a response from me. I may proceed to tell her in detail what I need to hear. This usually clears most things up without a shade of revelation on her part. I am usually asking her to tell me how wonderful I am and not to worry. She does.

I also learned from one of my most dramatic loves how a meaningful smile turneth away sticky words. The smile is infinitely more complex than tears, especially backlit in golden silence. Upon interrogation, my love's smiles come in: demure, dignified, patient, puzzled, sad/little, shocked, and weary. If I keep blundering on, she cocks her head, adds a mock "hands up" gesture, or possibly a glance both ways as crossing the information highway. She may follow her privacy smiles with a sympathetic, even searching look toward me. I have to be careful here, since this one look is apt to elicit startling information—from me. Maybe what they mean by "a noble silence" is learning to accept a quiet smile with good grace.

As there are coping alternatives to lying in love, there are also ways of making truths gently useful, not harshly barren. Foremost among these ways are the subtle, yet powerful sisters of timing and tact. No woman needs to be told at the very last moment that you are leaving on a long, romantic vacation with another woman, effectively barring her from compensatory arrangements and valid input. On the other hand, what woman needs to be told this possibly dismaying fact on the day she's also been harassed at work, sprained an ankle, and lost her cat? Watch for a good or better time to set a calmly focused scene. Then, using the balm of tact and reassurance, tell her your truths. Do anything to create a safe emotional field. When anxiety is high, all resources appear scarce.

Like any art, truth telling often takes ground work and time. Truth is like an enduring creative act, whereas lying tends to be a short-term fix, patched and repatched. Setting the scene and choosing the right word is only the beginning. One must allow enough time for the disclosure to sink in, for possible angers and pain to surface. The speaker should prepare herself to take heat and share pain until final resolution, if not acceptance. If the truth teller also gets angry for even one minute, it can take additional hours or days to deal with the consequences of her ill-considered outburst.

Raw, Spontaneous "Honesty"

Why not recognize that "truth telling" is more encompassing and richly textured than "honesty?" The concept of truth telling, distinguished from impulse honesty, goes a long way to ameliorating the old moral conflict of honesty vs. kindness. Lies break the heart, so can honesty. As Isak Dinesen observed, "Many people interpret truth in a negative sense: the person who does not lie tells the truth. So they go to their grave without ever having told a lie and without any idea at all of what the truth is." Hit-and-run honesty can sacrifice wider meaning and usefulness, often to coerce another woman to change, rather than emerge as an authentic attempt to clarify the speaker's position and identity.

Here is one type of sweeping, impulsive "honest" statement which probably covers up various realities and other valid ideals: "I like XX because she is so much more adventurous than you are." XX may also be more irresponsible, more stupid, or more malleable. Or, XX may indeed be purely more adventuresome with no negative sidebar. But what is the payoff for the "honest" comparison? To get two adventurous girlfriends by shaming one? Try again. Use specifics. "It gives me wonderful, stabilizing roots that we have a tranquil base and routines I can count on with you, but do you think we could try white-water rafting, the Lesbian sex club, guerrilla art on billboards, fire walking, etc." If still "Nope," spare her the honest opinion, then go out and make adventures until you need her to relax with.

I think most polyfidèles would ask only that you run this William Blake couplet through your loom before you express that forthright "honesty":

> *A truth that's told with bad intent*
> *Beats all the lies you can invent.*

Please do not be discouraged if truth telling in poly is arduous. So is managing that spider sac of lies, remember? If a truth can break the heart, more often it is the lie which does. Which wound takes longer to heal?

As Adrienne Rich wrote,

> *"An honorable human relationship—that is, one in which two people have the right to use the word 'love'—is a process, delicate, violent, often terrifying to both persons involved, a process of refining the truths they can tell each other... It isn't that to have an honorable relationship with you, I have to understand everything, or tell you everything at once, or that I can know, beforehand, everything I need to tell you. It means that most of the time I am eager, longing for the possibility of telling you. That these possibilities may seem frightening, but not destructive, to me. That I feel strong enough to hear your tentative and groping words. That we both know we are trying, all the time, to extend the possibilities of truth between us."*

Cuckoldery Clues

Offered in Penitence from My Own Days as Love's Double Agent

Trust your gut feelings and the Lesbian laydar™ on the right side of your brain which suggest your lover is fooling around or intends to. Whereas lie detectors are accurate far less than 25% of the time, Lesbian laydar™ is at least 90% efficient. The remaining 10% error factor is probably lust projection or a dusty crystal. Because humans have fairly predictable patterns, any change in typical personal habits and a schedule always flashes on the laydar™ screen.

Note the following bodily qualities of a lie. Smoothies do none of these things, but may leave a vapor trail of strange pheromones, soap, perfume, etc.

Eyes often avoid contact.

Smiles are less frequent. Real smiles create crinkly laugh lines around the eyes. Forced smiles do not.

Hands touch the face more when lying. Practiced liars keep hands hidden.

Voice may rise and end in questions. A voice may sound inappropriate to the occasion: too eager and urgent or too casual and restrained. Liars tend to sigh.

Diminished physical accessibility. Your lover is likely home less. There may be increased evening work and out-of-town trips. She begins to speak of "creating a more independent life."

Diminished psychic accessibility. This ranges from preoccupation and distance to obvious withdrawal. Moods may then swing into overly attentive relating. There can be a lower threshold of irritability with subtle or direct complaints—or uncharacteristic cheerfulness, including musical outbursts.

Unusual interest in grooming, clothes, weight, perfumes. Diminished sexual action—or just the opposite! Arousal is often accompanied by sudden variety in sexual repertoire, new toys, receptivity to erotic media.

Uncharacteristic offers to wash car, prepare dinner; accompanied by a flurry of presents, a.k.a. "guilt gifts."

Sudden interest in doing errands or walking the dog in order to make a private phone call or cruise by a new lover's home.

Often financially broke and "can't figure out where the money goes." Credit card receipts from unusual stores, restaurants, hostelries.

She describes having sexual fantasies about other women and asks if you do, a.k.a. "testing the waters."

Strange telephone calls, relative to what is normal in the household, of course. Incoming calls may take on a signal quality with sequential ringing or frequent hang-ups. Calls are often quickly terminated, *sotto voce*. Any itemized phone bill (*flagrante telephono*) is a snap to check, by the way. Use the name and address service in most large cities; ask your local operator. Or, use the criss cross directory—phone number to address—available in large public libraries. To get the cut of her jib, you may want to make the mystery lady a "survey call." Promise her a gift for her cooperation and address in answering "survey" questions. Do send a nice gift. A deal's a deal.

When confronted, your partner accuses you of being paranoid or involved yourself (projection).

Worst line when discovered, "I love you, but I'm not in love with you."

Best line when discovered, "Touch my breasts!"

How to Attract Truth Telling in Polyfidelity

Key: practice truth telling yourself.

Respect every confidence shared with you this side of bodily torture.

Go on record at least one hundred times that: The details of any intimate act performed in private by consenting adults are absolutely no one else's business. New lovers will feel safer with you, and you will not be expected to relate or receive scarlet stories.

Understand that a lover who is trying to tell you a difficult truth is respecting your power, rights and feelings, as well as honoring the long-term bond of trust you are both creating as passionate friends.

It takes two for the truth to be known: the speaker and the listener. Which is the more difficult role?

Note the most widespread lie is "I love you." It can also be the greatest truth. The most damaging lie is "Us" vs. "Them."

Take the care of a baby-bird-in-hand as you receive a lover's truth telling:

- Avoid critical, judgmental manhandling of a revelation.

- Resist the urge to spout advice. Do not try to "fix" what for you, an outsider, is too intricate for words.

- Marshall all your humor and self-acceptance to avoid being overly sensitive or dependent on anyone else's subjective, sometimes self-interested "honesty."

- Avoid jumping to conclusions, polarizing or taking sides. Her truths may change radically, so don't pin yourself down while she keeps moving. Today's lyrical love or corkscrew conflict may go *vice versa* tomorrow.

- Avoid any interruptions except for clarity. Truths are born in pregnant pauses.

"I'll Cheat You Fair"
A Closet Drama

This interview with Celine is about a polyfidelitous relationship characterized by that tart twist on honor called "mutual deception." Celine sent the interview to the other principal, Mara, at my suggestion. I hoped to interweave the supple tissues of memory. No response.

CW: Celine, when I first met you, you said that you took an instant aversion to monogamy. Why?

Celine: It saved me a lot of time *(laughing)*. Mainly, I'm uncomfortable with any doctrine like monogamy that is highly other-directed, rather than self-generated, self-directed, and self-evolving. Go ahead, be a patrioteer, or believer in Leviticus decrees, or an efficiency expert—but let your way be sufficient unto itself. Please don't tyrannize those of us who make other choices based on our own unique experiences and talents. Pure monogamy, not remotely prevalent, looks to me, where it even exists, like a full-blown fetish for one person. Okay. Just don't assume all of us should have that kink. I'll choose my own fetish; maybe it's the one called passion.

CW: Do your partners feel okay about your taking other lovers? Do you usually live together?

Celine: Well, I've lived with, let's see, four beautiful lovers over a couple of decades. Only Jeanne, my present live-in love, laughs at monogamy, but then she's French and a love child. We've lived and loved together for six years, refining the fires. Jeanne and I both take lovers and tell the other. When we first began, however, it was raggedy, especially when I fell in love with another woman, Mara, soon after Jeanne and I had met and moved in together.

CW: That was fast.

Celine: I suppose the moving in together tossed up my independence issues, as the therapists say. Plus my alchemy with Mara
fused like electric perfume. Most crucial, the practicalities
seemed in place. Mara was in a long-term, non-live-in relationship. She wanted some action and didn't care that I also loved
Jeanne and made a home with her. Besides, Mara smelled like
deep, worldly unlacings. Many decisions in my life are aromatic.

CW: Sounds like a nice bouquet, balanced.

Celine: It almost was, except that there was something out of kilter
for our three years together. Mara felt that she could never tell
her lover Heidi that I stayed with her every Saturday night and
all other times we could work in. She said Heidi would leave her
or overprocess the issue into a lifetime of utter misery. So we had
a vehicle for our relationship, but one wheel, Heidi, was connected only to Mara. This pulled Mara off, and sometimes we
careened, rather stupidly. I wonder if that wheel is still spinning.

CW: So you knew from the beginning that Mara could handle only
a hidden passion? You don't seem like a light under a bushel.

Celine: In the beginning, I didn't care. I was in the fugue of high
romance, etherized in bliss. The danger that Heidi would find
out added to the spice. I figured she would discover us someday,
then we would all just open up the form and roll along. I'm a
mutable sign. The secrecy also constructed strong boundaries
around our affair. We couldn't spend days in bed while everything else drifted. Heidi might enter any moment from the
wings. I'm goal oriented, so in one sense the boundaries worked
for me—as well as excited me.

CW: Did you feel guilty about duping Heidi?

Celine: Oh, I had my scruples, but they didn't stop me. I watched
myself almost as in a laboratory, experimenting with honor and
betrayal, lies and truths. At first, I was so afraid of Jeanne's hurt
and anger that I couldn't honestly wish *our* honesty on anyone!
Later, after Jeanne and I relaxed, what really became controlling

was an exquisite, paradoxical twist which Mara had worked out long beforehand with Heidi. It was to rule us. She and Heidi had a co-deceptive agreement regarding other lovers: "Our only sin is to lie poorly." They had both pledged not only utter discretion, but to actually lie when confronted with queries about another lover.

CW: Ah! The labyrinth of negative communication.

Celine: Mara may be the truest sophist/sapphist I've ever known. Her profession as a therapist is, after all, to use words to deconstruct words and "realities." She described herself to me in an early letter as a cool, chameleon-like creature merging into others' environments, changing as they did. She said this "skink" (shrink?) is most noted for her independent eye rotation, which provides her with alternating perspectives. The skink reorients herself quickly, depending on which eye and object she is favoring. Each perspective produces different behaviors. Most of the letter was about how, shall we say, she liked my warmth, which I thought was charming at the time.

CW: Did Heidi reorient herself as smoothly?

Celine: Well, as a hairstylist and dancer, I suppose she had the potential. But she often confided in Mara about her own lovers not working out. So it was kind of a three-legged agreement— or else maybe Heidi's affairs were idyllic, so she put up a smoke screen? The two women had agreed, after all, "Spare me facts, give me fiction."

CW: You said when Jeanne discovered your involvement she was not pleased.

Celine: Whew! She was hurt and she was furious. She didn't care if I had occasional recreational sex. When we first met, I was being sexual with a friend, which continued. Plus, I had told Jeanne from the first that I would never be faithful to anyone sexually. I promised I would try to be loyal, dependable and delightful in every other way. This is my code. She said fine and saw other women herself.

I, however, fell for Mara passionately, the real ju-ju. Initial infatuation tends to be one-pointed, so I wasn't terribly available for Jeanne. I felt like a jerk, hurting Jeanne, who had weapons herself, so I got hurt too. I began to think I needed to escape the whole living-together situation. Jeanne had to contend with a live-in romancer in the throes of delight as well as in the guilt and angst of distancing. Passion is the test of absolute maturity, and I am far from master. At least, I wasn't ready for an audience. Who in a manic episode is?

CW: Did you wonder if Jeanne would leave you?

Celine: Oh yes, because one of the most desirable women of my life and I had broken up over a *misalliance* of mine. Besides, Jeanne and I had a short history together, only six months. I was waiting for the other boot to drop. Perhaps one thing that saved us is that Jeanne is a painter, and she had built a fine studio in our home. A friend of mine said that it's harder to find a good studio than a good lover in San Francisco, so not to worry. But I twisted in the wind, feeling terribly mean about hurting Jeanne, yet unable, really unwilling, to fall out of passion with Mara.

CW: The pain of delight.

Celine: Well, suffering is not my game, but as a last ditch hope, I agreed to the most nerve-racking nostrum of all: to see a couples counselor with Jeanne. I also agreed not to see Mara for a month.

CW: Did it help?

Celine: Oh lord, first we had to interview a bevy of Lesbian therapists to make sure they didn't pathologize nonmonogamy, since no one in our little set was of the genus monogamous. Many therapists do pathologize nonmonogamy. Mara, however, got me a list of possible therapists, since this is her own successful professional specialty: Lesbian couples-counseling.

CW: *(laughing)* There should be decency limits on irony.

Celine: It gets even better. Meanwhile, neither Jeanne nor I had much faith in Lesbian psychotherapy as it's so expensively over-practiced. We, however, got a fine person. She was a merry, philosophical, calm presence. During the sessions, I really admired Jeanne for her spirit, eloquence, even the way she threw things. That therapist could duck.

CW: How long did you stay in therapy?

Celine: Not that long, maybe three months. What we enjoyed most and learned from was going out to dinner after therapy. We finally decided to just have a special dinner each week and a good time. Meanwhile this time had given us the opportunity to develop mutual respect and appreciation for one another, including our foibles. I recognized that Jeanne is a thoroughbred, a long-distance runner. We began to learn how to give one another a big meadow.

CW: Did all go as well with Mara?

Celine: Much of the time, yes. We are vastly different personalities, which fires passion. She is a dominator from the dominance/submission school. I'm a top, expelled from all schools. So we each had something to rub up against. Mara's postmodern, I'm still a romantic. I'm poor—if you can ever consider an artist poor—and Mara's wealthy and generous with her money. I do like white satin pajamas. Mara's a great conversationalist, a good lover. Her irreverence matches mine. I suppose I have more pride. I am proud of my pluralistic lifestyle, my aesthetic, my lovers and friends. Mara's motto is: "Act freely but in secret."

CW: Shades of "Don't tell. Don't ask. Don't pursue"? How did you personally have to collude in her agenda—besides not to go to Heidi and declare place?

Celine: Well, you must realize I truly wanted Heidi quite safely in place. Mara needs a lot from a lover, but I was with Jeanne much of the time and often into my writing, other work and

99

politics. I got nervous when Heidi left Mara because Mara would not share Heidi's mortgage or allow her more time. Mara never called her or processed anything. Heidi came back on the old terms. I was surprised, but quite relieved.

One splinter of duplicity for me was that I had to vaporize whenever Mara checked-in by phone with Heidi, which was at least twice a day. I called it her "electronic leash." We could be, say, in the alpenglow of lovemaking, and Mara would jump up to make a mundane call to Heidi, lying about who I thought we were, obliterating our warmth and intimacy. Watch sheets turn to alpen ice. I realize therapists learn to touch and go, concentrate and detach, a nice skill in many ways. Since I tend to have semipermeable membranes, I was both fascinated and shocked.

CW: Did you ever want to meet Heidi?

Celine: Not unless she knew who I was and where I, uh, fit. I did run into her, however, at the most appropriate event imaginable. Mara and I had tickets to the opening of "Portrait of a Marriage," the great Vita Sackville-West and Violet Trefusis fourplex film. I am a cross between Violet and Harold, I think. It turned out at the last minute that Heidi fell into disarray, so Mara had to be with her instead. And Heidi wanted to see "Portrait of a Marriage." I decided to go anyway, since I had been counting on seeing it and already had tickets.

I saw Mara and Heidi come walking up the ticket line. Heidi was tucked into Mara's down-jacketed arm like a small bird. Their tableau, this deep protective bond, etched into my consciousness. Passion is only a shooting star by comparison. Mara saw me, looked agitated but in control and pulled Heidi tighter from my view. I tipped my bowler hat to them and turned to face the wind.

CW: What if Heidi had just dropped over to Mara's when you were there?

Celine: She wasn't allowed to have keys, only the electronic leash.

Besides she lived in another county. But the electronic chokechain meant Mara and I couldn't travel without leaving elaborate cover-ups and check-ins for Heidi. Sometimes Mara would have to rush home from our getaways to comfort Heidi in crises. When I had crises of my own, Mara would be unavailable unless all suspicions could be neutralized. The therapist made *some* house calls, but not others. When I had a lumpectomy, I wanted to be able to reach Mara anywhere, even at Heidi's, pretending of course to be a client. Mara would not give me Heidi's number. Always family fictions first. I easily got Heidi's number elsewhere, but never did use it.

I'm a pretty low-maintenance lover, plus I have a circle of real friends and confidantes. I don't mind being a contingent lover, but I began to want to change the secret, rigid boundaries. I also realized that Mara, as a therapist, was sick of hearing about everyone's problems as well as usually working on Heidi's. I was to be her "fun" gal. She loved this riddle I told her: "Your wife and your mistress are each clutching the edge of a crumbling cliff. You can save only one. Who will you save? Answer: Your wife, because your mistress will understand."

CW: How did your friends relate to all of this?

Celine: Well, we originally had entirely separate social circles and then different tastes in friends, so there were very few women who ever met both Heidi and me. One couple who were themselves poly, psychiatrist friends of Mara's, had met us both and found it all very amusing. For Mara's birthday one year, they gave her seven pairs of beautifully air-brushed cotton panties, each reading one day of the week with the name of the woman Mara regularly saw that day. I was "Celine, Saturday," and "Celine, Sometimes Thursday." Sundays and Wednesdays were painted with "Heidi." Mara's racquetball partner, Liana, who was always used as my courtly cover-up, was memorialized by "Liana, Friday." Friday, they actually did play, though Heidi was told Saturday was racquetball with Liana as a ruse. To maintain

family fictions, Mara had to dispose of the "Heidi" panties, so
she gave them to me, cotton control panel and all. This was too
bizarre to handle, so I gave the panties to my beautiful acupuncturist whose name is Heidi, whom I sometimes saw
on Wednesdays.

CW: So you never left any trail, or is it tail?

Celine: *(laughing)* They call me the silver fox. Before I had always
left a few clothes and cosmetics at a lover's; it's a bother to
remember what to bring and to lug things around on the bus.
All had to be scrupulously hidden at Mara's so Heidi of the
Sunday night panties wouldn't see my Saturday's. When I left
for home on Sunday afternoon, there was a humiliating inspec-
tion, wherein we carefully removed any strand of my visible
presence, especially these long silver hairs. My photo was hidden
face down, and Heidi's went up again. After a couple of years,
I got queasy watching the obliteration, so I sat outside as the
weekend was being clear-cut.

CW: Great space wars.

Celine: Once I had a sort of waking dream: the four of us, Jeanne
and Heidi, Mara and I sat around a green baize gaming table.
Who would win the Queen of Hearts when the Joker is wild?
Who indeed was the Queen of Hearts? Now I will ask you. You
see these four masked Lesbians at play. Because we are fortunate
and adept Lesbians, we played in a rich casino blessed by Our
Lady. It is the kind of place where Higher Selves brush by their
players with perfumed sleeves, gently touching a shoulder, kissing a neck, hoping a player may notice their presence.

I introduce you first to Jeanne, whom we call the Sky Painter.
She, you will admit, is the most sporting because pluralism was
never the passion play she came to attend at the casino. She
came to love and to gambol with one of the Lesbians, the one
who gambles inveterately with hearts. Still, the Sky Painter
plays, even when the stakes are dangerously high. Sometimes

she plays a furious hand, sometimes a generous one, thereby stepping up the passion. It's a big sky.

Next there is the Soul Sifter, a skilled and delighted player. She is loved by two of the players, one who can sometimes look her in the roving eye, as well as the one who sits very closely beside her. In her day job as croupier, the Soul Sifter is privileged to observe hundreds of such highly stylized games. She is tempered to carefully weigh the various cost-benefit ratios in her hand and has developed a system which brings in what she needs. When the Joker is wild, she bets low or waits out the hand. She plays for amusement, ecstasy is beyond her limit.

Then we have the Dancer, an enigmatic, graceful player. She, like the Sky Painter, is swept up in a game she never choreographed, but did choose. The Dancer plays despite a profound handicap: many of her cards are not what they seem, nor can she even see two of the players! She can see and loves the Soul Sifter who sits next to her, keeping her from being too distraught by the game's bluffs and feints. The Dancer carefully discards the images she can see, sometimes waivers, but parlays high cards to win. She takes many intermissions, dancing in lace, which is, after all, the art of the hole.

Finally, there is the adventurous Scribe, the oldest player at this game, yet the least cautious. The Scribe devotedly loves two of the players, so she wants to play on and on, far past her own bedtime. A typical bipolar, she wins big and loses big, birthing and dying in her own flame. If she understood what the game meant, there would be no point in writing circles about it, artist of wholes.

We have reached the moment when one player is finally willing to toss in her vast fortune cookie, to open its "secret script." This would effectively end the game for this particular foursome, whether she herself wins or loses. Let's say you are invited to make a side bet, whose hand is best? The Joker is wild.

CW: Oh dear, it's not exactly the "Joy Luck Club." I think whoever lost here would win.

Celine: I gave Mara the parable. She replied simply that no one
ever leaves the green baize table. She said the question for the
risk-taker here is really whether the game will continue "with
pleasing tension and respect" or will deteriorate into a post-
game revealing the blank surfaces of everyone's cards. She asked
why a stylized and dignified exchange should turn into embittered volleys of the disillusioned? Mara, as a postmodern player,
said she believes value, and consequently love, reside entirely in
the imagination, in attribution, mirroring and bluff. There is no
game possible once the cards are revealed. Her only determina-
tion is to avoid this horror. She concluded that we can, however,
choose whether Kali will be a card or a co-player.

CW: You should try the "Marvelous Mah-jongg Game." I think
Kwan-Yin is your co-pilot.

Celine: *(laughing)* Too much fun. We decided on Kali——in the form
of couple-counseling—AAARGH! Mara and me! How would you
like to have not one, but two, therapists battling for your soul?

CW: You must be crazy!

Celine: Quite, but what can you do in a mid-wife crisis? I would
try anything to help Mara tell Heidi and persuade Mara to stay,
playing the designated alpha mate. In the office, the therapy
pros carefully sniffed around each other. Mara enjoyed the sessions enormously because she said it was great to unload her
problems, rather than slosh around in everyone else's. She wanted more appreciation for being "caretaker," providing the
house, her paid housekeeper's services, any car transportation,
travel and dining expenses. She did give me vast credit for "special effects." While Mara basked in the attention, I shriveled.
I liked the other therapist's eyes, but I felt humiliated, a closet
collaborator, a sex covert. Who could love a half-truth?

We each felt the therapist favored our own particular side of the
honesty conflict, which says something for her diplomacy and our
projection. I was pleased that she had a neat label for our frenzied
activity around Heidi: "maintaining the illusion of primacy."

Jeanne had given me a simple golden ring before we began our therapy together to symbolize a vision of wholeness or purpose we might share. I guess I was again crying for a vision. Mara kept saying, "This is as good as it gets."

After a particularly grueling session, I up and left—Heidi. I decided that one solution would be to simply leave the wretched codependent relationship I had with a total stranger. Super-co! Whereas Heidi's every move and conflict had been my concern, Heidi never worried about me in the slightest, couldn't possibly wish me well. In fact, I didn't really know her either, only my projections from Mara's introjections. I realized what a fudpucker I'd been to watch videos of Heidi dancing, listen to her on the answering machine, dutifully co-diagnose her actions and problems.

I certainly wouldn't forbid Mara to discuss Heidi, since she was a key player in her life, but I never asked about her again. When she came up, I didn't react, ask questions, invest energy. I listened. When Mara talked about Heidi, she was talking about herself in many ways.

CW: So you got rid of Heidi?

Celine: It seemed so. Best breakup I ever had. No loneliness. No one was mad at me. Sometimes I felt a ghostly smile. Then, after an especially nice weekend fling, Mara unexpectedly flashed me "Heidi" in print. She proudly showed me a letter she had written to the daily newspaper publicly joining Heidi's and her name. Heidi had nothing to do with the letter, disliked it, but let it go. It related to an issue I pointed out to Mara over the Sunday paper during one of our weekend lovefests.

In itself, it was nothing. But the underground cable snapped, and I knew I was through censoring, disempowering myself. One reason I am on this Earthwalk is be aloud. So the lying fields were my killing fields. When I slipped my photo from its sad little halfway house, Mara went into dominator mode. I seemed to hear the refrain of an old country and western song:

"You gotta know when to hold 'em, Know when to fold 'em, Know when to walk away, And know when to run…"

I ran from Shamelot. I packed up my hidden cache of cosmetics, leaving only the finger cots to fickle fate. I wrote across the huge bathroom mirror in silvered soap: "May all your illusions of primacy come true. Love, Celine." I hung the "Celine, Sometimes Thursday" panties on the mirror's top corner.

Mara waited in the living room to drive me to the dark streetcar tunnel where I was to be dumped in a fit of pique. I, however, left our backstairs romance by the backdoor, bucked over the fence and down the hills. Exhilaration. I had gone about a mile when Mara drove up. She yelled only: "Fuck you, you son of a bitch!" and drove off in a cloud of carbon monoxide, leaving me on the edge of the freeway. I enjoyed the "fuck" part and being the son of a butch after all.

CW: Did you ever see her again?

Celine: I waited a season to see if she would, just once, offer her hand. Then, I'm an activist; I contacted her three times, which is the number of times the faerie people make a request. I missed her, Violet to Vida. Devastatio. I would have tried to work out a way of being where we didn't have to lie to anyone. I could outlove her, that was my strong suit in our game of chance. Meanwhile, my self-value was blooming like a perfumed garden. It was so fine not to be serving coffee and doughnuts at the "Rescue from Reality Mission." Jeanne was great. I could grieve openly, if not lugubriously. Mara's fragrance began to blend into the sky.

CW: So she never responded to your faerie overtures?

Celine: It was no process, no access. She was true to to a comment she once made that if I ever violated the secret form or left, she would have no liaison, laughter or friendship with me. I discounted such clear indications of pretensive love on Mara's part. In some ways, an exquisite forgery, using many of love's words and symbols so well. People betray us by carefully hiding how little they care.

One thing happened which amused me by being so inevitable. One of Jeanne's lovers decided she wanted to process being sexual as a teen with her family's gardener. She unwittingly chose Mara as her therapist. Her current garden, of course, burst forth in all its local color. Mara instructed this woman to confide all in her, but to reveal to intimates nothing going on in therapy sessions. Still the Great Editor. Jeanne's lover was too much the dramatist to narrow her audience, so she decamped.

CW: Do you miss Mara at all?

Celine: Oh, a few things. The perfect moments. The possibilities. The insouciant sex and sensibility. I suppose I have the quality of never quite falling out of love, being ever captivated by a special fragrance on the wind. We three told the truth as well as we could at the time, but we each lied to ourselves. Because a woman lies about certain things does not mean she does not have truths to tell. Mara made me more fruitful. What better can you receive of a lover—or a therapist?

Besides, I rather like unrequited love. It can last so much longer than the other kind.

I guess one lover, Jeanne, gave me a special courage, and Mara gave me a special fear—both of which I need to be on my way. The whole experience fulfilled itself for me as a kind of initiation, I suppose. And, I'm lucky, Jeanne and I are extraordinarily happy, and I'm with other lovers who are open and welcoming as sunshine. Isn't a love affair ideal when one makes contact with her highest ideals, if not at first, at last?

Now, I can also marvel at the paradox of my own folly. I didn't fully understand that to be loyal, faithful to myself, I cannot necessarily be loyal to a beloved. An ironic thing was that Mara and I had flip-side fears. Mara's greatest fear is of being seen in love, mine is of not being seen. In any event, I got away with it.

CW: Never being discovered by Heidi!

Celine: No. I got away with loving Mara. The perfect crime.

Polyfidelity 101
Questions and Answers

The remainder of *Lesbian Polyfidelity* responds to questions my survey respondents most frequently posed, our discussions of double-digit dilemmas. There has been little intelligent re-conceptualization of the "The Lesbian Relationship" in our few decades of openness, so please don't expect "author"-itarian answers on polyfidelity here. Oh, and time for the obligatory disclaimer to my dear present and future lovers: As you do not expect a professor of trigonometry to be a triangle, please do not expect a professor of polyfidelity to be polyperfect.

We Lesbians will refine polyfidelity as we've done the Boston Marriage, butch/fem roles, and mighty monogamy. My beginning poly volley is exploratory and happily idiosyncratic. Here we offer awarenesses as we have lived issues. You can't buy wisdom, based on dear experience that it is, for fifteen dollars, but here is a nudge of hope and a wink in the right direction. All you may have to change is the way you think, feel and behave, so invent yourself as you go. For polyfidelity to maximize pleasure and minimize social wounding, I'm sure there will be means more skillful, ways more appropriate, and analysis more cogent, so send in your tips, and I'll do a polysequel. Meantide, in responding to the wonderful women who contacted me, I turned for inspiration to the newly discovered *Woman's Book of Changes, The Nous Ching. The Nous Ching* tweaks the old *Chi Ting: Manual of Monogamy.*

Query: How may I present polyfidelity in this life and in this book without premature endings and false middles? In answer, I threw:

PENTAGRAM #555: *Mo'an,* Wise Folly

ABOVE: Ho – Fire, Sun Seed in Mother of Pearl

BELOW: Hum – The Earth, Glittering Darkness

THE JUDGMENT: None, Praise the Goddess

THE IMAGE: Darkness melts before striking rivers of fire

Shock! The Arousing. Welcome to non-prophet status. Fumbling words and fingers bring success. In the moon-tower of the jeweled palace, the Superior Woman makes herself into her own hero. Ha! The monkey of merriment kisses the golden phoenix. Smack! Polyfidelity is a leveraged buyout, the promissory note in every fortune cookie. Perseverance furthers, so does silver. Ho! Backstairs sex, the abyss. Lovers can be a false path. Then again, it depends on where you are going. Compost and grow on. Polyfidelity is a bridge of hair over a chasm of fire, a harp of stars. Play on, play on.

INVENT YOURSELF AS YOU GO!

Jealousy: Polyfidelity's Shadow — or Its Compost?

Query: When I approach the topic of polyfidelity with lovers and friends, many say that they essentially do favor poly for quite a variety of reasons, be they social, sexual, political, spiritual, economic or whatever. Their big stumbling block, however, and one which continues to jerk me around, is the jealousy "specter." Don't most women believe that jealousy is an inescapable, innate condition of human nature, one to be provoked upon pain of rage and despair? If human beings are actually wired for jealousy, is there a way to minimize jealousy's danger, especially in polyfidelity, where it seems to be the dark and certain shadow side?

— *In the Dark, Concord, California*

Excuse me, is not jealousy more certain to be the fallout of monogamy? Monogamy dictates that sexual ownership is good. Therefore, monogamy actively foments a jealous aversion the sexual sharing to which we are literally so prone. Only one thing is certain: modern *Homo sapiens* is the most psychologically insecure species of the entire biota. How many of us worry where our carefully constructed stage and props will be tomorrow, not to mention the whereabouts of our lover's panties right now? Empirically, however, no one has yet found the jealousy gene—not even among the fabled green-eyed women.

The reality, in contrast, is that anthropologists have exhaustively documented that entire recent cultures, from Polynesia to the frozen tundra, simply neither exhibit nor act on sexual jealousy.[16] Prehistoric, premonogamous extended families of the Neolithic era and before, as we have shown, had few jealousy triggers. That one human being could—or would want—to own another human body for sexual expression is the baleful tenet of an androcentric five-thousand-year history of humanity's five million. Externally ownable genitalia is a concept as newly ideological as that of "landlording" a piece of the Earth's body. We have seen what has happened since land and body access devolved from personal caretaking into ownership. Boundless ownership by the few certainly means neither universal pleasure nor widespread harmony.* One can hardly prove, therefore, that sexual ownership with its analog, sexual jealousy, is universal, eternal and productive for our species. The possessor class, of course, argues that jealousy is as "natural" as their status quo.

We know further that sexual jealousy is rarely expressed in the same way by women as by men or by different classes; nor in a consistent manner over the centuries since jealousy has held sway in certain cultures. Today, jealous males tend to exhibit overt anger toward the others involved and to abandon the relationship with little negotiation. Men are much more likely to beat and kill their partner and/or the lover. In contrast, women of all classes tend to blame themselves in the case of a perceived rival. We are more likely to try to patch things up, especially if economic security is involved for ourselves or our children. The rise of the economically independent woman of the 1970's, however, is shifting this gender difference. Women with bargaining power are beginning to flex it and to leave—or remain in the relationship for a piece of the real action like Eleanor Roosevelt and Hillary Rodham Clinton have done when faced with adultery. Lesbians, usually being more independent-everything, seem more likely than hets to walk if a perceived rival appears. Lesbians, like most women, may also tend to be somewhat confrontation-phobic, which may also lead to split and run.

One definitely welcome change in today's jealousy perspective relates to its old "crime of passion" defense in criminal law. Not that long ago, jealousy was a powerful, useful legal defense for a

---

* According to United Nations' surveys, males control 99% of the world's resources. No, I'm not jealous. I am appalled. I fully imagine that if the world's richest men met to divide all their money among themselves, there would not be enough to go around.

killer or batterer. Now such violence appears for what it is: hate and control-driven pathology. Since our Lesbian poly is a new-paradigm-kind-of-gal, who eschews common blood' n' thunder mayhem, let us leave extreme, psychotic jealousy to the tabloid papers and tv-casters who glorify and feed upon jealous extremes.

The two types of jealousy which polys commonly meet are ordinary, useful jealousy and dysfunctional, delusional jealousy. Neither is terribly easy on peace of mind. Both useful and delusory jealousies may even combine forces for a neat twist of the dagger. Each reflects a similar stew of uncomfortable emotions. The most common jealousy emotions are anger, hostility, shame, greed, lust, fear and attachment/love. It is important to emphasize that *in polyfidelity jealousy is drained of the fierce poison of betrayal*. Our jealousy is not embittered by broken monogamous vows. Since polyfidèles are committed to one another's sexual freedom, we can only assume that each woman, in acknowledging the right to her desires, may possibly act on them. In polyfidelity, we escape the sickening horror that our love life is a sham, that we are dupes of a vow dishonored. To be wounded by stealth hugely magnifies jealousy's anger and pain. Thus, jealousy is likely to be more manageable in polyfidelity where the shock of deceit is not present to unleash emotional counter defenses.

This does not mean, however, jealousy isn't a wild brew in anybody's breast. Most jealousy specialists* agree that the jealousy emotions are generated by our reaction to the *perceived threat of losing something very precious to us*. My own complex brew of jealousy may be as tormenting as yours, we may even express jealousy in the same manner, but this does not mean that our root causes of a jealousy bout are remotely the same. This is why the one-size-fits-all "cures" for jealousy are rarely successful, as in the fashionable therapizing line, "Jealousy is a self-esteem issue." Well, most of the jealous women I've been with (yeow!) are highly individual, powerful

---

* And former raving jealousoids like myself who have somewhat sublimated our J-rush via intense scrutiny and commentary. See also Baumgart, Clanton & Smith, Pines, Salovey, White & Mullen in Bibliography, page 329.

personalities whose jealousy may have little to do with self-esteem, but with a thousand other mood swings. Jealous moods often vary, depending on the cast of characters involved and specific scenarios. Jealousy itself is more likely to cause a droop in self-esteem than the other way around. Just recall some of your jealous antics.

For example, my own jealousy, as provoked by one certain flamboyant love may be composed of one part public image threat: "How could she (as everyone tells me) makeout with that woman all over town?" Pour in one part of desire: "What if we can't spend as much social/sensual time together now?" Add a dollop of dependency: "Suppose we lose our economic partnership?" With yet another love, my jealousy scenario may be more composed of fear-of-abandonment: "She's so much like my father and first lover that she may leave me with absolutely no warning like they did." Lash in a typical portion of righteous anger: "After all the time and resources I've invested in her..." Shake it all up with a sweet binder like passion/compassion: "I love her fiery genius. But how will XX treat her during her stark burnouts?"

Occasionally, a jealousy torment can hurl me into an abyss of all Hell's circles, but this is usually when other areas of my life are in upheaval too, and if my roots are torn. Other times, same jealousy provocations, but guess what? I remain almost comfortable, allowing that my love life is like the weather, far from 100% predictable, but at least I live in San Francisco, not Greenland. I frame my jealousy as a mere blip in the great Commedia Lesbiana. I may even be prompted to do some juggling myself, and can be almost cheerfully debonair toward the antics of the other actors. In one of these lighter times, I penned an embossed invitation to a well-known "couple-cracker" (we'll get to these no-friends-of-poly later).

> *Pistols for two,*
> *Coffee for one,*
> *On the terrace at dawn.*

Or, I just take a couple of *lattés* and go to bed, not necessarily alone.

Useful Jealousy

While we are, for this genial moment, considering *jalousie de bonne grâce*, let us speak of useful jealousy. Jealousy may well be the alarm system for immediate tending and mending of a relationship at risk. If jealousy is defined as "a perceived threat to the loss of something precious," your perception may, in fact, be quite accurate, and precisely why the alarm tripped. Perhaps, while life is short, you have been taking your precious love quite for granted. In contrast, someone else's attentions become a fragrant conservatory of care. Or maybe your lights seem on, but you are never really home for her. Meanwhile, Mlle. XX is invariably, dazzlingly present, a tender and sympathetic host. Or, horror of horrors, you are so hypercritical, grumpy and picky that she'd be a fool not to find someone who makes her feel she's mainly adorable. In short, not to lose something precious, a new awareness and behavioral change are in order. If jealousy is the java that awakens you to such circumstances, drink it down and get moving.

The odd woman need never destroy a solid, joyful relationship, but she may indeed be a messenger, the catalyst of change, or even remain on the scene as a bargaining chip. Say you've reneged on an agreement: another woman is brought in as a flex of power to arouse performance—or else. Something like this happened to a friend of mine who had promised her longtime lover a co-tenancy share in their house. In other conflicts about the relationship, however, she procrastinated on the paper work legalities. Her lover begins gazing out the window at another woman. Negotiations quickly ensue: no extracurricular passions, name on deed. And the odd woman walks away with the moonshine. (More about the perks and perils of the odd woman's enormous range of roles in her own chapter, pages 161-180.)

A new player also frequently appears on the scene when one or both partners in a relationship haven't the foggiest mutual understanding in regard to rights, responsibilities and boundaries. Beyond mere assumptions and words, one partner decides to test the waters. Here is an opportunity to actively define or redefine your relationship and thereby strengthen it. No one should continually have to suffer a terrifying vagueness about whether her lover is coming or going. One lover may have completed a long, intense focus on school, art or career and now has time for more lovers, or begins a new activity where she meets many available women. So, we usually need to keep checking the sail to decide what is the most comfortable, free and easy way to enjoy the 'ship. Begin by being as familiar as possible with everyone's jealousy rigging. Sincere, open discussions about the role of other women in your growing relationship is a tribute to each other as very special people and to what you have already created together. Thus, jealousy's provocations are not all to be decried. The problem is in not examining jealousy at all, or, even worse, getting stuck in it.

More companionably, your own jealousy can actually be used as a homeopathic remedy from love's great apothecary! Try using a tiny pinch of your own flavored jealousy curry to compliment the buffet you share. In very—that's VERY—small amounts, a lover will usually find your jealousy to be a deliciously colorful enhancer. Consider how only a few slim strands of golden saffron permeate a vastness of rice. Everyone knows that a thread of saffron, the fragile, tiny sex stigma of purple crocus, packs a wallop as both flavor and dye. Just a dash of jealousy, like saffron's bright flash, goes a very—that's VERY—long way. Try it, she'll probably like it. You get to be creatively expressive, no histrionics. The spice of jealousy also serves as a great reality check on who's more or less alive at the banquet.

Allow only the most precise and loving expression of your perceived threat to be spoken aloud. As in: "I would terribly miss our wonderful Friday evenings together since XX seems so attracted to you…Of course, no wonder she wants you…but how I love our end-of-the-week sunset walks." A shower of poetic remembrances and delicious future commitments help rejuvenate old ties and emphasize value. Go effusively on record, especially in writing. Cards and letters have the value of repeating themselves when you cannot be on the scene. They can stake out a kind of territorial presence for everyone to note. Jealousy's delicate seasoning heralds your love's worth for all to know. In contrast to rude, ballistic and sarcastic jealousy, lightly, quietly expressed sensibilities of fear and value can strengthen bonds and heal wounds. Soft jealousy is as flattering to everyone as candlelight. Many women also find it as sexually exciting as a good fire. Dangerous, but contained.

By the way, most friends who observe your measured and gallant response to jealousy award you with amazed respect. Need expressed, but with a noble or laughing side, touches others with a regard for you, which is great for self-esteem.

Note yes, that humor is great—if a bit tricky with jealousy. Keep those witty lines focused on your own foibles to retain membership in the First Church of the Last Laugh. In love triangles, quatrefoils, etc., one angle volleying jokes at another may come across as too acute, or plain obtuse. Polyfidelity is such a fertile field of social comedy, you will never lack material for above and below the belt jokes on yourself. Jealousy-born merriment lightens the air, but any definitely mordant lines are best expressed to uninvolved friends. One could go so far as to say that while a sense of humor isn't everything in polyfidelity, it's probably 90% of everything. So try to make sure that 90% of all the women with whom you are involved have a sense thereof. Since, however, we do tend to fall in love with the earnestly serious 10% as well, the next chapters deal with jealousy's dark causes and its hard-won cures. Please also allow yourself at least 10% hollowness of the heart, at least 10% of the time. You can always use any spaciousness you can find. Jealousy is still the common cold of human intercourse, even among women who share the nonpossessive values of polyfidelity. Jealousy can be greatly immunized and healed, if not entirely tamed. Poly is one way to gain experience in playing this wild card of love.

Most people upset by jealousy hunt for the roots of the malady, hoping to understand ways to overturn the brew. Four current approaches, or schools of thought, emphasize a different jealousy taproot as the one to expose and take care of. I'll deal in separate chapters with these four most popular approaches to jealousy:

I.   *The Sociobiology Tenets* hold that we are born jealous, born to lose. Sociobiology maintains that jealousy is genetically programmed, hard-wired into your being. With these guys, and it is usually guys, emotions of the violent hue, like jealousy, are instinct, base instinct. Thus, sociobiology makes a neat apologia for poor impulse management, the control crazies, and low-down meanness.

II. *General Systems Theory* sees jealousy as a special interdynamic energy which particular personalities in a relationship create among each another. It factors in unique situations as well as the powerful values, beliefs and customs of family, culture and society.

III. A form of psychodrama, more accurately, *Melodrama*, treats jealousy as a lone individual's quirky imbalance and relies on "talk-therapy," or, if you are lucky, with her sister

IV. *ACT-UP! Behaviorism*, which encourages you to take jealousy by the scented lapels and dance her breathless.

MYRIAD COMPONENTS OF
"the JEALOUSY RUSH"

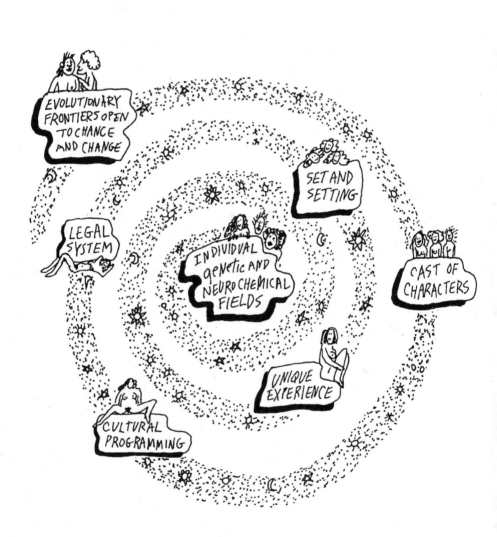

Jealousy as an Evolutionary Mechanism—Not!

The four above-mentioned clinical approaches are useful in ameliorating jealousy with the general exception of sociobiology,
so I'll dispense with it first. It is especially important to deal with
sociobiology's theories on jealousy because so many of you otherwise free-living and rational Lesbians are fooled by this grim
androcratic and deterministic ideology. Sociobiology has recently
been dressed up by academicians in the robe of "evolutionary psychology" since sociobiology's decidedly reactionary bias drew so
much fire. Sociobiology is an odd bird with colorful natural science
plumage, often quite fascinating in its analogies of human and animal behavior. I myself have been known to use biological studies
to point out that the vast majority of nature is not and never has
been monogamous, but poly. See previous chapter, "Evolutionary
History Tells Us…"

Sociobiologists and evolutionary psychologists unfortunately tend
to push the envelope of genetic determinism. They often use the
natural selection, survival of the fittest, circular argument: "XX
must be an evolutionary mechanism because it's so prevalent
(*i.e.* rule by white males, jealous possessiveness), so everything not
only will continue to be, but should be (ruled by males and possessiveness). Sociobiology first presumes its nature observations
are accurate, though there is a lot of slippage in their data.
Certain bird species, for example, declared to be monogamous
from time immemorial, are now found to have been poorly
tracked, to actually exhibit amazingly adulterous wanderlust.
Sociobiology, as widely practiced, overlays heavy ideology on its
so-called empirical methodology. Guess why? Most researchers
and studies are paid for by the system now on top. How often,

for example, has a study been funded on all the Lesbian or bisexual practices among Earth's female flora and fauna?*

Sociobiology tends to claim that sexual jealousy provides "natural" support for evolutionary "progress," and so sees jealousy as universal, not aberrational. Since humans are sexually jealous, the ideology goes, there must be a useful evolutionary reason why the jealous survived and passed along their jealous proclivities. Whoops. This observation is totally discredited by many anthropological studies documenting that sexual jealousy is far from cross-cultural. Nor, as we have mentioned, is jealousy alike in its expression throughout the records of all human societies. It must, in fact, have been atypical during our millions of years of prehistory spent in extended family polygamy. For most of human evolutionary time, there was no ongoing pair bond to defend by jealousy. Be that as it may, sociobiology goes on to claim that human survival, and our genetic replication itself, depend on our jealousy alarm system going off upon any suspicion of competition for personal attention.

The theory goes that an infant animal howls if its protector appears to divert food or security in favor of its own self-interest, or to a sibling, mate, etc. Any tiny, helpless creature who does not jockey for its just desserts perishes, doomed never to reproduce its non-jealous genes. Sociobiology thus assigns the mixed-emotion label of "jealousy" to a baby's response to physical stimulations like hunger or cold or wet. Simplistic? Reductionistic? While in the survival game, sociobiology rarely focuses on the equally complex emotions of altruism. Generosity is, however, exhibited by a range of folk, including siblings, who often nurture an infant, and who, it could be argued, have reason to be in competition for resources.

Jealousy seems quite incidental as a survival mechanism, compared to the powers of generosity, good fortune and coincidence. I survived largely because of my mother's good will, health, intel-

---

* We can but give a nod to the massive, if renegade, horticultural research enabling the Lesbian/Sensimilla plant takeover of the marijuana market. Yet, here too, billions of dollars are at stake driving biogenetic studies. I hope someone will research how well organic, music-bathed sensimilla mellows jealousy among Lesbian polyfidèles.

ligence, and resources, along with the critical fact that I was born in Pocatello, Idaho, and not, say, in Hiroshima in 1945. After our father's early suicide and family's economic plunge, sharing seemed better than jealous competition as a survival strategy.

 Further along in life, the sociobiology story goes, our sexually active "jealous-gene" utilizes its jolt of discomforting jealousy to keep a sexual partner in tow just as we tyrannized our early protectors. The master tenet of sociobiology is that competitive genetic replication, after personal survival, is the core drive of all living beings. Thus jealousy helps guarantee one's unique genetic replication by blasting away rivals. The right-wing survivalist and anti-choice movement zealots are amazing examples of what emerges from belief in a competitive "genes-ho!" premise. I have often wondered why we assess all behavior developments *after* birth? What about our primal intimacy, that period of participation, when we were one with our world as a life sharing our mother's womb? Why are we not as imprinted with the sense of belonging as with the sense of isolation that underlies jealousy?

Many Lesbians and gay men intuitively know that there is something seriously amiss in this survive-to-breed theory of jealousy. I cannot deny that I bellowed and bullied, charmed and pleasured my beautiful mother into feeding and protecting me from the elements. But why categorize my agitated baby reaction to various uncomfortable physical stimuli as being a valuable sexual reproduction mechanism hardwired for life, now labeled "jealousy?" This leap of logic splashes directly into the puddle of make-believe for any gay person. Let's just be accurate and say that all we can really observe is that most babies do the best they can to eat when hungry and avoid what feels disturbing to their sensitive little bodies. (How some adults lose this knack is another line of inquiry.) Suffice it to say that humans can and do use our giant brains to assign "meaning" to any physical stimulus/response. We create gobs of subjective labels and categories arising from our variously crafted language conventions and cultures. With language, humans have been creating virtual reality for millennia.

Of course, I'm still at it, maximizing survival comforts, while pursuing the delights and benefits of attention, all the while busy labeling the whole flow even after it is long gone. To this day, I bloom whenever my mother or another beloved makes me feel special and loves me along with anyone in the extended family. When any incident disrupts this idyll, and plenty do, I've noted that bellowing doesn't work terribly well any more. So, if anxious or threatened, I try to negotiate and charm everyone around to my desired status quo again. Motive: loving attention. Means: whatever works best for my own relational well-being and continuing success.

But, oh, Dr. Sociobio, this does not mean that sexual jealousy is predestined and profitable to the race. Look: my jealousy is triggered by only some people and then only sometimes. The exact same act, like one partner making a date with a new girl, does not necessarily trigger my critical need for attention. It may, but my entire personal gestalt of the day, maniacal or mellow, combines with biochemical, family, neighborhood, planetary and cosmic events to form a full deck. I may fancy myself the dealer, but the cards usually arrange surprises. Surely circumstances more than genes make the difference between lighthearted or blood-rushing jealousy? But that is our next chapter, the mutual systems theory of jealousy.

A further flaw in the sociobiology theory is that I, like a multitude of gays and childless or child-limiting others, have never given a fig for what sociobiology considers our primo biological compulsion: exact gene replication on this planet, as often and as long as we can sustain it. It is clear that decisively non-parenting queers, transsexuals, and celibates constitute a flaming fact of life sociobiology can in no way explain. Many of us deeply believe, in contrast to mainstream breeders, that there are myriads of ways to be fruitful and multiply. We thus energize the arts and the spirit. Where it is legal, we often become foster parents on a planet screaming in red alert due to overpopulation with millions of unwanted, uncared for children. Besides, it is obvious that my family's "line," should it be strung with genetic pearls beyond compare, is prancing onward in all my nieces and nephews, thanks to my sisters. Evolution and I are thus at peace.

Need it also be noted that my sisters and nieces never pause for one jealous moment to wonder if their particular genetic strand is replicated in their own pregnant wombs. For women, gene replication emphatically goes with the territory. Roosters crow; hens deliver. So the sociobiologists can be, at most, merely half right that *all* humans need to jealously police our mate in order not to lose a gene replication site. Only men could possibly "need" to be equipped with vigilant jealousy to guard their own reproductive success. Indeed, surveys show jealous men are far and away more obsessed with the exact sexual performance and "tools" of their rival, in typical size-queen fixation. Women, in contrast, tend to be anxious over the nature of their rover's emotional commitment and loyalty to any others. Women are more concerned with exactly who actual "family" is—who has intimacy, ritual, resource use and custody. If confident of such privileges, many a het woman allows mistress after mistress to alight, even to remain. Men, in what appears suspiciously like venus envy, can rarely endure the ongoing presence of a declared male competitor. Look at the two great games of aristocratic adultery on film, Ophuls' "The Earrings of Madame de…" and Frears' "Dangerous Liaisons." It is ultimately the gentlemen who cannot sustain the glittering chess-like war of nerves. Lacking the emotional stamina and intelligence of the women, each flees toward a duelist's death to "solve" the quandary of sexual jealousy.

Can males, as sociobiologists aver, really be so obsessed they may be "cuckolded," cheated into wasting their parental investment on a child with "cuckoo genes"? As everyone—but the birds— knows, a cuckoo blithely lays her eggs in another couple's nest to raise, going her merry way. Men over the ages have indeed made the cuckold male a nervous laughter theme in life and literature. But men are deadly serious: it is women they have historically battered and executed for betraying "paternal confidence." Here again, it seems that the so-called innate genetic programming stance is a rationalization. It is yet another attempt by a dominant group to justify its possessiveness and exclusivity by terrorism. Remember when a man could not be expected to control his "instincts" to rape any unprotected woman in provocative dress? Only a perpetrator would argue that genetic programming is all-powerful, that we are programmed creatures with little cognitive and emotional skills. Human consciousness (including, I hope, male) has the distinctive feature of being able to choose, to change direction, to wake up.

So, I ask, dear Lesbian, is your overriding evolutionary fear that of being fooled into supporting tiny babies impersonating your genes? If not, then you do not need sociobiology's inane innatisms. You need not to be sentenced to a lifelong jealousy supposedly implanted from your gamete days. If you are attracted to sociobiology's helix of logic and enjoy wild animal and insect stories, please note that biologically women should have an easier time than men with jealousy, and therefore polyfidelity. If biology is destiny as sociobiology infers (and feminism rebuts), be glad biological females tend to exhibit less sexual rage. (But take warning, bisexual poly women, today's swinger guy may lose it like the gentlemen of *Les Liaisons Dangereuses*.) Further, we have natural science's recently documented facticity regarding the virtual universality of female promiscuity—just as soon as we are free of the pregnancy and infant dependency cycle. To cap it, sociobiology implies that women could deactivate jealousy, being the sex pregnant with absolutely secure knowledge regarding our own genetic replication.

So, you may ask, why these jealous flare-ups with full-blown pulse-100 bouts of sleepless dementia? Let us enter the dynamic of . . .

Jealousy in the Jeweled Net of Indra*

Systems theory is savory because it allows one to see sexual jealousy in all its wraparound, 3-D, hologram, sparkling "Net of Indra" co-arisings.* I also like systems thinking about jealousy because, in badass fashion, I can come devilishly close to holding someone or something else *also* accountable for me being such a spoilsport in love. With righteousness, I emote, "This MAKES me so jealous," in contrast to "I AM so jealous." The former stimulus/response event is a fact, but one with circuits of contingency and possible escape routes. "I am a jealous person" brands one as a victim of jealous adversity for life, as one socially disabled. Many people, likewise, are much better able to deal with anger, often a large component of jealousy, if they do the same kind of reframing. "I have anger" along with a host of other qualities, rather than being ruled by total identification with anger.

Systems thinking will be a favorite with environmental Lesbians, all the gentle souls who bike on dates or try to recycle romance rather than hoard or trash it. Here, then , is how the plot widens in the jealousy-as-a-system dynamic. Jealousy becomes an active, intricate network of provocation and response, with fascinating patterns rising and passing away. Systems thinking holds a promise of surcease from jealousy, unlike sociobiology's jealousy gene-imprint. It is systems theory, of course, which informs the entire science of ecology, a philosophy of nature which views Earth not as one enclosed, inert hunk of matter, but as a nest of myriad reverberating systems, interacting to yield life and change. Systems theory may be translated into human intercourse as "We don't have to go it alone. In fact, we can't." It is not just that "we are all in it together." We all *are* it, rising and falling as one living body. Thus, intelligent couple and family counselors assume all relationship is, well, relational,

---

* The "Jeweled Net of Indra" is a vision of inter-reality beloved by Buddhists. Each being, as a gem set in a net's every nexus, reflects every other gem— even as it is also being reflected by the myriad of others. As part of the Net, one "eye" also contains the whole of it, as a dewdrop holds the moon.

that relationships are constantly being created and reinvented by the interactions of all players and environments upon one another. No single individual is cast as "Unmoved Mover;" even the supreme autocrat/top relies on the energy and response of the governed/bottom. Conversely, the seemingly powerless, no matter how tightly reined, expresses some degree of adaptive feedback which affects the balance of the entire system—and may ultimately even topple it. Remember how Anita Hill's testimony shifted the deeply entrenched structure of sexual harassment—presently in nervous backlash, *à la* systems theory, too.

Intimate partners situate along various power continua to happily complement—or unhappily sabotage—one another. Woman-to-woman relationships tend to vibrate along the more egalitarian, freedom-to-act spectrum in regard to economic, social, and work activities. Few can deny, however, that a typical Lesbian relationship system is hair-trigger sensitive and highly reactive to emotional eddies and currents. The introduction of extra lover(s), for example, can be an action-packed game of Fruit Basket Upset. As we know, no new player flies below laydar™ for long. Notice there are never only the two laser bolts (A & B) in a new poly romance, but exponentially at least six social energies beaming up and coalescing with one another in light show flux. (A to B & C; B to A & C; C to A & B.) Plus, we have all the friends, acquaintances, counselors, and gossips who may also critically influence color and motion. Linear causality behavior is out the window.

This focus in systems thought is on present, fluid patterns of action, rather than a past "primary cause," and only one "treatable." No agent in the system operates in a vacuum, all are calmed or stimulated and, in turn, affect the whole field of actors and setting. This explains why, when your lover's attentions wander, you are sometimes awash with jealousy and other times less affected. For example, even women who have a long fuse for jealousy can become extremely provoked if the odd woman plays the roles of both co-worker as well as co-lover. Perhaps a perception of the two others' co-creative survival/success bond overpowers the more "domesticated" partner. Maybe the time (and "overtime") allocation is infuriatingly unclear. Are they now at work or pleasure?

Many of the women who responded to my interview seem more likely to feel jealous if the odd woman is perceived as having some kind of higher status than themselves in talent, resources, etc. Then again, some are more upset to find the odd woman "just a floozy" or even "plain." This latter type feels the perceived lower status of her rival lowers her own. "How do I rate if her taste in women seems this lousy?"

Moreover, there are situational jealousy provocations—like actually witnessing your lover's caressing looks or hands on the rove. I sustain only minor turmoil as long as the toothsome twosome skip the "overts" in my presence. Even then, my peace of mind is not utterly doomed if I've got a life. Some of my loves, however, have been more tactful than others regarding the odd woman. "Indiscretion has always seemed to me one of the privileges of tact," the most famous pageboy of polyfidelity, Natalie Barney, once noted. This diplomatic give bland, matter-of-fact, low-profile commentary on their adventures, just the basic whens and whereabouts. There is a bare-bones, never bare-body, *précis* on the state of *amorosa*. The diplomats will reply lightly when queried, rather than blurt adventures or drag competitor classics into any already tense conversation. Other lovers, in contrast, can be lightning rods of passion and drama, or walk about in a stone-soul picnic, too spacey to even turn off the tea kettle. These totally expressionistic types, with their jarring energies or detailed accounts, can load the cannons of jealousy. Be advised that the whole world, even in polyfidelity, does not necessarily love a lover. This is especially true of the less requited lover if she also has PMS, a hard day, or a tendency toward existential dread. So, please observe the verbal skill of "selective sharing," designed to reassure, never to inflame.

Of course, it is not only your immediate personal actions which may inflame jealousy. Systems theory acknowledges that the social, political and cultural worlds of which we are also a part deluge us with messages to possess and to exclude. Look at how deeply we are programmed to selfishly own and monopolize a mere automobile. The era and culture we live in tells us not only what to perceive with jealous eyes, but in what manner it is permissible to exhibit jealousy. Men can be conditioned to physically boil over in jealous rage if "their" woman's face is unveiled to another male. Then they are taught to feel pride in torturing and killing the woman for want of a veil. In Euro-American culture, it is hard not to internalize the constant propaganda upholding belief in an economy of scarcity and of possessiveness. Since we glorify the heroic "lone individual" battling a hostile world, privatization of resources becomes a form of security and pride.

Such a sordid notion of social relations is hopefully being eroded as many people grow in the wisdom of cross-culture, feminist and spiritual commitments. Yet most of us were brought up on the exciting fare of sexual jealousy, and the J-rush is hard to dismiss. The battle over another person's body as sexual property is, after all, a grand theme of both popular and highbrow culture. Most of us are so psychically mediated into a jealousy frame, that we never consider the "why" of sexual possession, only the juicy details of "how. " It is quite to be expected that the most lucrative purveyor of Lesbian novels is nicknamed "Dyad Press" for its copycat portrayal of het-conditioned sexual responses like rote jealousy. Lesbian radical sexuality has, however, survived everything from self-hate mass-cult pulp novels through lobotomy, electro-shock and aversion therapy. Someday, may we leap over our pervasive jealousy conditioning too.

Using the Feedback Loop

This brings up the useful "feedback loop" of systems theory. No successful, healthy system survives in nature unless it can monitor, process and communicate information. Every ecological network, from ocean and marsh through alpine flora and fauna, maintains an optimum state via open, translational consciousness. This living consciousness is informed by an ever adaptive feed-back loop, a circuit which embraces both the external world and that which perceives it. We can visualize the human community as made up of transformative beings touched by vast, interconnecting waterways of emotion, among other energies. Emotions' fertile cauldrons bubble with the changing colors of life. Our teeming emotional marshes continually screen the total environment for information to optimally maintain their own systems. The emotional stimulus of jealousy, as we have seen, signals momentary, or possibly long-term, change in the system.

It makes eco-logical sense to keep the feedback loop open, to access significance of new data, negative or positive. So, to maintain balance and harmony, ask your lovers exactly what you *need* to know to quiet jealousy's active imagination and to take care of yourself. "How much time in the week do you want with her right now so I can make plans for myself? While you both are in first blush, would it be best for all of us if you just stay over at her place awhile rather than come and go at our house?" Do forbear, even for a moment, processing the hugely speculative, sweeping pronouncements of your roving lovers who fantasize aloud such whoo-whoo as "She understands me perfectly." Especially forbear pursuing any corrosive, system-clogging details like, "Guess what she wears to bed?"

Systems-oriented jealousy points out that a couple can also recognize and interrupt the old counter-communication blame loops which exacerbate any jealousy bout. These habituated patterns impede authentic feedback loops by shutting down one or both partners in anger or hopelessness. The nifty dynamic is that if even one woman disconnects from a counterproductive jealousy discourse of blame or defensiveness, the cycle, which functions on reciprocity, cannot proceed. You can always author a new plot, a new scenario, a different system.

One exercise that helps to avoid blowing a verbal fuse is the following one adapted from jealousy maven Ayala Pines' book *Romantic Jealousy*. Give each person on your love circuit one empty page with three columns marked to fill in, which her lover(s) will read and try to respect. The page is for a love-pair to share, not the entire network, unless so desired.

Column I is to list all your own unique "Jealousy Triggers," so women don't play with fire without a warning! Remember, as jealousy origins are wildly different, so are triggers. I am forever astounded at the variety of things I may do to provoke jealousy, but can easily avoid once I know.

Column II is "Pains in Being a Jealousy Target." These are the unendurable hassles you, as a rover, fear being subjected to by a jealous lover. The jealousy target is a largely overlooked role, one which merits important discussion, so a whole chapter is devoted to her later. See pages 149-159.

Column III is the helpful part on "Wishes Out of Jealousy Land." Make these wishes active, positive behavior you profoundly wish lovers would do to assuage the slings and arrows of outrageous jealousy. Note these are nonthreatening "wishes," no way to be construed as "demands," so dwell in gratitude, if you are lucky, not expectation. Treat each wish as a possible gift, as a performable "do," not as a forbidden "do not." This way you too will breathe easier when you see your lover's wishes. Make wishes extremely detailed, observable behavior like, "Tell me you love to be with me when we go out." Nip any sweeping, vague generalities like, "Make me feel sexy," or "Convince me that you won't leave." Here are some composite columns we've written or received.

I. Jealousy Triggers	II. Jealousy Target Problems	III. Wishes
You talk about X's great career and her terrible childhood when we are in bed.	You are silent and sullen for more than a day when I go out with other lovers.	For our "special" nights, you be the one to make the arrangements at least once a month.
I actually hear you make "the pitch" to someone else.	You make fun of my girlfriends.	Tell me you trust me. Time and time again.
I see you've bought her flowers but nothing for me.	You nose around in my personal papers.	Allow me to be left alone for a few hours when I come home from an outing with X.
You tell me at the last minute you have a date, so I have scant time for alternate plans.	You blow hot, blow cold: polyfidelity is great; poly is unendurable.	In groups, just once during the time, hold hands with me or put your arm around me.

Above all, notice that jealousy, like everything else—matter and energy, words and information—is a flow-through phenomenon. As an emotion, jealousy is as transient as the weather, but can be just as transforming, depending on the rest of the environment. One reason women have a horror of jealousy, with its brew of anger, fear, or longing, is that we are sure when first hit that the discomfort will never end. It is the old case of being so deep in the emotional soup that we literally cannot see any way to climb out. We obsessively assimilate every jealousy ingredient, hypnotized by its energy.

The trance, however, breaks when the ingredients begin to dissolve, as they always do. This may be sooner if the environment doesn't particularly support jealousy, later if everything around us goads jealousy. You'll probably be out of the jealousy soup by nightfall if the alternate love nest keeps a low profile, and if your basic survival needs are fairly independent. You'll be out if you aren't hooked on control-queen behaviors. You'll be out if you have developed a variety of means to express and receive love. Sleep may be uneven for a while, but your body's intrinsically self-correcting systems will make sure you never die of insomnia. One day you will wonder, "How could I have ever made myself sick about Marigold and Ms. X? Marigold's been through five crushes since, and I'm still in the pollen."

Permanent jealousy, with its crotchety, timeworn circuit, is only as permanent as its payoff. In open, self-organizing mutual systems, transformation is always possible. Synergies of woman energy can bloom in corollas and colors never before seen. Why opt for a closed system because of that old circuit breaker, jealousy? Rather than be a mere fuse-box on a neck, we can open as a transmitter of the organic, integrated passions of life. A self in process, not short-wired. Feel that surge of jealousy energize rather than shut you down.

Villain in Your Own Jealousy Melodrama

What people refer to as psychotherapy, psychoanalysis, and psychodynamics could more accurately be termed "psychodrama," or better, "melodrama." For the going rate, every understudy becomes the prima donna in her own life for a fifty-minute hour. The director/therapist, besides running the show, also acts the part of *claqueuse* to your past, your problems, and your emerging character. The directing therapist coaches you into character by exposing your tyrannical "unconscious," hopefully moving you into plot control, which you are out of, or you wouldn't be here in the first place. The show may include a replay of dreams, fantasies, biographical sketches, transference and its shadow, counter-transference, and, for the ham in us all, role playing. How these soul directors are able to dive into your unconscious from their conscious is possible via their own long stay in state-accredited institutions. The prerequisite for training is an amazing arrogance for shooting the unconscious rapids of other creatures at will. Oh, and a keen faculty for labeling. Three guesses what I am? "Hostile!" Go to the head of the Melodrama Department.

Dr. Freud and Dr. Jung are the melodramatists who presented modern Western culture with the theater of our seething "unconscious." Their unconscious seemingly replaced our more transcendent, transformative consciousness of yore. Jung's rather polyfidelitous "collective unconscious" is my favorite of the two. This is not only because Jung was such a major adulterer himself, but because Jung tends to be arty and exotic, abounding in multivalent archetypes with action-packed shadowlands, populated with friends in disguise, such as wolves who run with women in distress. In contrast, Freud's unconscious is largely a slough of base biological instinct, snarling with eternally unresolved parental and childhood fuck-ups. Dr. Freud, unskilled in cross-cultural studies, did vividly dramatize the insane asylums and drawing rooms of old Vienna. He deemed the Viennese jealousy he saw to be a "universal drive," rooted in the unconscious via childhood trauma. Freud held we have a limited amount of libido to bestow, therefore sexual hoarding and jealousy are "natural." Neo-Freudians roll up the curtain to explore your violently jealous Oedipus/Electra complexes, your double-dealing hidden motives, your deep-seated, aggressive and neurotic sexualities. Freud himself had to look over his shoulder while seducing his wife's sister in the family home. At twenty cigars a day, could you smell him coming? If all this sounds lurid as a coke-fiend's rap, it is. Dr. Freud popped holes in his nose from excessive cocaine use before dying of tobacco-related cancer.

Not to worry. One of the more zealous reformations always at play in the theater of melodrama cleans up the mess of the master. Enter the seventies "recovery movement," still acting out. Millions became galvanized by the fierce melodrama of a psyche not only unconscious, but unsober. Moreover, in the no-fee theaters of recovery, you can play *o solo mio* before entire groups of people, almost any hour of the day, for a long-term run and, what's more, be paid in plastic chips. Alternatively, you can invest $8,000 a month and receive star-attention in sensational company on a recovery dude ranch. Alas, for the jealous, there are no jealaholic meetings on the recovery roster. Who knows what hanky-panky could be going on while you're away in a church basement or at a recovery farm?

So, it's back to traditional duodrama with jealousy. Amazingly enough, the *Diagnostic and Statistical Manual of Mental Disorders*, which earnestly and officially labels many of the psyche's demons for therapists, has no entry whatsoever for sexual or romantic jealousy! So what that this state of mind is responsible for one third of the murders in this country, not to mention its role in battery, suicide, and destruction of property. The *DSM* does list a certain pink elephant called "Alcoholic Jealousy," about which "too little is known to be documented." And you thought your life was on the rocks? No matter.

In melodrama, sexual jealousy is dealt with as another deflating character defect, the product of the mind of an isolated personality in response to long-standing psychological and behavioral problems. As Freud's basic instinct, a drive located in the unconscious, all you can do is suppress jealousy, and try to remain nonviolent for the sake of civilization. Melodramatic transactional analysts cast jealousy as one more trick of that little rascal, "the inner child," kicking up a ruckus. Extricate the kid, love her regularly, perhaps in stuffed animal epiphany, then put her out with the cats at night. With the inner child scenario, you are a babe in the "original triangle" with your parents, and kid, you lost. ("Lost is right," says the incest survivor, but that's another story.) Still smarting from parental jilt, please continue through the rubble of childhood outrage. You, as powerless youth, had other love rivals who bested you in battle. Today's neurotic response to perceived intimacy loss is a defensive habit which became ingrained. But there is hope. Since baby-you started it, big-you can fix it. Rational you can handle jealousy because you are a champ now. What? You don't feel so great? Then we'll work on your low self-esteem problem for a few years. Shame on you for not feeling good enough!

Thus, we use jealousy, already a self-focused, self-centered torment to descend into more "inner work." If melodrama therapy is dialogue-driven with little action, its "cure" will be largely ineffective or short-lived. When is a maelstrom of strong emotions like jealousy erased by mental efforts or eliminated by the dawning of insight? Awareness is not quite enough. When self-understanding masters the emotions, the meek will inherit the Earth. Philosophy, psychology, and even religion's greatest enigma is not how to explain the human condition, but to ascertain what moves us to actually change our ground of being. If you think change takes a shot of spirituality combined with experience-laden action, welcome to. . .

Jealousy in the ACT-UP World of Behaviorism

*B*ehaviorist psychotherapy tells us to get into the act by playing new, never before performed roles. Try experimental theater. Behaviorists declare that you can sift through the archaeology of jealousy forever. Why and how you can possibly internalize that another human being is your personal property constitutes an endless onion stew of causality. Even as layers are peeling back, the living bulb of soul continues to grow and reform. Silvery layers of sense and sensibility rise and slough off as long as there is life, continuously creating new story lines to analyze. As we've seen, jealousy packs in one ancient hominid's grab-and-hoard act that sparked another grab-and-hoard act *ad infinitum*. It is butressed by monotheism's proudly proclaimed Jealous God to inspire me-me-me behavior. Jealousy is further plumped up by the body ownership ideologies of sexism, serfdom, and slavery. It is supported by economic propaganda which valorizes competition and private possession. Then, showered with sparks from personal childhood losses and adolescent sensitivities, jealousy's causes flame on and on and on… How to break the spell?

To displace and calm frequent flare-ups of jealousy, behaviorist psychodrama stresses a faith in change over defeatism. Behaviorist methodology involves DOING observable acts to counter jealousy, limiting eternal analysis. Energetic action indeed helps to calm jealousy in me, along with the more revelatory shake-up of two lovers dying of cancer and old age respectively. No mere mortal will ever run so far away with one's lover as the Dark Goddess. I thus came to measure all loss in terms of the ultimate.

Not, however, wishing to recommend death as the best jealousy cure, the more vital behaviorist antidote is my favorite. For example, what shifts when just once a day you make an effort to share a possession? What moves in the world when you share with it? What moves inside? Watch how behavior wags the tail of feelings, instead of it always being the other way around. Western psychotherapy's obsession with feeling is a roundabout course on life. Acknowledge any jealous feelings without shame. But like anger, you do not have to express or suppress jealousy. As one of my favorite teachers said, "You don't have to be a Buddha; even for one breath, just act like one." If you are sick with jealousy inside, actually do something physically expressive and positive; you'll begin to get unstuck.

For example, change your daily routine even slightly to please or pamper yourself. Hey, even change your routine to please someone else. During a recent jealousy jag, instead of always reading the paper in the morning, I picked apples and flowers from "our" garden and delivered them with a note to a different neighbor each day. One neighbor perked my interest in growing herbs from cuttings she gifted me with in return. Only when I began reading about her old-fashioned herb called rue, did I remember I was supposed to be unhappy.

The idea is to accept that your feelings aren't so hot AND to get on with your best purposes in life. Your attention may jump erratically back to jealousy, especially at first, but the mind's disc simply cannot hold two tracks at once: inner referencing OR taking in the world of color and motion and fragrance. The world needs your gifts, loves your appreciation, your caring—even if one woman doesn't right now. Psychotherapy often beams its energy into shoring up personal love dyads. What about courting the world as lover, world as self? What if the masters of psychotherapy fitted us for the rewards of being active in community and causes larger than "The Relationship?" Is there not more to life than being a solitary, successful couple?

Since the root of the word *jealous* is the Greek *zelos*, also mother of our word zeal, jealousy implies action. The behaviorists may indeed be onto something. The first act I suggest, however, is:

RELAX. *Via negativa*. Do the most with the very least. Rub a drop of calming lavender oil in that special hollow at your neck surely designed to hold fragrance in your honor. Then, in a comfortable place, relax on the flat of your back. Your legs are outstretched, hands palm-open at your sides like the grateful dead. This is the delicious *savasana*, or "corpse pose" in yoga. My cats call it the "compost pose." *Savasana* seems one of the only yoga poses cats cannot do, so they often purr atop you in admiration.

Meanwhile, you are breathing slowly and deeply, each breath purring peace within. Now move gently into deepening relaxation: focus on the feet to release all energy from them, then into the calves, the thighs, the arms. Now be conscious of your whole trunk relaxing. Relax the buddha belly, the buns, the sides of the chest, the shoulders, the distraught heart. Feel all the generous spaciousness which actually comprises the entire body. Explore your honeycomb bones, loosening your muscles. Surrender the churning thoughts. "All these I give unto the hands of peace." Feel the breath in the nostrils. As your calm deepens, be aware of your consciousness becoming centered at the stillpoint between your eyebrows.

To quiet the squirrel cage of the jealous mind and move toward gentle detachment, many spiritual traditions use some version of a mantra or simply count breaths from one to ten and back. This focus displaces worrisome mind chatter since the mind can script only on its free track. Use of a mantra is also comforting and easy. Just pick a focus word or very short phrase that is firmly rooted in your belief system. Repeat the words silently on each inhalation and exhalation. Don't worry if you often lose your mantra to the old chatterbox. Gently go back, time and time again, to your chosen words and breath. Mantra examples are "Blessed Be," or "Shalom," or something like the formal mantra of the great female Buddhas: the *Om Tare Tutare Ture Soha* of Tara and the *Om Mane Padme Hum* of Kwan Yin. Healing phrases are:

"I breathe in spaciousness."
"I feel free."
(Or, simply inhale the word "Spaciousness" and exhale "Free.")

"Breathing in, I calm my body."
"Breathing out, I smile."
(Inhale "Calm," exhale "Smile.")

"I breathe flowers."
"I feel fresh."
(Inhale "Flowers," exhale "Fresh.")

Inhale Moon   Exhale Stars

Here is the place to move into Tantric consciousness described below, or, it's lovely just to drift into...

SLEEP. Sleep truly does knit the raveled sleeve of care. But should you remain a whiplash of adrenaline, insomnia bruising circles under your eyes, feel free to...

SELF-MEDICATE. Stay away from reliance on any pharmacopoeia that deaden self-awareness and self-healing, like booze and prescription drugs. Go by a natural food and remedy store to obtain the Vitamin B family and Vitamin E, which are great for the nerves. There will be an array of natural remedies for anxiety and insomnia like valerian, skullcap, and ironically, passionflower. Packagers often combine natural remedies into one blissful "calm tab" for the afflicted. Tasty herb teas like chamomile ease the furies. In troubled times, I take the ginseng tonics and teas, even chew pieces of this heroic root, because ginseng can make one feel like an Empress on holiday. You may indeed want to take time off to...

ESCAPE. It's okay to jump the fence, if you can, and leave the whole scene for awhile. Certainly escape the remotest observation of the two new lovers' infatuation together. Head for new scenes, new sights, new music. In difficult emotional times, body tissue tenses. To ease this, twist towels, take long walks. Long walks are quiet avenues to distinguish useful feelings from racket feelings. The longer the walk, the more your mind sweeps clear of blamemongering. In its place, you can summon. . .

LAUGHTER to fortify your amuse system. If you can find humor in anything, you can survive it, which is called "Remirthing." A sense of absurdity disperses hot energy. Laughter in despair acts as a release, a space where hope can come in. In the wild script you're enacting with jealousy, laughter acknowledges a frame break. Did you know that a healthy infant laughs around 200 times a day, an adult only twelve? We seem to have forgotten that the joke is on us. As I begin to relearn to laugh at myself, I realize I will never cease to be amused, which makes for some lasting security in this old world after all. As Romain Gary remarked, "Humor is an affirmation of dignity, a declaration of our superiority to all that befalls us." Perhaps it is as important to know what is *not* serious as to know what is. Jealousy is a good trainer in this department. Don't believe that if you mock jealousy, however, you can slay it. The yoginis suggest that you may actually want to. . .

TRANSFORM JEALOUSY. Try this skilled alchemy when you and the savasana pose mentioned above become a regular item. Now you can actually invite the dread jealousy to float *with* you in your stillness. In the winking practice of Tantric Buddhism, the discipline is to align yourself with patterns of emo/thought—whatever they may be.* Imagine those bright delta-women signs on the highway that spell out one word: "Yield." Among other teachings, Tantra involves the judo-like play of moving through "negative" energy rather than resisting it. You are probably more familiar with the application of Tantra in sex, moving in deep, slow flow

---

* The Tantric teachings originated in India and the Himalayas in the seventh through the twelfth centuries C.E. The Sanskrit word *Tantra* comes from the verbal stem meaning "to weave." *Tantra* is a spiritual path which weaves, or integrates, every aspect of life. It includes all daily activities, such as the intense energy of intimacy and sex, into the path of awakening.

with the pleasure iridians, while not immediately grasping at orgasm. Women, especially Lesbians, are natural *Tantrikas* in regard to the pleasures of sexual ecstasy, where the senses are paths to the sacred. But Tantra also utilizes pain as well as pleasure to catalyze the transmutation of dross into gold, of dimness into awareness. In Tantra, you can rise by that which you may fall. A tantric flip rolls with the punch of life, so that you flip the problem onto its kazoo to get on with the dance.

To illustrate, it is said that a Tantrika does not come to a stand of poison ivy—like jealousy—and turn back, nor does she even tiptoe around the ivy to get back on the trail. The Tantrika plunges directly into the ivy—"So be it!"—even, my dears, if this takes her off her apparent path! Tantra is like using a thorn to extract a thorn. Tantra holds that we can shift an imbalance of emo/thought emanations back into their mother reservoir of energy, one of primordial luminosity and intelligence. In the Tantric philosophy, it is sheer energy which gives impetus to both the enlightened and confused states of mind, which are grouped into the great "Five Families" of mental energy. Thus, Tantra holds that anger is the flip of the incisive, penetrating wisdom contained in the *vajra* (diamond) family. Pride is seen as the tantric flip of equanimity; grasping passion has its impulse toward union; dullness of emotion opens into all-encompassing spaciousness. These are the great families of *ratna, padma,* and *buddha,* respectively.

Jealousy and envy in Tantric Buddhism are members of the rousing family of *karma,* a Sanskrit word meaning "action," much as jealousy's root *zelos* in Greek calls forth a whirlwind of power. In its confused form, the karma family emerges as the absolute paranoia we recognize in extreme jealousy. But karma transformed is marvelous potency, the ability to be keenly aware of what needs to be done, with the power to touch everything in its path. The karma family is associated with the element of wind. Wind doesn't usually scurry in all directions; its great cheeks blow one way. Such is the one-note direction and control typical of jealousy. Yet, a monsoon energy can also generate power in fulfilling greater purpose.

In its form of the energy "to do," the overweening self-conscious-ness of jealousy is absent, but the wings of power are strong and steady. We are able to see possibilities and take the appropriate course with single-pointed efficiency. It is as though we had been walking through life and now have a bike. Thus, ignition of the karma family can torpedo a psyche into jealousy or be the great stamina for birth and growth. Each of the five Tantric families shines with a particular color, shown by the five bright stripes of the Buddhist flag. The family karma, with its components of jeal-ousy and envy, is associated with the color of green, as jealousy is in the West. Green is also the aura of springtide, of arousal and fresh, new formation. With all this energy pulsing, will jealousy blow us into tumult and disarray? If not, how does the wondrous trans-formation take place from turbulence and torment into successful activity? Only one way:

BE BOLD. You need to pause, to enter the wildness of the jealous emotions and feel their naked quality, with no veil between you. Enter jealousy as a lover, not as an alien. It does not work to treat this emotion as an unruly employee, either to be disciplined or dismissed. The best way to enter jealousy is to sit alone with her for a time. I have had tea with jealousy morning after morning, and I imagine I always will. She holds a profound sweetness under her bitterness; why, it is not hard to fathom, considering the emo-tions of hope and love which preceded her. Jealousy also has the vivid imagination of a great tragic novelist. Appreciate what a tale-spinner she is.

Now taste along her continuum, experience her texture, her color, heat, and cold. Most of my life I had never really visited with jeal-ousy. Instead, I reacted in vehemence or victimhood: talking, talk-ing—with everyone except jealousy herself. We have been taught, after all, that jealousy is an enemy. It's avoidance at all costs, and so we resist her very being, try to push her away. If actually caught by her, we focus our aversion toward her, then go on to blame our-selves and others.

Since jealousy is a complex of feelings, your Lady J will surely be a different figure from my own. My jealousy usually comes first as a volcanic wind, roaring in my ears, a hot tempest quite capable of blowing everything to bits. Gradually, as I move into thinking and labeling such extraordinary stimulation, the jealousy chills. It dips into an even more frightening wind, arctic, biting. No one dares come near my fuming dry-ice planet. Meanwhile, my intense concentration on a partner's every act, expression and mannerism flashes like the sun on an icy branch.

I really can't sustain these burning/freezing extremes, once I take tea face-to-face with wild-eyed jealousy. But I still feel swept like a ship, far from the hemisphere I once knew, far from the navigable stars I once had. So I often summon up (gads!) my favorite image of Greta Garbo, as the magnificent, once rollicking Queen Christina. She stands alone at the end of the film, now countryless and loverless, her cape billowing before the ship's mast. In one of the most exquisitely stark, vulnerable and heroic close-ups of film history, Greta Garbo faces into the wind. "Yes. We will sail. The wind is with us." World beckons afresh to the daring.*

Not that I don't continue to huff and puff. But entering a one-pointed "touching" with jealousy herself, the craziest squalls begin to level out. My volcanic storms move into warm, if insistent Chinooks. The nor'easter becomes more bracing than biting. I begin to remember that if I can't change the weather, I sure can set the sail. Let the jealousies become *dakinis*, the dancing energies of life. Was it not high on karma green that I had the momentum to begin this book? You, too, can

WRITE JEALOUSY AROUND. Like the rest of us, when jealousy is organized, she is more productive. Use what is left of your mind to list all the paranoid speculations and imaginings which now regale your love life. A well-organized woman can be comfortable

---

* Garbo was of course asked what in the world she focused upon in order to summon such a portrait of silent, soaring intensity. Garbo replied: "Nothing."

even in hell. Be specific. "They are laughing at me." "I'll be left in the lurch to do all the child care." "I won't have anyone to go out with on week-ends." The wilder the better. "She will use the recipes I created for a seduction dinner for XX." You'll realize that jealousy is like all emotions, a quicksilver feeling, which is why we don't call it a fact. Run your rampant speculations by anyone whom you love or trust. While you are at it, make a list of all the mean and thoughtless acts that have *actually* been perpetrated against you by the renegade couple. Take any outrages that constitute actual harm to life, liberty or property to a lawyer or to a vigilante society of your friends. I am serious. One errant lover gave her new girlfriend her live-in lover's credit card for an "emergency." Girlfriend racked up $6,500. After noting all such felonies, let any other meanies from the other couple's antics, if any, be loosely categorized as your own monogrammed "resentments." Burn these chronicled audacities on pieces of paper under the full moon; they are injurious to your health. Do not go so far as to number them, paint the numbers on stones, then throw them at the offending parties. Such stones however, are fun to throw into the waters of oblivion. Any such ACT-UP ritual you can create to inspire and reify your transformation of jealousy into clearing action can be a powerful catalyst. The mind needs concrete evidence to rearrange its patterns. The word, "e-motion" bespeaks "motion," energy-in-motion.

Finally, outline the minimum participation from your lover you are willing to live with right now, subject to changing conditions and time, of course. Once crystallized, the terms may be easy and agreeable to all concerned. Don't depend on mind-reading from anyone, especially early on when delusion may be high in general. You might, for example,

- Set fun, intimate time once a week.
- Honor all economic and public commitments.
- Agree to perform all the usual chores.
- Call for a wide birth between you and her new girl for the present.

143

Be sure to confine your requirements and concerns to your *own* relationship. This is the only one you can hope to organize, never mind control. Considering your long-term best interests, think through what action you might take if your minimum requirements are not possible now, are not possible for a few weeks, are not possible ever. No threats please, just contingency planning. Once you've got your own act together, you can more easily. . .

SECURE THE SOCIAL SECURITY DEPARTMENT. Take special time each and every moment you can to reaffirm the love and trust you have in your lover! A wild patience has carried you this far. You two are the ones with the history of real alliance. History usually outranks mere infatuation. Enjoy full tilt reminiscing about great moments of your romance, about deep moments shared. Mythologize with shameless creativity. Emphasize that:

- You want to remain in her life, to grow together with new possibilities.
- While commitments may now extend to others, the original commitment to each other is a living creature to be enjoyed and cared for in its changing forms.
- You continue to place both partners' truth-telling as the keystone of polyfidelity and hope she feels the same.
- You continue to value sensual variety, sexual positivism and discovery as part of every woman's right. Repressive monogamy memories often fade when polyfidelity negotiations get tough. Monogamy's false security and happy-ever-afters can easily become a comforting fantasy again. Be careful a momentary loss of nerve doesn't hurtle you into pledging sexual ownership.
- You want to work with your love to create and re-create whatever social structure will support your mutual ideals in polyfidelity.

While it is important to spend time affirming and clarifying "The Relationship," eschew constant, obsessive processing. Invest most of your time together in pleasure and support, which is why you got together in the first place. Process the odd woman with your lover as little as possible. Consider, however, whether to. . .

CONFRONT THE ODD WOMAN? The odd woman in polyfidelity may become somewhat analogous to your lover's family. The reality is that you fell in love with your lover, not her family, nor any of her friends for that matter. Some women enjoy relating to a love's family; others are better off anywhere but in that family's bosom. All you "owe" a partner's family and intimates is agreeing to an introduction and to extend polite, positive energy during the time you are all in the same room. Some of these people may become halos around your existence. If you are predisposed to feel good about someone, they aren't apt to become the bane of your bone—especially in small doses. You do have a right to *extremely* small doses.

I believe it is wise to meet the odd woman at least once if it seems she is to remain on the scene a while. I always imagine the O.W. to be a dazzling W.O.W. Valkyrie with the talent and intelligence of a Redgrave. I think it is important for her to get the cut of my jib too, especially that "I count." "Here I stand" is a tip of the hat to reality. I like to meet the odd woman on my territory, somewhere I feel comfortable, like my home or favorite café, without a crowd of knowing acquaintances observing the action. If meet in public we must, I'd of course prefer an event where I'm important or well-connected or knowledgeable.

It rarely seems to happen this way. I usually do the honors of welcoming or being welcomed to the dance at just the moment much of my dignity and self-possession are mere facade. We have had to meet at the site of *her* famous reading, or in the embarrassment of four of us turning up by chance at the sex club. Then there was the time I had really been meaning to wash my hair and was wearing the most maladroit pair of overalls. . . My usual policy is simply to give the odd woman the benefit of the doubt and interact if she wishes, within reason. When this woman makes my lover happy and respects my existence, we've had really good times together and actually shared a lot of practical wealth. For one woman in particular, I still praise the day when she—by extension—came walking into my life.

I have also had run-ins with a type of woman I call the "couple-cracker." She is not really polyfidelitous. She feels alive only by stirring up drama and messy conflict. She tries to destroy relationships in order to hold sway for awhile, then moves on to the next target. Your don't get this type among polys as much because there isn't the clandestine excitement, the adulterous angst of monogamy for her to feed on. If a couple cracker comes to call, by all means confront her. She is not able to read minds either, and may have picked up a lot of nonsense about polyfidelitous relationships. She was not born understanding your rights and feelings.

You can simply call the woman to ask her what in the world her intentions are with your love, since you understand she's been suggesting "breakup." Say you do not understand what is going on and repeat that you want to know her intentions. Stop. Listen carefully here. Do not be hasty, nasty or blaming. Do not interrupt. This is a communications call. It is best not to react at all to the couple-cracker's excuses, except to calmly repeat, "Is it so?" or variations thereof. You may get a lot of information or nothing at all. It does not matter. If you let yourself enmesh with the couple-cracker, you get stuck with her emotionaholic agenda, which is decidedly not yours. Your aim is to put her on the spot and for her to consciously take responsibility for her actions.

Move on to the most important part. Tell her you appreciate her honesty and that you would also like the opportunity to speak honestly, without interruption. Give her the truth to live with: You are deeply in love with your partner, and while you are polyfidelitous, you do not intend to trade her in to someone else, which is the antithesis of polyfidelity. Say you are hurt and confused. Declare that you aren't yet sure what you are going to do, but you wanted to give her the benefit of a hearing. End the conversation. Such a point blank "I count" will scare off many a deluded woman, be a wedge to crack her notion that you are a fade-out. No hysterics. No loss of face. No verbal violence or flying debris. In a potentially harmful situation, you are a clarifying rather than a destructive force. This deserves respect. Now spend your energy where it really counts. . .

EXPRESSING ALL KINDS OF LOVE & AFFECTION & SENSUAL INTEREST in your rapscallion philanderer. This is much more fun than processing and haggling. If genital sex seems too sensitive at present, it is as sensual to listen, touch, see, smell, speak and reflect on your love with shimmering attention and joy. Above all, express no verbal judgments about her until you've walked in her ramblin' flip-flops. If she is at first not terribly responsive, you can always slip into. . .

SELF-DELIGHT. When a lover steps out, it's a green light that you now have the time for the self-indulgence and self-appreciation you may have been neglecting. Not to mention the time you now have to bask in the social support of old friends and to cultivate the social approval of new ones. You can also take a leaf from the *Lesbian Swinger's Notebook*: imagine all the exciting sexual acts you can have with your partner when she is back in your arms. It is an irony, that swinger or not, sex with other people increases interest and attention in each other. Polyfidelity is often used expressly for this purpose, among others. So, let us leave this gusty chapter with a cheer for. . .

THE MARVELS OF MANIA. Consider that it is possessive daddy culture which says the conflagration of jealousy means to give up hope and go weird. Rather than using your powers for armor or battle, take a deep breath to open your heart for the one ray of love you must have or you wouldn't care at all. Then give away this love, this ever-renewable energy. Give to yourself. Give to your friends and families. Give the flower of a smile. Give to a passerby. Give to the brave planet. Give your labor, your talent, your art. Give your receptive presence to the broken or the lost. Give away all you can. If you don't feel like giving, so what? With the beating wings of karma, you can do it anyway.

With all this juice on the loose, go ahead and receive too. Lap it up. Allow others to give to you. Open to reassurance. Learn from every creature, the kitten and the maple and the whole whirling slipstream. Receive the joys of companionship and caring. Receive the gift of work well done. Receive the gift of spirit and divine mystery. Receive the vitality of breath and the exhilaration of motion. Accept every gift as it comes, without judgment. What to do with the weeds of the mind? Bury them near the plant to give nourishment. Receive jealousy and take tea together.

Didn't she come to bring you a sense of wonder?

So What's the Target of a Jealous Rampage to Do?

*Q*uery: I've worked pretty hard on becoming a low-level jealousy person, phasing out my old, ruinous rages. Lots of effort later, I'm happy to be giving love pretty much without strings, and I have a couple of girl friends here and on my travels. My biggest problem now is that my lovers often go into ballistic—or heart broken—jealousy with me, even though they know I'm a rambler. I dread the whining, the resentments, the old courtroom drama. What do I do to help a woman not to worry? How can I feel less fear and anger myself when I'm the target of sexual jealousy?

— Mandy Torpedos, Fort Kent, Maine

*D*oggone it! Jus' keep that target movin' and you'll be over the fence in no time. Really, more than a soupçon of jealousy (the delicious kind we talked about previously) is unacceptable. There is real risk in being a jealousy target, whether physical, psychological, economic or social. Many jealousy targets act as if their lover's jealousy were a wooden leg, a responsibility-free, lifelong disability. They get kicked around the block. Jealousy and rudeness go together. Who wants to be on the receiving end? Ugly, possessive harassment is not acceptable behavior, with its debilitating hash of accusation and defensiveness. Ask a woman to help work out an alternative or be clear that you'll leave the reservation.

But before you play this tough-love hand, try asking yourself "How do I contribute to this jealous dynamic?" Do you perhaps *like* to keep your loves a little jealous? Hummm? Do you cock a jealousy trigger when you need a self-esteem boost? Does her jealousy make you feel more desirable? At first we may not discern how mean-minded jealousy can be because it often hits a flattery nerve. Massive jealousy, however, rather than being a gift of love, rises high on the tide of selfishness. Then again, perhaps her jealousy gives you a feeling of power in the sense of making it clear that you "can always go elsewhere." Is provoking jealousy something you do for revenge or punishment? Or does jealousy perhaps add to your sexual dynamic as a couple, via sexual fantasy or in dominance/submission games?

Let's say jealousy provocation is not a power play on your part. But maybe you are taking her for granted? Perhaps you are not keeping polyfidelity agreements? Fidelity does not mean monogamy, the often twisted usage of the word. Fidelity means that you make an agreement and you are as good as your word. Fidelity and loyalty are also demonstrated in polyfidelity by not betraying confidences or violating privacy, nor parading grievances in public, as so-called "faithful" monogamists are so painfully wont to do. Then again, perhaps you actually are directing too many resources elsewhere, be they temporal, sensual, economic, etc. Consider whether her jealousy is merely situational. For the moment, you may have a sexy new lover, but your jealous love now has, well, just you. Things usually even out when the lover balance does.

Maybe, a faint maybe, there is for you little payoff at all in a woman's jealousy. But the payoff for the jealous one is, first and foremost, ATTENTION. Attention is always coveted, much more than mere sexuality. Jealousy, however expressed, in fire, ice or tears, is above all, the dramatization of the self. Perhaps her self is being overlooked by you, or is not receiving considerate, respectful treatment. Maybe all her jealous self wants is to reaffirm love and loyalty, to clarify what guidelines are operating, or just to have you validate her emotional turmoil. As a woman declaring herself a Lesbian does not instantly eradicate all her homophobia, neither can one adopt polyfidelity and erase a whole lifetime of jealousy conditioning.

No jealousee, however, can "rescue" the jealous. Relationship changes are rarely accomplished by one partner doing something to another. So-called help administered unilaterally from one being to another is usually a power play, which doesn't work for long to reshape behavior. Since we weary of the term "co-dependence," let us call it emotional slavery to act only to provoke someone else's response, whether jealous or jealousee. There are, however, ways to take the edge off being targeted in jealousy. Announce once and for all—well make that several times —that jealousy does not get the job done. Let her know quite clearly that if she wants you closer, her jealousy is aversive and drives you away. Point out that jealousy is a proven method for getting rid of everything one is afraid to lose.

Then express the other truth: loads of love and affection. This woman deeply needs to feel "special." Is she not special to you? Remember all those times when you have feared loss of love? Respond as you would like to have been treated. Focus on all the things you do have together, not on what's missing. Review all the mutual love and trust you share. Admire all the benefits and supports you currently provide to one another. Dramatize the place she holds in your life. Set up great dates, excursions, and projects for the future. Concrete future plans are far more reassuring than the flat statement that you want to stay together. For what? Color in anticipation and detail.

But you have talked enough. This jealous woman wants to be validated. To validate is to bear witness and to empathize. To validate, it is not necessary to agree one iota. "I can see you are hurt and angry." Find out what type of loss she fears. This could be loss of love, loss of face, loss of material resources. Who in heaven knows until you ask? Be sure to also find out what she expects. Some lovers have perilously unclear arrangements about polyfidelity. I finally made an agreement not to romance any of my lover's "family" of friends. She never cross-examined me again.* Take the time(s) to give your lady a fair and loving hearing. Everyone deserves to unravel jealousy, and society at large won't help a whit.

---

* I was young and hadn't realized this is a very deep boundary issue for many Lesbians. After all, friends literally equal family for women who have lost biological ties due to rejection. Thus women speak of a confused circle of lover/friends as "incestuous."

By the way, when a lover tries to blame her own sexual jealousy on you, get support for yourself, especially from single friends. Talk to a monogamous couple and you're likely to hit their nerve of jealous insecurity; they can be dismissive or blaming.

If there is any physically violent behavior against you, tell all your friends, while getting out of the relationship. An unexpected violent eruption of jealousy may come from someone who merely agreed to polyfidelity to get you in bed in the first place. Many bisexual women mentioned this to me regarding their male lovers. You can sometimes deflect any potential for violence by expressing no overt disdain, ridicule or rejection in the heat of argument. People who erupt in violent jealousy have huge control needs, yet are deeply dependent on their lover for self-image. They may use violence as a misguided way of gaining back their control. Often seeing things rigidly in terms of black or white, control *habitues* may feel that there is nothing left to lose—and thus destroy. Recognize that these people likely have immense problems with shame, that the worst thing you can do is humiliate them further when they get threatening. Express, by all means, whatever respect you can for affection you shared in the past. People who are contemptuously jilted with absolutely no attempt made to respect their feelings may be on the road to revenge. If you ever set up such a theater of cruelty and blame, you may regret it.

Break off from an "I" place: I am too busy, too volatile, too old-fashioned, whatever. Even adopt a character deficiency you cannot get rid of, but will apologize for. "Yes, I am a workaholic. I know what I am losing." Endings are as important as beginnings. The Sacred Mother gave you the gift of creativity and memory to make roses in December. Protect a lover's self-respect and your own, and you may be on the way to the joys of *après-deux*.

Many women who would have no qualms about negotiating themselves out of physical violence never set up guidelines for negotiation when ordinary conflict and tension rise to verbal violence. Think about this when a jealous argument begins. What is your usual m.o.? Angry defensiveness or withdrawal? Why not the careful steps of negotiation? Negotiation is not a contest in which both women must give up what they want. It is a means of working out a problem like jealousy so that both are satisfied. "Mixed couples," wherein one woman wants to be monogamous and one wants to be poly, have even been known to work things out by the negotiation suggestions below.

Concerted, focused love negotiations are yet another way to maintain the mutuality so valued in Lesbian relationships. As men are conditioned to compete win/lose, women learn to negotiate win/win. So, most of you will be naturals at jealousy negotiating, once you internalize a few dependable guidelines for the sake of emergencies and flare-ups. The reason for practiced guidelines is that when emotions run high having a structure helps everyone keep perspective, as for example, when a jealous person is making demands and finding fault. The guidelines suggested below take a good deal of practice. Change may be slow. Set-backs do not mean failure. The only failure is not to try. These guidelines are very useful for jealousy, but are generic to most conflict.

How to Argue in Peace

Make a no-distraction appointment for discussion later if faced with a serious outburst or seeming dead-end polarization. This provides a period for you to create a clear "I" position. Deal with yourself first. Take some time alone to understand what you are feeling and why. "When she comes at me like this over XX, does it mean she wants to leave? I didn't betray her. Why am I defensive?" Be sure to focus on your own goals to stay on track. Otherwise, if the going gets tough, you can fall into merely reacting to her emo/thoughts.

Set a time limit on the discussion from five to thirty minutes! If you don't get anywhere, negotiate for more time or set up another meeting. A time limit sets focus, curtails meandering. It also prevents "wear down" tactics. Someone bullied into an agreement rarely makes much effort to keep it.

Begin with compliments and affirmations. You can always, no matter how disaffected, say you appreciate being with a woman who is generously open and committed to positive conflict resolution.

Touching is VERY helpful during the process. People often feel competitive and alienated during conflict, whereas touching arouses well-being, trust, and intimacy. As a woman is stroked, more hemoglobin is actually released into the blood, refreshing her with oxygen. It has been noted that European friends touch each other about a hundred times an hour, Americans rarely more than three or four times. In thirty cultures studied, the more touching, the less violence, according to Helen Colton in *The Gift of Touch*.

Move into defining the exact issue, breathing deeply every time you feel a defensive prickle. Define the issue as shared, as *we* do not agree, as *our* problem. No matter how irrationally jealous she is, you're the one she's dumping on, so you have a problem, too.

Each of you get equal time to speak without interruption. Go over precisely what each woman thinks are the exact discomforting actions. Isolate components. Stay in the here and now. Never express contempt for anyone's (perhaps oddball) feelings. Forget old wars or you'll never wind down the current one. If one woman doesn't want to speak at her turns, sit together quietly. I've always used this part the most, the still waters.

When you do speak, describe the emotions said actions arouse in you and your ego position. This admission of feeling can be quite vulnerable, not necessarily being your dream reaction. Every time you come from the "I" position it leads to clarity. Say the word "you," and blame rolls. Listening stops. Try stating your position as a fear which you would be delighted to give up. This is more likely to make your lady feel like a lady, helpful, rather than hostile or defensive. "When you come home late or not at all without calling me, I'm afraid you're hurt or that you are making plans to leave."

Then LISTEN—with all the egolessness you can muster. Do not interrupt except for essential clarification. You can't fake listening. It shows.

Guess what? Neither woman has to defend herself or justify her actions. She does not have to satisfy the other's questions on old stuff. We are creating a new game here.

You can get really fancy and do things like role-reversals after all the informational and emotional cards have been dealt. In role reversal, you keep trying to describe the other's point of view until she is satisfied you understand her position. You can't imagine how validating it is to hear your position being revitalized from another's lips, or what switching roles does for the empathy of the "opponent" now turned "advocate."

Finally, comes the pitch for change. Ask for 100% of what you want. You can do trade-offs later, but maybe you won't have to. Negotiate to change behavior, not feelings. Do not regale her with all the things that you do not like and want ended. This quickly degenerates into the blame game again. "I want you to please call me as soon as you know you won't be here." Note this is stated as a "want," not as an or/else demand.

Hey! You're still speaking and you've reached the settlement stage. Brainstorm to get something for everyone. "When I phone that I'm not coming home, just thank me for calling and tell me what's new," *i. e.,* nip the angst and disappointment as though there is a broken agreement.

Don't hold out for total agreement or for an apology with bells on. Accept what is reasonable, not perfect. Quit while you're ahead.

Use a thirty-minute cooling-off period for any negotiation that's a really tough one. "I don't want you to see XX on the weekends." (Gasp.)

Write out the solution and its implementation process when the conflict is a very thorny one. Even the most honest among us often filter memories to remember only what we want to. If solutions are not adhered to, even when it is quite clear what was agreed, something is awry, and it's back to the bargaining table. When your partner regularly agrees to one thing but never implements her part of the bargain, she is an infantile model who should perhaps be traded in for a responsible adult.

Evaluate yourselves on how you communicated and how to improve. Any below the belt tactics? Here and now focus, specificity, humor, affection? Is there now a decrease of hurt and fear? An increase of information, trust or caring?

End with affirmative closure, for heaven's sake. Thank each other for *trying* and for any solutions proposed. Do forget that "one last word." Kiss her instead. Be sure to recognize that people react differently after a heavy discussion. One woman may need continuing reassurance; the other may take hours of time alone.

Immediately arrange something fun to do together where no relationship issues are raised.

Jealousy? Is It More a Question of Loyalty?

Let me raise one last, yet critical issue I wish every target of sexual jealousy might crystallize for herself. This is the issue of loyalty, a jeweled essential of the good life, whether person-to-person loyalty, loyalty to a group, an ideal, an aesthetic, creed or idea. Who happens to touch whose nookie, and when, is surely not a vital concern in comparison to the deep vaults of loyalty, eternally renewable.

The fact is we don't need sexual exclusivity at all from a lover. What we usually do need is our lovers to be steadfast allies. Such allegiance, of course, can only be built over time by exhibiting trustworthiness through all the rhythms of intimacy, especially those which involve the weathering of crises. Here are the heartfelt questions of loyalty: "Will you hear me, consider me, care for me, be open to me? Are we creating a garden of specialness in a field of trust?" To be a loyal lover, a fidelitous one: show up when you say you will; pay attention to whatever happens; tell the truth; and be open to the outcome. When I am a jealousy target, I cannot help but wonder how loyal a woman is to me who considers me the radiant light of her life at 9:30 am, realizes I am with another woman at 10:00, so at 10:05 deems my precious self a monster. But then, one of the more mundane tests of loyalty is, "Can I keep the faith even when she behaves badly?"

Loyalty is a great meditation because we can also look at all the old loyalties pushed upon us from birth. These "coerced loyalties" are more like conditioned reflexes. We are totally unquestioning of their origin and useful purpose today. For example, how many American Buddhists or Goddess worshippers will still pause before sitting a baby on a fat *Bible* to give her a little more height at table? On sweltering days, how many of us continue to wear clothes, even when alone? How many feel loyal and duty-bound to pay taxes to non-supportive, in fact ruinous, governments, to genuflect to hierarchies of unfair privilege? People are loyal to imaginary geographical lines, to compulsory heterosexuality, to sexually closed relationships, but they can't remember why.

We are conditioned to think of loyalty in terms of dualistic black or white, and in terms of scarcity. Friend/Enemy. Insider/Outsider. Yet carefully considered loyalty is a fluid living trust touching different shores of circumstance. Perception of rigid here/there dualistic loyalty gives rise to the fears of "loyalty conflict," which the idea of multiple lovers can bring up. Sexual jealousy pales in contrast to loyalty conflict. Fear of conflicting loyalties invariably comes up when for some reason we are struck with catastrophic anxieties of "what if. . ." about the future. "What if both lovers get cancer at the same time? Will you be there for me—or her?" Well, no one likes to envision one suffering friend, not to mention two, three or four, but consider and reiterate that women are creative and strong in personal crises. Women have been the ones to handle whole households of crises! Just as gay men summon strength in the face of massive AIDS losses, Lesbians are proving we can do the same for AIDS *and* cancer.

The best way to diffuse cataclysmic fears for women who will not be put off by the "long odds" reply is to carefully go over possible contingency plans in detail, like we do in San Francisco with earth-quake preparedness, or when people draw up post-operative care schedules. Make as honest and as clear commitments as you can. "I think I could promise to come over one full day or night a week, prepare dinners, and will do my best to help organize others to do the same. Haven't I come through for you before?" There is noth-ing like a mutual support pact to make everyone feel lots safer and better about everything in this dangerous life. How many people fear death only because they are afraid there will be no one to sit with them?

I bet half the time you are targeted ostensibly for sexual jealousy, it is because a woman is feeling major anxiety over where your *loyalty* is, not your vulva. Loyalty is much more pervasive in the fabric of a relationship for women than for men. We tend to see relationships as some kind of great cooperative union. Among men, steeped in team hierarchy and outward aggression, loyalty is usually a code of the negative, to simply avoid harm. Thus, John Mitchell, a "man's man," was "loyal" to Richard Nixon, as the only conspirator not to squeal on Nixon's felonies—in contrast to the way Ollie squealed on Ronnie. For women, loyalty is more apt to mean a caring, positive effort to demonstrate specialness. Our loy-alty is woven with empathy. If we hold someone to be special, we are there for them in support, in defense. This involves duty and dedication. It is shown by women overwhelmingly being the ones to care for the sick, old and dying in a family. We tend to value loyalty in our promises to a lover. "I'll call you" means "I'll call you." Men complain in amazement that women actually take these three words seriously.

So return your calls. Stay loyal and true to yourself. If the principle of polyfidelity with its personal bill of rights is part of your code, remain loyal to it. You'll find the right woman to belong *with*, not belong to. Do not worry unduly about minor jealousy flare-ups, especially when the relationship is young. Do you really want anyone who is so securely arrogant as to be immune to all jealousy?

Warnings for Wantons

Experience is knowing the price you have to pay.

Intimacy does not equal intensity. Question extreme emotions while treating them to tea, conversation and delicious refreshment.

Conventional sin is no excuse for bad manners.
Keep agreements. Keep agreements. Keep agreements.

"One does not discover new lands without consenting to lose sight of the shore for a very long time." — Gide

Focus on this moment's joy and adventure. No expectations.

Find composure in the truth of impermanence
and the depth of true joy.

Rejection of joy is the only blasphemy.

Deep commitment to two lovers may be the max
unless you're unemployed. Heed the Law of Raspberry Jam:
"The thinner you spread it, the milder the tart."

All advances depend on timing.

Kind form and resilient schedule lead to equipoise.

Polyfidelity depends on lightness and on friendship,
dedication to passion and to community.

Leave only the trace a bird tracks in the sky. "Wander, but don't flaunt," is the wise rambler's Principle of Least Obtrusiveness.

Domesticated Homo sapiens' favorite thing is to complain.
Don't be tamed by it.
In contrast, no wild thing suffers from self-pity.

Life herself is a scandal.

The Odd Woman:
Pragmatic Romantic

Query: What's with all the demonization of women who prefer love affairs to love nests? Women who see each Lesbian as a sensual individual, not as a stump, neutered and shackled by coupledom? No breakup treachery on my mind, either. I enjoy being in a co-housing community, so am not looking for that "just one anchor" to shore me up in this (yup) absurd, isolating world. I've been having a great time with a married woman whose Lesbian partner seems gracious and tolerant toward me. Sometimes I do worry I'll get hurt, but I want to make this last. Any suggestions?
— *Freida Buck, Asheville, North Carolina*

¡Brava!

No one has any right to consider you tainted (adulterated?) unless betrayal is afoot in your liaison. Still, you are upsetting current Lesbian social convention and many private assumptions. Good medicine for the smug, I'd say. Some carpers could be envious that you all have a passionate, companionate arrangement with few of the freedom restrictions they have. People may have "single phobia" too. Many couples agree to curtail sexual, self-actualizing adventures out of their own clinging emptiness. Whatever it takes not to be alone. You're single, swinging—yet partnered. Forget the milligrubs. The dogs bark, the caravan moves on. You have, however, hitched your wagon to a star, and I would not for one moment underestimate the ecstasy—and the effort—of the odd woman's transit around coupledom.

I note you hope to "make this last." On the sexualove continuum, from casual to serious, your long lasting approach places you in what social scientists call a "parallel relationship." Parallel play is a long-term liaison conducted alongside a marriage. The spouse knows, accepts, and often approves that another lover exists. This sort of longer-term liaison is usually well directed by customs, agreements, and habits: the kind of *bravissima* designer arrangements *Lesbian Polyfidelity* chronicles and celebrates.

As sensual interest comes to embrace the beloved's authentic person and character, ongoing care and commitment usually deepen. Meanwhile, at the other pole of the sexualove spectrum is the lighthearted, recreational affair. Here players revel in sensual activities for their own sake. Thus, we have the more person-centered "liaison" in contrast to the more act-centered brief "affair." Each lover's version of the connection, its relational/recreational mix, could be represented by two, perhaps differing, yin/yang spheres. Each would show moving, melding, but distinct areas for sensuality and for commitment. Woe to lovers who initially misjudge, then continue to misinterpret one another's sensuality/commitment ratio in a relationship equation. I bring this up because the odd woman seems to be the person most often misled—or to misread—what is actually going on in her married lover's sphere of intent. Is her married love seeking open relationships or just open beds?

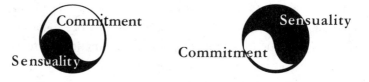

We sometimes hold parties for the local odd women from my poly-fidelity survey. These odd women prefer parties to some sort of support group because most already have powerful support and safety nets in place. If this were not the case, the odd woman rarely survives more than a brief showing in the Triad Olympics. Besides, a typical support group's motherly milieu or blame game resentments don't exactly inspire the flirtation gambits in which most odd women delight. At one gathering we once determined that an affair usually buds around one of four common functions from the point of view of the partnered woman. It is important to note one cannot really define an affair, except possibly by function. The only generalization we agreed upon is that an affair is a form of self-expression. Of these four types of affairs, only one is ideal for the odd woman to pursue. This one is a romance with a partnered woman who is seeking variety and/or connection for its own sake. A truly catered affair! More of this all-systems-go ride later.

Riptide Affair Warnings

Please shy away from the others: the "out-the-door" affair; the conflict-avoidance affair; and the intimacy-avoidance affair. You can take a tumble, while your lover remains sitting pretty. An out-the-door affair means you are being used to provide the provocation, drama and alibi for a couple breakup. Scenes, scenes, scenes. If this doesn't throw your life into tizzy enough, you are also being sucked for momentous shots of rescuer energy. The partnered woman, lovely damsel in distress as she seems to be, usually does not have the honesty to examine and declare exactly to her partner what isn't working in their relationship. She may not have the creativity and energy to co-process a solution. Or, in a proven stalemate, she can't find the respect and self-direction to leave by herself, as bravely and kindly as possible. She sets you up in a "pre-bound" relationship, about as crazy to be involved in as a rebound one. The usual problem with such a lover is her failure of nerve. She is likely to bed and wed you to repeat the same cycle. You'll be luckier if she leaves—which often happens—as soon as you've delivered the passion necessary to spring her. So, please stay away from any couple on the rocks, unless you are a drama queen. Truly polyfidelitous couples are usually deliciously companionate, in passionate delight with one another.

Be also wary of a woman enticing you into a "conflict-avoidance affair" as a way to manipulate rather than confront her partner. Her focus is really on her spouse, with you as the foil. These can be affairs set up for revenge. Ugly. They are also the ones in which you are the lover's bargaining chip to manipulate more spousal time and attention. Or, your presence pressures the spouse to change behavior, as in provoking more material generosity from her. You are, in short, the other bidder in auction, not of love, but of power.

The "intimacy-avoidance affair," a seeming oxymoron, is more het male than Lesbian. It is also rare where betrayal is absent. It may occur, however, when one woman easily feels engulfed by intimacy, fears for her own selfhood due to physical and psychic merging with a partner. Sexual meandering, with any accompanying conflict, can provoke distance. Even in honest relations, the odd woman may spark partner arguments. These create distance. The odd woman beckoning certainly necessitates actual physical distance apart from the spouse. Thus, the rover may feel curiously independent, "her own" woman, the more arms that hold her. None of this boundary-setting is necessarily a misfortune for the odd woman. Just be careful of extreme coldness where no one is ever allowed to get really close, if your goal as odd woman is intimacy as well as recreation.

The craziest reason, of course, for having an affair is no reason at all.

Surf's Up!

Thus endeth the riptide affair warnings. Now let us float on less sinister waves in the bounder's main. Select a woman who just wants to have a great time romancin' and dancin', with no ulterior agenda except maybe becoming one of your delicious intimates. You'll know in a few weeks if you're headed for the briny deep or for surfing in the sun. By creating a liaison with a woman who already has a "helpmate," your role can be about as close to pure pleasure as conceivable. If marriage is emotional work, the liaison is emotional play. When your domesticated lover is sick and crabby, someone else is in charge of the ward. You see your lover at her best. There are few unpleasant or mundane demands. You all do not spend time together scouring the oven, worrying about bills and the in-laws, haggling over who cleans the kitty litter or washes the dirty socks. Yours is the time to make love, make laughter, to share the beating of hearts.

Your shorter, limited time makes for compressed intimacy. Here, some realities are obliterated, the workaday flotsam and jetsam. Other realities are illuminated, your talent for sensual play, for storytelling and listening, for enjoyment and relaxation, for learning new things, going on adventures. Ah, the excitement of self-exploration via the inland passages of another. Both the child and the adult are freed on the wings of romance. Limited time is sexually arousing, with its special intensity and excitement. Lovers appreciate one another more, knowing the moment is fleeting. Precious time is not as likely to be misspent in trivial argument, faultfinding or moodiness.

The liaison re-narrates lives. Your relationship is experienced not as constraining, but enabling. Or it can be viewed as light relief, a fantasy world within the control of the dreamers. The odd woman almost has it all: a sexually charged, romantic and lust-filled friendship. You attain the high level of comfort engendered by a regular *amoureuse*, with little daily irritation or drudgery. The *quality* of the involvement offsets the quantity of involvement. What's more, the odd woman is still free to fool around or to go home to acres of lovely privacy and alone time.

Sure, the purse-lipped Calvinists aver that you have no right to skim the creme or keep the mundane from the door. Well, let their teacups rattle in their saucers. I wonder how many an odd woman on her dying day will lament, "I wish my life had been more possessive and less passionate, more stale and less sensual?" Can you imagine her confessing, "I so regret my fine hobbies of gardening, theater, and lovely swims, of being absorbed in good books and conversation. Most, I regret my similiar attachment to honeymoon pleasures with women I would never own. "

Perhaps the credo of every happy odd woman is "I want," rather than "I need"; "I let go," rather than "I keep." What are the essential qualities of a woman who does not feel that to share a lovely woman is a second-rate pastime? For openers, the authentic odd woman prizes individual freedom over couple security. She is able to compartmentalize her sensuality from her householder life. Her greatest key to success, however, may be when the odd woman is *already married.* Yes. She is usually wedded to a cause, a career, a first family or extended one, or to a passion, like art. She can, of course, actually be married, playing the role of spouse in her own polyfidelitous relationship, as well as of the odd woman to another relationship. This is the famed quadrangle of Lesbian love which provides an excellent balance in need and role sharing.

In any event, it is absolutely essential that the odd woman have vigorous focus apart from her love affair to avoid the notorious "odd woman out" syndrome. The odd woman cannot be moping about when her married love is unavailable. She is instead deeply engrossed, delighted in her own time to pursue another passion. Besides being extremely self-directed, the successful odd woman has developed a harmony of being, a cohesive self that enjoys life apart from the love merge. She is probably a dynamite self-soother. She knows herself and her issues. These issues may feel something like: best to live alone to indulge my shameless quirks; keep responsibilities lean in order to travel; build the business first; major in the kids or the academic degree; spread commitment among several sexual and heart friends.

Another quality of the practiced odd woman is her *noblesse oblige* around sharing, which requires discretion, planning and the ability to foresee practical as well as emotional dimensions. She certainly has to respect her lover's home base, usually treating this provence like a dull private forest, with respect and a wide berth. Our form of adultery is not the "lawless region" Hawthorne calls it in *The Scarlet Letter*. It is a balancing act, well-governed by territorial boundaries and other fine-tuned customs.

But is it not lonely, rarely having full immersion in your beloved's living space? Yes and no, depending on the situation. She may, after all, have Laura Ashley tastes or mangy dogs. I know odd women who are insomniacs if not on a certain side of their own bed in their own home. Still, as odd woman, it may be hard not to want a trace of yourself in her boudoir. There are ways. I figure that my love inhales around 10^{22} atoms per breath; lots of these are mine. I literally dance in her heart wherever she lays her head.

Yet, let's be clear regarding the power dynamics of a relationship based on frank structural inequality, even if in all other ways it is fair and generous. The fact is that the odd woman's lover spends most of her waking and sleeping hours with someone else. Although the odd woman may have aura, the spouse usually has the territorial, temporal and social status. Further, if your relationship gets touchy, the married lover has another stash and can more easily fold. She can walk out on you to be lavishly embosomed as the prodigal wanderer. But where does the odd woman go to for caresses immediately after a breakup—unless the arrangement has been quadrangle or she too has loving friends on call?

Our self-actualizing odd woman, pragmatic romantic that she is, must be a born risk-taker. All liaisons, of course, are a calculated risk, a prime reason they are so exciting and sexy. So the wise odd woman recognizes that just because a liaison ends, does not mean it is a failure. It means it has run its course. I have never known a love affair to end without something of the vibration remaining to enrich my existence. I honor this rainbow parachute I've woven of everything that's broken. But, just so you won't have to bail out as the odd woman, here are some final cautionary notes.

The Three Way. Both in bed with you at the same time, the couple is often using you as a dildo. Later they get to process everything, while alone you may be feeling sexually colonized, then marginalized. While it is lovely to be a respected guest in a relationship, three-ways can easily make you feel like the tool or toy. Bisexual three-ways seem to last longer than Lesbian ones. Lesbian three-ways are usually so emotionally flammable they can split atoms— and blow up relationships. Three-ways can be hot, no doubt about this. They can also be flustered and alienating, much sexier on the smoothly choreographed fantasy level. Swinging gals advise it's best to play with two-plus sexy *strangers*, passing in the night. There is no intimacy power struggle tomorrow, just a lingering bouquet of bodies and throbbing memories.

The Exclusive. Here—and it's common—your married love actually suggests you save your lips for her alone. A typical line goes, "You know that I'm certainly not playing around with everyone. I can't bear for you to." In this double standard she gets it at home and for dine-out. Nuts. This is contrary to every tenet of polyfidelity. It will kill your social life, make you cross and cross-eyed.

WARNING! WARNING! Danger! Mayhem! Fucking with your married lover's spouse or any lover's long-term heart friends can be fatal unless everyone has ardently taken the vows of Lesbian group marriage, a creature scarce as hens' teeth. The emotional overload of a close community's conflicting loyalties may come crashing and burning around your sweet ass. Havens of confidentiality are no longer safe because everyone is in the loop. Taking lovers from different friendship networks makes good evolutionary sense. Nature seems to prefer a far-flung variety of genes for the sake of innovation and inter-tribal alliance building.

Secrecy Will Entomb You. Initially, you may love an intrigue's dangerous excitement and the bond creation with the guilty spouse. Then you'll begin to hate yourself for collaborating in this closet of false shame. Anyone who asks you to hide does not respect you, herself or passion. See previous chapters on truth telling.

The Fatigue Factor. Your married love can empty out emotionally and physically from trying to keep all her women satisfied. Polyfidelity takes a practiced equilibrium. Being willing does not always mean she's able. Give her a loving intermission. Life should be full of intermissions. This is one reason I've enjoyed being the odd woman. We automatically have intermissions to roll around in.

The Classic Dangle. Soap opera stuff you shouldn't ever be involved with because, remember, you don't get hooked by estranged couples. But the dangle can come down the line. It may go on for years. Your lover one day confesses that "things are hard at home," so she may be considering a little trade-in, like for you. Pay no attention. There are always times when one partner doesn't much like the other. These tiffs are rarely permanent. Emotional fidelity is constantly shifting depending on who you are with and the tide of events. Stay out of a couple's haggles. Do not take sides, since you've heard only one. Never compete with the spouse. Her seat is taken, and your position to her is not superior or inferior, just different. Keep it this way. To help understand the advantages, you may want to brush up on the timeless techniques of ye old. . .

Courtly Love

Virtually all the happy, satisfied odd women I interviewed or have met along the garden path are students or naturals in the great tradition of *l'amour courtois*, "courtly love." Our thousand-year legacy of courtly love not only perfumes but permeates Western civilization. It is therefore amazing how few Lesbians have delighted in exploring its roots, variants, ideals, and inspirations, if even to understand courtly love's unfortunate debasement, as well. As the women's spirituality movement has gone back to archeologically mine the very bones of the Sacred Mother, as political Lesbians unearth our heroism "before Stonewall," I suggest the wise odd woman journey back in time to the fragrant lavender capital of the world, Provence, France. Listen to the songs here of the twelfth century *troubadour* and the female *trobairitz*; study the powerful women who cultivated courtly love as *salonnières* do art. Such arbiters of courtly love as Queen Eleanor of Aquitaine and Marie, Countess of Champagne, secured a sexualove revolution which many historians argue is more influential than the Renaissance.* Here was a social philosophy which grips moderns today as powerfully as organized religion or material rationalism—and heartily-

---

*   "Courtly love effected a change which has left no corner of our ethics, our imagination, our daily life untouched, and thus erected impassable barriers between us and the classical past or oriental present. Compared with this revolution, the Renaissance is a mere ripple." —*C.S. Lewis* contradicts both. Certainly the pleasure and passion of modern gay liberation, not to mention seventeenth through nineteenth century Lesbian love, would have been inconceivable had the aesthetic of courtly love not arisen. Polyfidelity, of course, is a direct heir of courtly love's "wisdom of adultery" as a positively sacred calling.

It would take yet another book to recount the history, aesthetic, and influence of courtly love on those of us bearing the knightly colors of Lesbian outlaw. Lesbians are a heresy within the heresy of courtly love, its evolutionary apogee. Who does not long to unite with her beloved as the emanation of the Beloved? As with any spiritual quest, courtly love is variously applauded and derided. It is constantly being purified, while as consistently being profaned and twisted, depending on the era and agenda of the practitioner. Courtly love is indeed replete with excess, folly, misguided dualism, and sheer absurdity, much like our other social arts and sciences. Courtly love, along with these, reveals the Sky-God vs. Earth Mother ambiguity toward sex and love, our amazing approach/avoidance in the sexualove dance.

Detractors of courtly love, like Denis de Rougemont, even link courtly love with incest desire. They point to courtly love's displays of a glorious madonna figure entwined with a subservient, adoring lover. De Rougemont also sees courtly love as a promotion of suffering and death. All such old boys who get it up for control and reason see absolute shipwreck in courtly love. True, an aspect of courtly love links love with suffering, as well as love with death, at least metaphorically. This may not be a neurotic, but a realistic acceptance of the high and low tides of passion and idealism. A lure of the sea of passion is to plunge us into its unsettling intensity, its pungent, salty incense of change. In this ocean's presence, we are hopefully not out of order, but we are deliciously out of control. And who does not agree that the love relationship is mortal? Love and lovers die. Loving friendship blooms and fades. Death is not a failure. It means something has let go to open yet another cycle.

So, let us explore the courtly love inspirations of use to the Lesbian freelance, the odd woman, who is courtly love's dashing heir and acolyte. One can't help but be historically fond of courtly love because, like Lesbianism, it is a loving movement which also promotes heresy and social disorder. Courtly love was a predominately woman-led revolution of the emotions. Its medieval roots lie in the hideously persecuted heresy of Catharism. Its ancient roots draw from western Manicheanism and Platonism, stern soil oddly disinclined to hybridize flesh and spirit as one. Yet homosexual Platonism glorified love as a stairway to spiritual excellence, love as a union of souls leading to wholeness. Platonic dualism was offset in the early Middle Ages by courtly love's Eastern roots. The Crusaders brought back Moorish and Asian beliefs, like Sufism, Tantra and Taoism, which presented sex *per se* as sacred ennobling energy, with woman as transcendent Goddess. From these poly-roots, courtly love amazingly flowered on the bleak fields of feudal barbarism and misogyny. Here the Catholic Church obsessively cultivated the fear that sexual love was a trapdoor to hell. Women were land to be tilled, mere lust and child bearers. The economic and political contracts of arranged marriages engendered loveless fornication with the added weight of sin. Astoundingly, courtly love began to exalt adultery with special ethical and spiritual values at the same time adultery was a capital offense. Adultery, which had been in classical times a grave private matter, became an act of sedition, punished by the ruling state and sealed with eternal damnation of the Church. Romantic love defied the edict that female flesh is a male property right.

Meanwhile, on parallel tracks, other developments prepared the way for our profligate flower of change. Among the ruling classes, wealth opened up leisure. Leisure unfurled the delights of pleasure, games and art. As the Crusades and wars quieted down, a surplus of noble young sons came on the market, only to find a scarcity of land and ladies not already wedlocked. At the same time, there was a growing revulsion to the barren, harsh God of the Patriarchs. The deification of Mary was sweeping Europe, the return of the ancient Earth Goddess of Ten Thousand Names. The "Mother of God" was becoming "God the Mother" again. This heresy of "Mariolatry" was later to be formally suppressed, but never destroyed. Men looked afresh at the madonnas walking about on Earth in magnificent courtly raiment. Hymns to the Madonna became lighthearted songs and poetry to a lofty married lady. What had begun as a game and literary conceit was to become a way of life.

Social historians argue whether or not courtly love was, in practice, actually consummated, much as Lesbian historians debate the question of physical orgasm in women's lush, effusive friendships of past centuries. Both the cults of courtly love and female romantic friendship, in all probability, held a spectrum of behaviors. Some lovers reveled in earthy lust, others tantalized one another with chaste intimacies. There are written accounts, journals and letters to "prove" each position—and all those in between. Note that it was essential for both cults to at least feign innocence in the face of massive social taboo. Don't "just say no." Just say, like our politicians, you do, but... you don't come.

Whatever sexual seizures did or did not occur in courtly love, one thing is certain, the techniques of human sexuality were thoroughly refined. Mere two-minute rutting was considered disrespectful of the beloved, as well as vulgar. Sipping all the senses was celebrated in a delicious courtship spiral of foreplay, with nary a nod to procreation. The poetics of foreplay, ecstasy, and afterglow were memorialized in verse. The separation necessitated by adultery was endured with exquisite longing, only to cycle afresh when the lovers could rendezvous again. Long sessions of fondling nude in bed are succulently described. Here, a quick drive to orgasm is scorned in favor of playful and prayerful adoration of the beloved's body, with no penile entry. This well-known practice is known as *amor puris* in courtly love. Fingers and tongue were not verboten. Sound familiar?

Courtly love held, quite perceptively, that romance and passion usually thrive on separation and uncertainty, thus its preference for the obstacle of the triangle, with its unpredictable and changing climates. It was further understood that the soaring adulation of a mere mortal is unsuited to the irritations and pressures inherent in household mundanities. Marriage and romantic love were seen as a complete contradiction. The lover was, in fact, usually unmarriageable. So, create a parallel fantasy for two, where the focus is unharried adoration and theatrical adventure. Thus, idealized love or infatuation, far from being considered, as by the ancients, a form of madness, came to be considered an ennobling pastime.

Courtly love promised generosity of the soul and actualization of the spirit. Its quest demanded discipline: the cultivation of awareness, of sharing, of gentleness, strength and courage. This care appeared not only in gallantries, but in major duties to the beloved, like championing the weak in the face of the powerful. Under duress, one need observe a noble constancy, a profound fidelity to one's love muse. The chivalric virtues were adopted for the sake of pleasing and of pleasure, and in the name of a higher law than daily feudal oppressions.

Conscience became, for the first time, related to passion in delightful "Courts of Love." These Courts, inspired by women's leadership and wisdom in all matters of love, explored the ethics and proprieties of love in public dialogue. For the first time in the Western world, unmarried lovers adopted an ethical code to guide them on what they considered to be a spiritual quest toward the grail of the body, soul and oversoul.

Such courtly sensual play and questing was later to become vastly tamed by bourgeois morality and individualism. Alas, the merchant-mind prefers certainty. Yet, the ideal of a wildly sensual *cum* quasi-mystical union remains as a marvelous dream, far outshining the Catholic and Calvinist procreation dictates. "The Myth of the Romantic Marriage" is reflected in our tandem polygamy, our fetish of the twentieth century romantic dating ritual, our preoccupation with adulteries in fact as well as in fiction. Tepid as a Westerner's sensibility may be in many realms, the deep blush of thirteenth century courtly love still colors our pair bonding. Never mind that attraction may be a complex pattern of passionate hunger plus the desire for security and comfort. Whatever purpose for choosing a person, "passionate love" is the only acceptable publicly voiced reason. The frailty of our bourgeois hybrid "romantic marriage" is revealed in frumpy *Reader's Digest et al.* umpteenth millionth checklist on how to wedge the romance back into marriage.

The odd woman—like the adulterous *courtière*—asks, "Why bother with marriage doldrums at all? Why try to make a silk purse out of a sow's ear, when both have their place?" Apart from northern Euro-American cultures (and our media), this reasoning indeed prevails. "Falling in love" is rarely deemed the prelude to marriage. In most cultures, marriage is usually viewed as a highly valued, but humdrum, practical business. Why not acknowledge playing to the power of three precisely because it kindles challenge, longing and excitement? Keep it offbeat, outside the norms. Here the short, charged hours together are awash with appreciation, awareness and totally alive intensity. The odd woman knows her blend may be more artifice than reality, more peak moments than reruns. Oh, there may be the devil to pay. She can afford it—always with both eyes open.

La Belle Dame de Psyche

Thus, we have the rich, historic conceit of courtly love, both fashioning and inspiring the odd woman who beckons from afar. Lesbians have actually taken things a step further, creating a conceit within a conceit. The allure for the odd woman, the purely attentive, but not quite possessable one is eternally seductive. If she doesn't appear, Lesbians often invent, or should I say hire, her—in a more proper and professional, more malleable version, of course. Who else is the ubiquitous Lesbian therapist but a safe odd woman? The parallels are staggering: therapist as ever-yearned-for, idealized odd woman, our transcendent intimate, mental hands on one another's knees. That's "therapist," not "the rapist" of orderly manners and morals is she, but a professional of discretion and breeding, abiding by vocational restraints.

Light and consensual therapy, what the trade calls, "sport therapy," is largely an erotic construct. (I am not, of course, describing the deeply disorienting madness treated in mental institutions run by the white shirts.) What do we ardently desire in this odd woman whom we are prohibited to touch or feel too inexperienced to pursue? Exactly what I found in a classic definition of consensual therapy: "an external stimulus to replace one array of internal feelings by stirring up others." You may be crazy to visit a therapist, but then again you may be crazy not to partake of a professional odd woman at least for courtly love practice if your insurance pays.

Come with me. Let's book a session.

The desired one may advertise near the personals, practically supporting feminist newspapers like *Sojourner*. We set our rendezvous at a carefully prearranged time, allowing the light excitement of anticipation. We are encouraged to meet once a week, but can easily make that two or three times. I know women who spend more time bathing and preparing for their therapy "date" than they do for work. Many women make love less with their partner once they start seeing a therapist. She is likely to consume vast reaches of our emotional and intellectual life. We meet our lady for a one-on-one assignation, doors so tightly closed they could be locked; sometimes they are. No interruptions are permitted as we search the Esperanto of one another's eyes and hands.

There is an emotional pledge of utter confidentiality as well as loyalty. After all, sexually charged events, hot fantasies and dreams, especially taboos, may be explored together. This is called "safe sex" because while the client revels in both indiscretion and inhibition, the therapist is gallant in the face of every shame. Uptown therapists (that's Sacramento Street and Pacific Heights in San Francisco) sensualize their environments with valuable, changing objets d'art. Lavish bouquets advertise what flowers always do—sexual display.

Set and setting encourage delight, pleasure, and swollen emotions sans physical performance anxiety. We also may relax with tea, soft music, and perhaps incense, candles or aromatic oils. Here we will return, with our shield or on it, always welcomed home from the quests upon which Lady Therapy inspires us to embark.

Sociologists and psychologists who study affairs and liaisons note one common thread in all their variety: *a drama atmosphere*. The script may be one of suffering or joy, lofty or dreadful, but an engrossing narrative it is to the creator. We revise, re-narrate our lives to give them meaning, to create change and motion. Likewise, a skilled therapist taps into your story. Lady T not only attends your story, but will co-create a new one with you.

We admit we choose a therapist for her narrative style: playful, spiritual, bulldagger swagger, motherly, dominatrix, egalitarian. We also breathe her pheromones. To be frank, Lesbians care more about these sexual sentinels and styles than any purported therapeutic orientation. Women, especially Lesbians, instantly track a therapist's sexual aura, quickly note unspoken, subtle sexual charges. A therapist confided to me that she is aroused by occasionally entertaining a lover (non-client) in her professional suite. Invariably, clients, even hours later, remark on the room's vibrational waves—indirectly of course. "The flowers seem to pulse with excitement today." "How alive" or "young" our therapist looks. "It's different in here," they repeat in some variation with happy, quizzical smiles.

So let the intense intimacy roll with Lady Therapy. Here is the relationship you dreamed of. You decide by one phone call when it begins and when to break it off. Ooops—early warning signal: therapist breakups can conjure all the sweet, widely-broadcast suffering of true courtly love. The most public melodrama of a client/therapist breakup is the controversial saga of Lesbian Episcopal priest Carter Heyward. The voluable Heyward wrote an entire book, *When Boundaries Betray Us,* on the steamy etiology of courtship and parting from her, shall we say, impenetrable

Lesbian psychiatrist. Finger-touching explorations by candlelight, but no—horrors! s-e-x.

Can this marriage be saved? No, because there was none, no consummation in biblical terms, that is. Was the pure, transcendent love worth it? Yes! For Carter, precisely because of the ordeal, the longing and ecstasy, plus the ongoing media attention. Had Carter brushed up on the tradition of courtly love her therapist had internalized, she would have fashioned *Boundaries* as a glorious paean to Lady T, overriding any taint of petulance. Reframing it all as lifelong poetic longing, no telling what this preacher cum *trobairitz* could have tasted with Lady T by now. There is an old saying in courtly love: "It is easier to mount a dragon than to leap off." But don't worry, there are loads of other books, less truculent, on how to leave your therapist. Somehow we don't tremble, needing advice on how to leave our acupuncturist, coach, minister, lawyer or gardener. Why? Because we do not usually share with them that shimmering romantic love we do with a therapist.

So, forewarned, please enjoy the meanwhile: Lady T's polished role in delivering an accepting, downright warming relationship. Her training in the sensual arts is to become a living example of optimum attachment for you. Thus, your relationship unfolds in an atmosphere of safe, yet heightened suggestion and openness. Intimate, vulnerable revelations subtly disrobe you more naked than naked, exposed beyond flesh. With the absolute attention of prayer, Lady T takes it all in—and remembers each detail! Like antiquity's sacred prostitute, she tolerates unorthodox desires while remaining a serene, goddess-like creature of wisdom and power.

By now we are in the fabled, primeval forest of "transference." Nothing if not inflammatory, the theory of transference holds that the bewitched client attributes the attitudes or behavior of significant people in her life to the therapist as well. Thus the client will reenact her patterns of interplay and conflict, her needs and desires, while now in a safe, teaching environment. Transference is held to be good practice, useful for brushing up on wholesome skills and exposing neurotic delusions. You are supposed to fall in love with Lady T!

Lady T is not, however, supposed to fall in love with you. Your flattery and her power are refreshing enough. Her mutually expressed desire would be a variation of "countertransference," distorting the client's reactions for the therapist's own uses and needs. I asked my therapist friends if they ever loved their clients anyway. As Freud once remarked about a scandal of Jung's, "In view of the kind of matter we deal with, it will never be possible to avoid little laboratory explosions." I found out that most successful therapists are "serial lovers," just as I may "love" people whose writing I am editing. Editors, too, attentively draw their authors out, protect them, amuse them, polish them up, often share their deepest feelings, hopes, crises. Author's victories inspire us. We celebrate together. Brilliant authors fall in love with great editors and will follow them from publishing house to publishing house. Together, quest after quest, we delight one another. But in publishing, unlike the therapy arena, we are quite clear that we also depend on one another for economic survival. If authors and editors have sex, it may break that romantic, idealized flow, which is also cash-driven. Lady T, however, as the perceived "top," never alludes to how economically and perhaps emotionally dependent she is on a client's keeping her best bottom forward.

Speaking of which, perhaps we should pause for a commercial break. Ain't it supposed to be god-awful to pay for intimacy, good conversation, understanding and love? To pay for sex talk, a private, suggestive milieu in elite company, with maybe some "play" or good old body work? As it is impossible to prohibit adultery, the most society can do is charge admission. Why not indulge if you've got the coin? Because current gender ideology emphatically denies "good" women can do what men have done for millennia. Women are deeply conditioned not to seek sensual *hetaerae*, talented mistresses. (Save them for the guys?) But it was Sappho who first used the word *hetaera*, not the boys. *Hetaera* means "companion," "intimate female friend." Much later the word was appropriated to mean a paid, educated courtesan for males. Via "wholesome" Lesbian therapy we get to luxuriate in *hetaerae* again. All it takes is a small attention deficit at home and an income over four figures.

Lesbian mavericks (wealthy ones) are now engaging actual sex workers for attention, leaving the mask of neurosis behind. In San Francisco, it is around $200 an hour for a woman you would love to dine with and discuss fractals or Tae Kwon Do—as well as caress later. Many sex workers say they do a sliding scale for women (yay, sisterhood!). As one remarked, "Don't we wish all clients were women?" So you may get down around $150, and a house call at that. These ladies of pleasure receive two or three calls per month from Lesbians, lots more from bisexual couples. So if you prorate the therapist's fee of around $50 to $100, it all comes down to how many senses you want to curl up with in a session. Also how you consider the question: why is sex the only human activity in which the professional has lower status than the amateur?

Of course, we know that a therapist, unlike an editor or sex worker, is absolutely prohibited by law, if not common sense, from delving deep into your wordless mysteries. This is for the best because if Lady T does become your actual lover, problems will invariably ensue, just like in real life. Then you will have to go to another therapist simply to deal with your bad relationship with the first one. Yet another love potion may be drunk, and on and on. You'll probably never get over the "core issue" you desperately need to untangle in the first place.

Look at the Reverend Carter. She originally went into counseling devastated by a deep crisis of faith, something every minister, every questing knight, must fathom. But Carter got hot and bothered, full of entitlement during mere transference. Her Lady T, one of the strict constructionists in the continuum of courtly love, would go tantalizingly so far, but no farther. If the holy grail becomes mere possessive goal, will it ever reveal the vision, illuminate the quest, open a path? Lady T embodies a non-attachment vision, proving her devotion by not pursuing orgasm with her Lesbian knights.

Thus, the odd woman, hired or free form, stands not so much for unrequited love as for non-possessive pleasure, intimacy and love. As the prophet suggests, "Let there be spaces in your togetherness. Fill each other's cup but drink not from one cup." In the ecstatic/mystical tradition, you can have everything by letting it go. We wave the tide out, enabling us to relive the fresh taste of incoming love, time after time.

Bridges and Boundaries:
The River of Clarity

Query: One of my co-partners who also plays the s/m scene says that our polyfidelity arrangement demands as much attention to power dynamics, roles and explicit boundaries as s/m. She seems to be the one in our polyfidelity circle who most comfortably honors an agenda, asks for what she wants, and rarely processes the past. Do you think successful polyfidelity may be as highly stylized and disciplined as s/m?   —*Topsy Turvey, King of Prussia, Pennsylvania*

Well, I'm fit to be untied. The s/m girls usually call me a rollicking creampuff. At this news, and as my nether beard grows silver, shall I emerge as Dyke Daddy with all the trimings? I will bet my sweet candy-ass that the communities of poly and s/m could stand as allies with other erotic minorities in exploring radical intimacy and sexuality. Strange bedfellows unite? As a feminist I am far from nonchalant about the s/m comparison, but I note it is not the leather folk who denigrate my sexual style. Nor can I blame them for society's problems or my own. I just figure a use of freedom is to free someone else, rather than get tied up in tired dominance/submission cliches.

As I sit with your question, however, I realize certain concepts associated with s/m may indeed be present in polyfidelity. Perhaps the colorful, complex braids of the Promiscuous Weaver all intertwine somewhere. But guess what? Aspects I love of the Japanese Tea Ceremony are useful skills in polyfidelity too: its dramatic restraint, total focus, superb discipline, and conviviality. And what about a martial artist's boundary control, any fine craftperson's self-direction, self-discovery, and pursuit of clarity? Where will the analogs end? Why should they? Come with me to the Tea House of the August Mons. Everybody check your bamboo whips, masks, and hot wax behind the moon's pierced ear. Lettered over the Torii Gate is the famed s/m credo: "Safe, Sane, Consensual"—to which some-one has added "Joyful," and "Harmonious."

For safe and sane, we first drink a fragrant brew from superb earthenware bowls. There is warm, wild rose hip and hibiscus tea for the "just-say-now" guests. Sake with a morphine drip and coke sparkle is offered to the "just-say-no, I-do-not-want-to-be-here," guests, who drift off. The very first, wake-up sip in any polyfidèle circle is: *to win you must be present.* In polyfidelity, it is essential that various players' commitments, schedules, and territories are sensi-tively, patiently and skillfully handled. There are a variety of emotional whirlpools to deal with. Good judgment and clear per-ceptions are everything. No one is going to make it if they are swimming around half-looped. In poly, you get the opportunity to multi- process and rewrite all your old relationship lines like, "Control!" and "Escape!" Overdrug your script, and you'll lose the right mix of abandon and restraint.

The cachet "sane" seems a bit quaint to use in a society so routine-ly insane, where virtually all women and workers are socialized as bottoms. Why can't the world's controlling class hear the "safe" words the Earth's creatures cry to stop the battering? Few of us can be heard over the media dominatrix. Those who do cry loud enough can get their throats cut. So if you can find a tea house of sanity, an intimate circle where players responsibly honor safe words, soft, impermanent bodies, and the precious intensity of the present moment, cherish and visit this place often.

"Consensual." This is one of the dearest, most warm, silken and aromatic concepts at polyfidelity's heart. Monogamy restricts erot-ic consensus to a rigidly closed system: "I agree to love you IF you create sex only with me. To *deserve* your love, I will be sexually faithful in return." Polyfidelity holds that erotic consensuality flavors the entire world when we are so fortunate as to experience the miracle of direct desire. In polyfidelity, you are totally free to propose any delectable act to any woman alive. No shame. She is free to consent, yay, or reject, nay. (Rejection? In the land of consensuality, the only failure is never to propose.)

In conscious, sane polyfidelity, no woman is in the loop who does not want to be here. No one is powerless and no one controls. There is likely to be a rhythm of outflow counterpoised with receptivity. One reason multi-partner sex became taboo is that people got tricked non-consensually into a multi-person erotic system billed as monogamous. Here we sink to the typical adultery model, stained with anxiety, betrayal, and guilt. A non-consensual sex drama degenerates into melodrama, or, lacking all safety or sanity, into tragedy. Safe, sane and consensual poly is a heroicomedy. Its honest human foibles can bind us together in a freemasonry of discovery and humor.

Beware of forcing "pseudo-consensus." This is not funny. Remember pseudo-consensus from political affinity groups and Big Daddy nuke-families? Group members, out of frustration or fear in the face of overwhelming energy, "make nice" and *seem* to go along, only to withhold participation later however they can. Some Lesbians, often the partner of a rover or the odd woman involved, do not sincerely want to commit to a co-partner system. Liaisons happened spontaneously, not by their plans. They are biding their time or experimenting under pressure, thus may consciously or unconsciously try to subvert the system. Noncooperating partners are usually resenting a perceived lack of power. They are feeling threatened and insecure. In this scenario, relationship boundaries are often ambivalent or shifting, without clear understanding or agreement about what is moving and what is secure.

A miserable situation ensues when the multiply-involved partner herself does not clearly understand whether she is using another woman to transit out of the prior relationship or to renew/ restructure it. This often happens with a beginning, spontaneous polyfidèle. If you have no clear relationship commitment(s) within yourself, the only consensus possible is that you are on shifting sands, negotiating by crisis. Whoa. Take time to be with yourself and any suitable counsel you require. Negotiate a month at a time for arrangements everyone can live with until there is self-stability. Beginners' luck and a good heart will get you through this hellpit, but only after you clarify your own agenda and boundaries.

Ah, boundaries… limit-setting. Where do I begin and you leave off? Polyfidelity can be defined as a conscious, planned, *boundaried* alternative to monogamy. Few relationships are totally wide open. After all, everything in our universe consists of something organized, surrounded by a boundary. The most highly flexible boundary systems are called "alive." The operative word here is "flexible," neither completely permeable nor fixed. Healthy, flexible boundaries protect one from chaotic, distracting and dangerous interaction, but allow for optimal stimulus/stimulants. A psychic boundary is a symbolic membrane that prevents us (victim) from being controlled by others or us (offender) from controlling them. These invisible protective boundaries help to keep others from bursting into our personal space and getting us to do things against our best interests before we've had a chance to take our own counsel and speak to our own concerns. This is why maintaining one's psychic boundaries is like protecting one's immune system. Happily, our boundaries keep us aware of others' boundaries too, so that we respect their personal space rather than try to manipulate or control it. At birth, each of us is given three acres all our own: emotional, intellectual, and spiritual. As long as you don't invade anyone else's, you get to do with your three acres whatever you please.

Boundary maintenance seems to be a MAJOR issue in many Lesbian relationships. (Or did women ever have this symptom before the therapy industry?) Problems with Lesbian partners falling into "enmeshment," or "merging" is exhaustively—and exhaustingly—described by therapists, in clinical literature and relationship advice books. If you think of a boundary as a hula hoop or segment of a revolving door, in an emeshed relationship, both women are locked in the same space, having given up two private arenas of action and growth space. Look how Lesbians flock to co-dependency groups, always made up of 95% women anyway. If one Lesbian has incest or abuse trauma, support groups abound for her partner to deal with her own trauma in partnering the traumatized! Listen carefully to conversations Lesbians have about their relationship challenges. One preoccupation is attaining and holding individuality and autonomy. Heterosexual women, by contrast, usually focus on their eternal quest to attain closeness with intimacy-inept men.

Women are socialized to keenly observe flicker and nuance of another's emotional state, to immediately empathize, then to "fix" things if necessary, as one would care for an infant—or pacify a dangerous animal. Such behavior, after all, has been women's 5,000 year destiny: to protect the infant, to outmaneuver the batterer. It is a priceless ability that we can scan subtle signals, deduce a pattern of meaning, and respond with understanding. This is the famous "female intuition," which would be termed "intelligence" were it a male faculty. But what happens if our boundaries become so permeable that we don't take the essential time/space to respond appropriately to what we sense? What if we automatically click into the old "mommy" or "serving-girl" routine? This often happens if we simply re-act to another's experience as though it were happening to us. It's almost as if we've provided another person with a chair that says "Director," and become part of their storyline. Focusing excessively on their needs, we have lost ourselves in their script. When we neglect our own priorities, we usually try to recapture self-worth by pleasing or manipulating "The Director." "The Director" may not even be a person. It can be a cause, a goal, an image, even someone else's old tape.

It can, for Lesbians, be "The Ideal Relationship." In the perfect, ideal anything, there is great fear of any issue which may lead to differentiation and perhaps to conflict—therefore to change. Direct confrontation is assiduously avoided. Neither partner dares to deal with actual issues of major import because she is afraid the ensuing conflict will unleash emotions next to lethal. Thus, unique individuality is squashed. An enmeshed person, hiding differences for the sake of the perfect, unchanging relationship, is a person unknown. Hidden resentment seethes in lieu of open conflict. Bickering often plays like a radio to broadcast trivial or pseudo-problems. Here are examples of such a masquerade: her sloppiness leads to ants invading the kitchen (the someone's-to-blame game). Her extended long-distance conversations with mom are childish (therapizing). Her clothes are all wrong for a party (reflects on me). The large, real issues could be more like: "I hate doing so much of the cooking and cleanup since I can't try new dishes and new guests." "I really want a separate phone, phone number, and my own bed." "I can't reveal my attraction to another woman at this party or ask her out, even to talk."

In polyfidelity, healthy, stable boundaries are necessarily exercised, and I mean well-exercised, to support differentiation as well as to provide security. In the next chapters, I'll illustrate which boundaries serve to modulate fears of engulfment or abandonment, with suggestions from experience. Poly is, in fact, a superb strategy for learning all kinds of boundary development. Many women in the survey reported using polyfidelity expressly for this purpose. How so? Because one woman simply cannot make covert, casual assumptions in polyfidelity. Utter confusion would reign, with explanations due several people. Here we have several different individuals creating an optimum relationship system for everyone. Somewhere on its spectrum, each woman has a comfort zone, a wave length, her own hue and rhythm. She has rights and responsibilities to be set forth in flexible, but identifiable sanctions.

Each woman openly establishes:
Her own physical space, including, or course, sexual bounds
Her own territorial space
Her own temporal space
Her own emotional space
Her own intellectual space
Her own economic space
Her own vocational space
Her own social space
Her own spiritual space
So there.

If a woman isn't clear herself regarding her own sphere *and* skilled at maintaining it, she'll be dizzily swept into disarray. Inner issues and inner warfare become more visible the larger the arena of projection. If a polyfidèle's leaky boundaries allow meddling raids on others' space, she is more likely to be called on this. In a larger relationship system, it is harder to get away with control-queen antics. Your targets may slip away—or organize.

What is the process of healthy boundary setting? You physically feel a warm sense of loyalty to yourself. I often visualize my boundary as an energy force-field, a golden circle of light softly pulsing around me, sometimes expanding outward in laser force if alarmed. In tranquillity and intimacy, the circle diffuses, lightly misting me, sending rainbow bridges, sparks of pollen. Useful boundaries are appropriate to the situation, sometimes near and inviting, sometimes well-extended, marking wide berth. Good boundaries tighten to preserve individuality, then open to admit new perspectives. They are firm enough to keep values and priorities clear, yet extend arcs to communicate to appropriate people. Boundaries may have to intensify drastically to withstand trespass from the careless, the selfish, the mean—even the well-meaning. As Anne Katherine wrote in her excellent book *Boundaries*: supple, healthy boundaries protect without isolating, contain without imprisoning, preserve identity while permitting external connections.

One reason people are "in love with love" is that love can effortlessly transport us beyond our daily, predictable system of boundaries into newly creative ones. Each lover improvises music within a set of mutually stroked-in boundaries to create a delicious new harmony. Soloist becomes accompanist, to effortlessly change states again and again. When all is going well, we feel our boundaries at their most magical. Our constructed self-complex is beloved and secure while open in delightful discovery.

In contrast, we've all felt the anxiety of poor, leaky boundaries in uncomfortable situations. Here, we try to react immediately without fully digesting input, and things go awry. Sometimes we can feel overwhelmed with life, distracted with each new proposal or demand, easily harassed by another. It is hard to set priorities, much less to follow them. It is as though you just woke up as an infant triple-Gemini at the helm of a roaring speedboat. What is most conflicting, however, are the hodgepodge boundaries, first too permeable, then too rigid; these are part-time boundaries that are actually impaired.

They say that if a woman spends her time just surviving, she has little opportunity to develop a self with effective boundaries. Instead, she forms a hard, yet fragile shell whose inner self is waiting to be born. For now, it may be stuffed with other people's agendas and values, or with anger, fear, grief. One assuages all this with attempts at over-control, with compulsions, with hate, numbness, thrills—anything so as not to feel so empty. What is waiting to be born, of course can be born, and reborn. "Boundracides," such as ridicule, contempt, insecurity, battery, even atrocity can be healed. Nascent boundaries spring up again and again like the green realm pushing through concrete. As poet Wendell Berry writes, "For healing we have on our side one great force: the power of Creation, with good care and kindly use, to heal itself."

People without dependable boundaries often resort to walls. Defensive walls are built, over time, of tightly constructed, dense and impermeable emotions like anger, fear and grief. They seem to work, at least in the short run. They certainly block most invasion, but they also wall-out people who are not actual enemies, who truly wish us well or may be useful. Since walls mean zero relating, no one gets through. This means not even the multifaceted you. We are all holograms of many aspects, including the spirits of clarity, humor, self-interest, etc. None of these can travel through a wall of rage or panic. In contrast, even the martial artist's toughest boundaries hold a moving spaciousness which the fighter uses to maximize awareness and capture the wide angle. An odd dynamic occurs when a person with walls chooses a person with few boundaries in order to vicariously experience sharing without having to be vulnerable or to share themselves. Here, one does the emotional work of two, and usually exhausts herself. Or, a person with walls may seek another person with walls so no one has to risk sharing. In walled camps of any kind, control and manipulation games usually kick in to avoid any domination or shame.

What are useful ways to strengthen boundaries instead of create walls? First, welcome the relief, abandon the guilt, of saying "no" to others. Feel the freedom of saying "no" to compulsions. Savor the moment. Feel both the freedom and relief of saying "yes" to yourself as your best friend. Accept, then celebrate the fact that you are unique. You need not run with the herd, conventionally imprisoning your body to one gatekeeper.

Remember, boundaries are most easily impaired when you are fatigued and ill or lonely, afraid, and sad. Above all, notice that split second, that "turning point" between reacting, in contrast with *responding*, to an event. A few deep, spacious breaths will usually deliver this time and summon the functional boundaries you need. In this space/time, consciously choose what interpretation to give the data beaming at you. No matter how forcefully someone else is editorializing events, take time to ask: "What is true for me here? Are this person's words and actions actually about the world or really about themselves? Is any of it valid? To whom and why?"

To be able to cue into the extra breathing moment I need, I sometimes visualize my cat's bright, cool gaze helping me sweep in my boundary lines. While a dog has very near, open boundaries and leaps to human whim, my cat usually retains distinct, firm boundaries which say, "I am on cat business. I received your message and will get back to you later, perhaps much later." Even dozing, the cat can be aware of my every move, while easily maintaining her own sphere. Ever notice that after a cat's daily seventeen-hour rest and meditation period it may spend at least half the remaining hours on what we perceive as self-grooming? I was told privately by my cat Freyja that this is actually routine, careful "fence-mending," bio-electrical boundary maintenance. If necessary, she is even ready to put up a hair-raising electrical fence. "We have pet peeves too, you know," she reminds me.

In doing exactly as she pleases with royal, delicious practicality, Freyja reshapes the world to her own comfort and convenience. My polyfidelitious cat is domesticated only so far as it suits her special ends and convictions. She is one of these remarkable creatures who has the courage to live by her own standards. This is the reason there are no ordinary cats and the reason not one cat suffers from insomnia. Boundaries!

Hearts of Space:
Territorial Boundaries

Query: We're mainly enjoying polyfidelity, but the question of physical turf is confusing. Last month, I unexpectedly came home early from a trip. Since my partner wasn't expecting me, I barged into a love tryst right in our living room. We were all three really embarrassed, especially the new woman. Who should go to a hotel?

— *Kay Ottick, Portland, Oregon*

Hotels are a great boon to polyfidelèles—if you can afford one. But what you really want to do is avoid mixed-up reservations ever occurring on the home front in the first place. A *flagrante delicto* shock goes beyond mere event to create reverberations. In an intricately linked and balanced poly-system, one emotional collision can cause a chain reaction of pinball bells and lights.

Many things are simpler for the multi-relationship lover who lives alone. As mentioned, a reason polyfidelity is so acceptable in the Lesbian feminist utopian novels is that women often live singly in small homes while sharing communal space for dining, arts, work, etc. But even when you live alone, you may give out keys. Make it especially clear that, except in emergencies, lover visits are to be prearranged by invitation. Let everyone know that you appreciate phone-first requests for hospitality. Many Lesbians are quite patrician about their privacy, anyway, although I know some country, small town and Southern Lesbians who are likely to miss *laissez-faire* visiting. Push your luck if you want, but getting caught with your pants down is only funny months later.

Live-in lovers who entertain other romances absolutely must work out clear territorial guidelines, much as they do already with friends and biological family. I haven't met any Lesbian live-in partners who are totally debonair when face-to-face with extracurricular sexual shenanigans, nor any odd women who would be comfortable with plural lovers colliding. Few Lesbians have this kind of bland tolerance themselves or dare to ignite the emotional ballistics of lovers in unexpected confrontation. Such freedom of expression is seen more in het swingers and bisexual threesomes.

Space in polyamory, or any where else, is a subtle issue. Sometimes I wonder if this is because we don't really move in space. Maybe we are space touching itself? Thus there can be no rigid formulae regarding live-ins' territory. Women make enormously different arrangements. From my interviews, here are several ways for handling space smoothly, from the most conservative to the more easygoing.

We consider our home as the supremely safe, private space for our own relationship. In four years, none of our respective lovers have ever stayed overnight. We have only one bedroom. I don't relish Carol's lover rolling around in our bed or slipping into my bathrobe after a shower using our Valentine soap.

I don't mind if my live-in love has her lovers here as long as I am away, the lover stays out of my bedroom, and I can come home any time and be free of them. My partner really dislikes my entertaining overnights here. She laughingly admits she holds to "residential monogamy." So I have women over only for a few moments, like when they pick me up.

We've gone from the "continent away" house rule to the "state line" to the "night away" rule. At first we agreed that if either of us were across the country, the other could safely have lovers over so we'd never cross paths and have ludicrous conversations and scenes. Then we liberalized it to "across the state line" and finally decided that as long as either of us had plans to be away overnight, the house could be open to the other's pleasures. Coming and going times, of course, have to be scrupulously honored. Once my partner, Kady, got sick and had to come home early, when I had someone over. Kady simply called, and it was a fruit-basket upset, but I had her slippers at the door. My other lover was really funny and nice about it, and we both sent her flowers the next day.

I prefer to first meet my lover's loves briefly at our home, when they're on their way out for the evening. This is a matter of curiosity and for my self-protection, too. The woman sees my plumage on my turf. I feel much less threatened after I meet the other woman and get a sense of her style. Otherwise, my imagination can run away with me. She becomes a breathtaking Glamazon with infinite talents and powers of seduction.

My live-in partner and I thought we'd figured out everything about blending space, when here comes the recurring question of where to put other lovers' gifts and love tokens, even whether to put up their travel postcards on the refrigerator. To smooth the issue, I now try to receive a lot of stuff at the office, cards and so forth. We ultimately decided to keep other women's gifts out of our common space. When I got gift champagne, however, my partner put it in *our* refrigerator real fast.

Here's a plug for the enabling answering machine. The first thing to set up for live-in polyfidelity is separate electromagnetic space: your own telephone number and answering machine/service. This seems painfully obvious, since even being a receptionist for your partner's non-lovers is a drag—but wait until those breathless, dulcet tones cross the line. I don't see how multiple relationships were ever consummated without answering machines, discreet rendezvous scheduling and time consideration being of the essence. Plus the delights of "phonication!" Use of voice mail is utterly private and perhaps more sensible than a machine for polyfidèles. No indiscreet messages ever blast through the house as some may if an answering machine is turned up by accident or intention. You give up the machine's haughty option of screening calls however.

❦

We're pretty much open to everything—except to one of us being within a hundred paces of actually SEEING the caress or the "act" of our lover with someone else. Watching any physical exchange, I get a jealous adrenaline rush that rubies my eyes and cracks my contacts. And beat this—I'm a pacifist. But who said you can control your emotions; all you can do is perhaps rearrange them.

Therefore, we design it so that there's little possibility of crashing into a rendezvous at home. If either of us is entertaining a lover here and the other may come home—chances even one in a hundred— we tie a silk scarf on the front gate and one on the bedroom door. If I see that scarf, I can call and say I'll be home to another part of the flat, or hang out somewhere else, or at least gird my loins and avert my gaze.

❦

The space issue that has been rather unusual for us is that I live alone, but my lovers each have a live-in partner, so I go to their apartments only a few times a year when their lovers are away. This means I'm usually in the host/provider role with its cleaning, linen and towel maintenance, food, etc., responsibilities. My lovers add are both very sensitive to this and bring food, clear up and all. Still, I'd like changes in my erotic scenario, too, to get the variety they have coming here. So, now we're setting up a romantic getaway fund and doing friends' house-sitting for my change of scene.

❦

Territorial rights and responsibilities took us a while to work out, but it helped the relationship as a whole to develop a sense of delicacy around space. At first, we were very protective, "not in my house, you don't..." This seems natural because we were trying something new and needed to feel very safe while building up inner security around poly. Now I guess our basic guideline is: If more than one lover is on the scene—by design or accident—save all physical and romantic exhibition for private space. Upon meeting, no one has to prove possession, after all, or overt passion. It's often helpful to talk about everyone's assumptions regarding public meetings before they happen, then check out feelings afterwards.

From experience, we actually try to avoid all attending the same events, but if it happens, it happens. The woman whose two lovers are both present at an event often feels her emotions and attention bifurcated. I find this to be highly disconcerting when it's me. So, I focus on my breath a lot. Yet, I still get rattled trying to please two women at once, even though I know it's not my job to carry anyone else's emotional baggage. If close encounters occur, I'd still rather be one of the two swains in our lady's presence. And, it's back to the old rubric: exhibit no physical or romantic endearments at the time. Opportunity for these always rises again. (Okay, sometimes I try to get away with my "can't wait 'til we're alone together" smile.) When caught in any emotional crossfire of multiple-meetings, I usually place myself in sort of a French court mode, pretend I'm in a formal diplomatic encounter with volatile allies. What this means is that I smile a lot with my eyes, then try to get the hell out of Dodge.

Chance encounters are always a possibility, like where one woman is just shopping for bagels and runs into "the couple" of the moment, or when two contenders cross paths. Always be relieved if you aren't in the lingerie department. At such a moment, words fail me. To my fellow-travelers, I simply make a silent, formal zen bow with hands together. If I can bow from the heart, all is well. ☯

Mother Time: Polyfidelity in the Fourth Dimension

uery: I agree with the idea polyfidelity 100%, but where could I ever find the time for more than one lover? It is possible to be a polyfidèle and have a full-time job?

— *Wanda Rohm, New York City*

es, polyfidèles run the gamut from slackers to workaholics. Guess what? We all have the same number of hours per week: 168. Usually, when people declare they do not "have time" for an activity, it is a polite way of saying they do not truly prioritize said activity. Other things are, let's face it, more desirable or easier or safer. Hopefully, these other things are freely chosen, not forced upon one as is true of exploited peoples. Let's assume that most of the women reading this book are typical American working class, *i.e.*, ultimately you do not control the means or manner of production in your job. You are employed by the "owning class," a.k.a. the "protected class." Every mortal, however, from mogul to mudlark, owns her own 168 hours per week.

May I assume you use a seemingly inescapable fifty-six hours sleeping, fifty hours on the job (including commuting), eight hours on personal care, three hours of domestic care? This leaves you fifty-one hours per week to: visit with family, friends, lovers; care for dependents, like children, aged parents, the ill, and/or animals; play music; organize a revolution; meditate; work out; therapize; net surf; loaf; write a book on the above, etc. Take a moment to figure out the typical "floating time" in your week; it is a useful revelation! Beyond survival time, you can see you have XX hours to do a few choice things like some of the examples, not all of them, by any means. No way.

I respectfully suggest that you, my dear and busy Wanda, simply choose other things to do than have multiple lovers. You use the common excuse of "time deprivation" to evade the opportunity for loving more than one. Perhaps you are already a corporate bigamist who values an eighty-hour-a-week career, as loyal to the company as you are to your lover? Or you have a fifty-hour-per-week commitment to physical fitness and the Internet which you choose over intimate relationship(s)? After all, it is true, you cannot give quality attention to Lesbian Avengers, a potter's wheel, and a swooning lover all in one moment. But, unless you are in a health crisis, exploited by force, in a trance, or recently deceased, you do what you want to do. After your four survival basics are met—food, shelter, clothing, and health care—YOU DO WHAT YOU WANT TO DO.

I am not saying, however, that polyfidelity is simply a matter of prioritizing, budgeting hours, getting organized, and being disciplined. If this were the case, all you would need would be one of those expensive, prepackaged time management systems, which kill the spirit, not to mention romance. Polyfidelity, dear heart, is no less than leaving the grid of time for the circle of love.

Let's time travel a moment. We were brainwashed into the trick of clock-time before the age of five. Everyone, except mystics, ecstatics, and the un-American, was force-fed that clock-time is "reality." Clock-time, however, is merely a left-brain fictional system, extremely logical, only partly useful. I used it a page ago to make a cold mathematical point: you probably do have clock-time if you want it for polyfidelity or for stargazing or for deep-sea diving. But clock-time is never enough for the Great Matters of Life & Death, of which polyfidelity and all matters of the heart are primo. This is because clock-time is an invented artifact in the man-made economy of scarcity. Clock-time, by definition, is finite, a limited resource based on an exact number of hours to be somehow hoarded, then carefully spent. Americans tend to make so-called time deprivation a virtue. Busyness conveys self-importance, self-worth.

Clock-time is a notion of largely discredited seventeenth-century Cartesian and Newtonian "laws" of nature. Like any theory, clock-time explains certain things and is useful to certain classes, much as pioneering nuclear physics was. Remember "Atoms for Peace"? Seventeenth-century physics considered time to be something of an outside agitator. Its "time" was a foreign factor influencing "the machine" of the natural world, according to certain mathematical laws. The clock, in fact, was Descartes's model for the human body and the universe itself. Remember, the clock mechanism had recently been invented and was considered by technophiles as a miracle, much as we consider the computer. Clock-time is a relentlessly forward movement, orderly, unchanging, a linear cadence of seconds, minutes, and hours imposed upon our biorhythmic bodies like a grid.

Clock-time was seized upon by eighteenth-century industrialists who made fortunes from workers' assembly-line routines. Captains of Industry could not have workers coming in "after breakfast" or leaving "when they were tired," as normal creatures do. This would throw off sequential assembly-line movement and increase costs. Thus, time clocks have held us in thrall for three hundred years, attempting to erase the ancient rhythms and cycles of the universe. Watches became our watchers. Successful clock-time became defined as speed, as fast-forward. We continue to valorize any mechanism that will increase speed, even as it also increases our burden, like the fax machine, cellular phone and beeper all do.

Because clock-time can so easily be collapsed into that other fiction—money—by ukase of the White Rabbit of Capitalism, time now equals money, period. Minutes are coins; hours, dollars. Or, in the world of lawyers, whose official billing schedules are rigorously set into six-minute (!) intervals, minutes are dollars. (This is why it is unfortunate that our government has always been run by lawyers; lawyers think in short-term gain, rather than long-term effect.) If you are not somehow manipulating the fictional equation between money and clock-time, then go homeless and starve. Or go snort coke—coke is clock-time's way of saying you are not making *enough* money.

While clock-time as commodity time can be a useful concept, it is an incomplete, false description of how we actually experience time. Tests show most people are dismal failures at estimating the passage of even five minutes. If our sense of space were as poor, we would miss doorways and pour tea into laps. A clock cannot be time any more than a map can be undulating terrain and flowing waters. Because time is not a matter of numbers, most time-management books, seminars, and systems soon fail. They will certainly never give you polyfidelity. It is Mother Time who can.

Mother Time, dynamic Time with a capital T, is an unlimited flow of limitless energy. Time is an inhalent. Being all process, she has no destination. Mother Time is theater in the round, the unintentional timeless now of *all* seasons, past, present and future happening together. She may be perceived as a living net, a spun continuum connecting events, like jewels ever reflecting jewels. She is not a scarce, but a sacred source, our ever-abiding, natural habitat, surrounding us like water does fish, like sky does birds, indivisible. I watch my garden where Time moves successively and in a circle. Growth stages and entire environments succeed one another. There is, concurrently, an unbroken circular rhythm as life rises, bursts forth and dies, for the process to begin anew. This is Time as a wheel, moving along, yet spinning in the round.

You can't waste Time, only yourself. While so vast and fluid as to be uncontrollable, Mother Time is highly personal, never independent of me, yet inter-dependent, co-arising with you and you and you. She is not without a sense of humor. But just as there is no hand to catch Time, we do not always catch her amusing drift. She is quite beyond language and numbers, being both relative and Absolute. We need to trust the silver-rose river of Time to plumb her intuitive truth. Our difficulty in precisely conceptualizing Mother Time does not undercut the live experience we have intuiting her, ever-fresh. People thus speak of opening "a window of Time." We know her as now (ah!) and as eternity—in moments of perfect stillness, in ecstasy, or if certain drugs somehow melt the little clock hands wringing our nerves.

Mother Time is deeply interior. Invite her as your ally and you become inner-directed, moving with the larger story of your life purpose. Before all others, the great philosophical question to consider is, "What do I do in my Time?" If you study the question of death, it helps unlock your question of Time. What would you like said about you at your funeral, about your deepest being, all your doings, what you chose to connect with? Who will be moved enough to speak? Who will even show to celebrate how you opened your window of time? The essence of a truly accomplished life is one's emergence as loyal friend, delightful lover, and companion. What becomes extraordinarily significant as we look back are other living creatures, especially family and friends. Who are these intimates? Often, for Lesbians, they are our lovers in life. It is our lovers who shape and polish our souls. Take away love and Earth is already a tomb. Why would Mother Time limit lovers when there is a Time for every purpose under heaven?

Clock-time does indeed limit lovers. It considers simple human intercourse laborious and frivolous. We seize quick surrogates like watching an hour of tv actors spending time; we order leisure clothing from a catalog of beautiful country slackers looking past each other; we linger with no one over no-time factory foodstuffs. The fax is totally unequal to the slowly licked, scented love letter. Long, moon-washed courtships are out, so are recurring honeymoons, afternoon walks, heart-to-heart talks by the fire, romantic dinners, and dawn-to-noon sips of sensuality. Downtime? Unworthy? I think that if I were imprisoned for the rest of my life, these are moments that would sustain me. These moments remind me of humanity's heart and soul. They are an answer to why I am alive.

Since our ally, Mother Time, is so multi-ordinal, so multipurposeful, I often share with her my living-on-purpose ideas. What I do is important because I am exchanging my life for it. I threw out all the time-management bridles I always bit through no matter how artfully constructed and color coded. For NOW (all I have to worry about), I spend around twenty hours a week of my "beyond survival" time writing this book, and about the same entertaining lovers and friends and the possibilities thereof. I manage to be alone, to garden, to care for my larger community. Sometimes I drop a ball, knowing I will pick it up again one of my mornings with Mother Time. Perhaps Time is just nature's way of making it seem everything does not happen at once? Thus I try to be *semper fidelis* but flexible, especially since I don't have writing deadlines anymore. This is because I had a real deadline several years ago.

I was collaborating on a book with my great love Elsa Gidlow. She had had several serious strokes and I never knew from weekend to weekend whether I would see her again. Her sight, insight, and memory flowed in and out like the tide, quite seamlessly, often beautifully. But as soon as I left her garden on Sunday evenings for the city, I grieved ragged sobs on the trail. Finally, I talked about this with Elsa. We actually got to laughing about the word *deadline*, humor relying as it often does on a jolt of implacable truth. What is any deadline but an artful death? Elsa said, "If you will just work on my life story and don't panic, I can work on my own good death." All around the garden: lifelines, deadlines, lifelines, and on. Elsa was always a devotee of the poignant amusements. She laughed, "How can I possibly die before my life story is finished?"

We decided that if she died before the book were finished, at least we would be presented with a shorter book and clear last chapter, always the hardest one to write. If she flew off to eternity before The End, Elsa agreed I would stop and simply copy a common sign I saw along the Dipsea Trail as I walked to her: Trail Closed to Return to Nature.

The book, *ELSA: I Come With My Songs*, was published as the fragrant spring buckeyes blossomed along the Dipsea. How we all sang! By blackberry time, one of my trails was indeed closed, as Elsa's opened beyond. Whenever I meet a new woman, when I sense the wings of love beating again, I hear Elsa prompt, "Happy Trails" from the Tao of Time. ☯

Leisure Rhymes with Pleasure

uery: The line "Another day of delicious retirement" occurs again and again in the eighteenth century's luminous journal of Lesbian love, *The Ladies of Llangollen*. Do you think that polyfidelity can be a reality in the twenty-first century unless we have a leisure revolution?

— *Lotus Tarry, Austin, Texas*

It's true. Idleness is the root of all pleasure, including culture and art. Except for gay sensibility, eroticism seems to be a casualty of twentieth century stress, overwork, and toxics like prozac and tv. In New York, our busiest city, the letters for calling time on the phone are "NER-VOUS." In the gay Mecca of the world, San Francisco, the letters are a more jolly-time, "POP-CORN." Few ideologies strike a claim for leisure—but polyfidelity does with a great flourish, even a sound of trumpets! A transformation to polyfidelity rests in deep interior stirrings, on a new ideological, even metaphysical base: the way we approach time relates to how we care for others. The bright tricolour of polyfidelity is surely *Liberté, Éqilibré et Loisir*: liberty, equilibrium and leisure. We sometimes forget that in sonorous English "leisure" rhymes with "pleasure."

Another "Loisir" ideology to explore is one of the most charming and daring of spiritual paths, the ancient Chinese Taoist "Cult of Idleness." The Cult of Idleness is on the same languid contour as the slow smile of troubadour, bohemian, hippie and slacker. People revered the wandering Taoist sages and quiet Taoist hermitages where one lived in voluntary simplicity studying nature, eating when hungry, drinking when dry, and visiting all night when such auspicious coincidence presented itself. Taoist art still beckons us with its wild, worldly and timeless strokes. The few coins in the Taoist purse accompanied a great sense of beauty in the breast. Freedom-loving Taoists vowed not to let the art of living degenerate into the business of living. They kept their accounts on a thumb-nail. Thus, mundane concerns did not interfere with their soaring poetry and painting, their long meditations, afternoons of tea, or moons full of wine in love's dalliance. High Time.

As Oscar Wilde remarked, "I adore simple pleasures. They are the last refuge of the complex."

The Taoist romantic Cult of Idleness was essentially democratic. Forest dwelling Taoists considered obscurity a great virtue, holding a profound awareness of the handicaps of fame and eternal anxiety related to possession, ambition and power. The "nobody" can revel in existence. This is not possible for the wealthy, but only for the poor, "unsuccessful" scholar of life. Such simplicity is—simply—the highest expression of personal power. Look, Mom, no props. "Obscurity is dark, ample and free." As Virginia Woolf's pansexual Orlando notes, fame "is a braided coat which hampers the limbs; a jacket of silver which curbs the heart; a painted shield which covers a scarecrow." Mother Teresa smiles, "We do not do great things. We do small things with great love." How much care we banish and leisure we gain when we *do* something, rather than *be* someone.

Ancient Taoist writings on the unhurried arts of love, as first taught by women, design sexuality from the inside out, to be empty so to be full, like the Taoist concept of time. In the feast of life before us, Taoists value the appetite. The savoring appetite is the thing, not the feast itself, which ceaselessly dissolves into another form on time's Lazy Susan. Since everything is impermanent, go slow, go easy and melt into . . . this special time, this now.

Modern U. S. culture, in contrast, fears full-bodied, full-hearted, laze-about idleness, especially the long, delicious tides of sexuality. Why? Because lovers loving undermines our intense work imperative. Furthermore, erotically fulfilled people are hard to denigrate, subdue and exploit. Audre Lorde eloquently demonstrates this in her classic essay, "Uses of the Erotic, The Erotic as Power."[17] Creative Eros gives us the energy to pursue change, the fullness and satisfaction to continue the struggle. Countless analysts agree, from Emma Goldman to Michel Foucault plus all Roundheads of the right who want to stifle Eros. In Puritan Massachusetts, idleness was not only a sin but a punishable crime.

Would television have been a crime? I fondly hope so, given the Cotton Mather channel. Every great lover yearning to enter the leisure class: Pillor your tv. Forty percent of American leisure time drains down the tube. The average American will spend one quarter of their life married to the set. Marge Piercy's novel, *The Longings of Women*, was partially inspired by surveys which show that many people's most intense relationships are with tv characters and personalities. It indeed approaches the cult of the bizarre when a U. S. Vice President goes to war with a fictional tv character, Murphy Brown, and, of all things—loses!

The polyfidèles' nonfictional problem now, according to Harvard economist Juliet Schor in her brilliant book, *The Overworked American: The Unexpected Decline of Leisure*, is that during the last twenty years U. S. working hours have increased by the equivalent of one full month per year! Thanks to increasing productivity and unions, U. S. work hours were declining in the first half of the twentieth century. Nineteenth century paymasters had forced grueling seventy- to eighty-hour work weeks. Prior to this, of course, people worked in agrarian rhythms. The clock had not replaced sun or seasons. Medieval Europeans took off one-third of the year for saints' holidays. The Protestants nipped such idleness, of course. Anthropologists and economists, according to Helen Fisher of the American Museum of Natural History, are calling our ancestors "the original affluent society." It is one of corporate media's greatest hoaxes to sell us the myth that leisure is an invention of capitalist "progress." Ancient cultures worked only a couple of days a week on survival, then played, gossiped, wove folktales, worshiped, even gambled for fun. Of course, they gamboled too. Life may not have been always as easy and pleasant, but it certainly was leisurely.* Many societies and great cul-

---

* Life expectancy for the hunter-gatherer was around thirty years, so if you want to return to that time, many of you would be dead. At least you would not have lived a life of quiet desperation.

tures had no word for "hour," much less "minute." They had moment to moment intimacy.

Unlike all other industrialized countries today, Americans are choosing money over time. U.S. citizens are working two months more per year than our counterparts in France, Germany, Sweden, etc. A main reason is that while our production has doubled since 1948, so has our consumption. We spend two to three times as much time shopping as Western Europeans. By the fifties, the U.S. began a shopping and spending spree unequaled in the history of the world. Meanwhile, the government, the corporations and their media joined in a union busting program from which the labor movement has yet to recover. Unions are now riddled with many officials who identify more with the imperial corporate class than the workers. This is not true of many committed, idealistic labor organizers, but no matter—eighty percent of their possible constituency, corporate elite wannabes, identify with their glamorous bosses. Workers are inculcated with competitive insecurity to undermine their solidarity. Meanwhile consumerism lulls and diverts. Righteous confrontation with the owning class is not valorized in our media nor told in theme parks.

Few can dispute that a corporation monopolized economic system has given us maldistribution of wealth and well-being. Remember when Bill Clinton, Presidential candidate, told us that the rich U. S. ten percent at the top have more wealth that ninety percent of the rest of us? Sharpening this fact, the U. S. super-rich one percent own forty-eight percent of all U. S. financial wealth![18] Our concentration of wealth today makes Europe the land of equality; we are class ridden. The poorest fifty percent of all U. S. families, largely single moms and kids, hold roughly three cents of every dollar's worth of wealth in this country.[19] There are millions of beggars in our streets, sweatshops here and throughout the world. U. S. corporations and their politicians have created a seemingly permanent unemployed and under-employed class solely to keep workers docile. Too much leisure is not their problem, but too little money and dignity and opportunity. Meanwhile, everyone else, especially since real wages began to decline in the seventies, has too damn much to do.

What is the solution? How can you save your libido from an increasingly voracious workweek to invest in polyfidelity?

First, get out of the rat race while you can. Even if you win, as Lily Tomlin said, you're still a rat. The rat race is full of lashes like "fast track," and "rush hour" and "go-getting." Take a cut in job hours for a cut in pay if at all possible. If you earn as much as $22,000 a year, you are sixty-five times richer than half the human race, with one in every five human beings on earth being a scavenger.[20] Working fewer hours can mean a cut in professional status, but how many of your professional colleagues will care to drive in that fast lane to mourn at your funeral?

More easily, and well within your power, get off the work 'n' spend treadmill, where the loop of leisure is trampled to death by consumerism. Many of us are so unaware of our real needs, we multiply our wants. A polyfidèle, however, is a personalist over a materialist. Since this is a soft-core pleasure manual, I will not discuss here the sheer rapacity of U. S. consumerism and the monumental suffering it inflicts on the Earth and her creatures. It is enough to say that we have driven 100,000 species to extinction in the last few decades.[21] Take a Quaker saying to heart: "Live simply that others may simply live." Then like a Taoist, stay out of all shopping channels, except for food and real necessities. Shopping is the prime cultural activity of Americans. Even our museums, parks and highbrow performances have "acquisition opportunities." You probably own all the clothes you need for the rest of your life. The thirteen billion dollars we spend for sports clothing actually translates into a billion hours of work to pay for them. For variety, how about trading wardrobes with lovers? You already have more luxurious pleasures and goods than any queen of yore: running water, electricity, heat, music on demand, literature, antibiotics. Remember it was a queen who pleaded, "All my possessions for a moment of time"—the mighty Elizabeth I. The truly successful person cheerfully devotes time to paying back what she has been given.

You can certainly stop buying all the things that sell you a hollow fantasy of leisure and power while making you work like hell to pay for them. Sophisticated "green" consumers seem to collect exotic experiences over gross materialism. These include programmed adventures: tours to the Isle of Lesbos and shamanic sweat lodge "cures"; solitary computer games, electronic networks of arm's-length strangers and data glut, exorbitant, supplied states of being like virtual reality. Who is not aware of internalizing the computer industry's compulsory upgrade mania? A woman satisfied with a 1978 Volvo seemingly cannot get up in the morning without "Windows 95" and its obligatory string of add-ons. Often, even women who make comfortable salaries feel "poor." We get into hock up to our eyeballs for leisure surrogates like time-shares we rarely use and gardens we never lie in. We follow expensive, quick-improvement paths that go nowhere. We support restaurant and wine "environments." We suffer through personal beauty and fit-ness Olympics, stressful sports and spectator emotions. Enjoyment of real leisure, however, costs much less than the maintenance of these luxuries. Happy people are lousy consumers. Try it for just one week: joyous, conspicuous non-consumerism.

Instead of paying other people for your leisure, do something to get it for free. For example, medical insurance coverage is a chain that binds us as full-time slaves to the already protected owning class. Actively support a Canadian-style system of universal health care for all Americans, employed or not. Also join the culture of resistance to press for labor reform. Labor parties and unions are strong in Europe. U. S. bosses may offer you money, but rarely power with the rights of self-management. Help rebuild the U. S. labor movement by organizing however you can, even informally. United we bargain, divided we beg. A rights contract gives you the power to hold your job while protesting unfair labor practices, plus irrevocable sickness and old age benefits. If you are in man-agement, encourage part-time and flextime work, with full bene-fits, including pensions. Give workers an option to choose free time over raises. Provide sabbaticals, not trinkets, for work well done. Have a heart, your next lover may arise from the leisure class.

Lesbian moms, please beware of enormously upgraded parenting standards, ever on the rise from the nineteenth century idealization of "mother love." No one is urging child neglect, but our society now pushes the most intensive and expensive mothering program in human history. May our little dyke-tykes not be over processed, leisure-fearing creatures who will actually give up five days a week to live for two. My friend's little girl, doing arithmetic story-problems, figured that a typical company would use twenty-six years of her life for every year she got to keep. "What's the pay-off?" she asked. Note: if you are a full-time mom, you're worth a whopping $80,300 a year, according to the Institute for Women's Policy Research. To employ a cook, maid, chauffeur, baby-sitter and financial planner would cost about $1,500 a week. Ease up.

Above all, avoid falling prey to workaholism, "the pain we applaud," because our system equates work and responsibilities with goodness. Bosses love workaholics to set the standards of production. In the Cult of Idleness, you are precious if you can just get through the day harming no creature. Workaholism means one fears "the abyss" of free time. Deeply internalized thoughts and feelings may arise as soon as we are not being pounded by outside attentions. Stillness is indeed a pregnant void, which is why we now "learn" to meditate. The first unharried awarenesses may be of personal anxieties, even existential griefs. In busyness, they were never heeded nor accepted as guides, as transforming allies in conscious living. With open time, our logical, judgmental side finally quiets by getting a rest, too. We may begin to wander gently through our entire mode of existence to discover that only half the task is getting life to do what we want. The other half may be discovering where our life wants to go.

If you choose workaholic women as lovers, simply book dates with them far in advance. They will cheerfully assign you into their vast schedule. Be patient while you become permanent on the master agenda. Workaholics respond well to regular schedules (like "every

Wednesday") and gentle, appreciative reminders. Never try to change a workaholic yourself. The key that first wound up the machine is a flaming sword, and only the workaholic can cast it away. Smart love and a large, lazy cat of great presence have been known to help roll back a workaholic's time barrier.

Note: Workaholism is not about the joy of abandoning boundaries between work and play. Those for whom work and pleasure are one are Fortune's favorite children. If long work hours are not joy to you, decelerate just to see what happens. Remember leisure is like unoccupied floor space in homes: no crowded mess, no noise, nor lack of privacy. It is the realm of the privileged. You are holding spiritual frontage as one might own miles of ocean view.

Speaking of homes, a great place to win leisure is to drastically "downsize" domestic labor. Since the fifties, Americans have had an affair with the immaculate. House "wives" were literally kept at home to clean floors as though families ate off them. Housework will not necessarily kill you, but why take a chance?

Simplicity is always a clutter-buster. The less you own, the less you have to care for, the less you must be a mired domestic rather than a bounding lover. As you do use things, clear as you go, in "no-trace" simplicity. Handle everything as though you were handling your own eyes. Make your trail invisible as a bird's track in the sky, a zen aesthetic also much prized in polyfidelity. "No trace" creates no visible fall-out from past guests to intrude upon present ones. Moreover, many women are embarrassed to entertain when clutter becomes a thick-layered mess. So we waste a succulent block of time just clearing the decks or do not consider offering the outer hospitality where inner hospitality flourishes. Simple lifestyle is to polyfidelity what appreciation is to romance. Simplify. Simplify. Simplicity opens the gate to the leisure which nurtures life and love.

Sister, spare that spare time.

Schedules: To Love, Honor and Negotiate

Query: I've had co-partners for years, but I still have the most challenge in creating schedules. New women usually are concerned that scheduling wrecks spontaneity. All I know is that I have to organize my love time or everyone may want something at once. How else can I cope with a possible feeding frenzy?
— *Sonja Buttons-Zahn, Monterey, California*

The most harrowing thing for me was when all three lovers wanted to process relationship schedules in the same week I also had my period. I almost became a wandering menstrual. Luckily, I was seeing my bisexual love bimonthly, so later, by the time I was ovulating, she had forgotten the problem. I barely managed to negotiate with the second love, but by the third I had learned from the second, so we had a solution. Whew.

Just because you've taken the "Pledge of Alleisure" and understand the spirals of yogic Time as well as clock-time, doesn't mean you can gloss over rendezvous preplanning and scheduling. In successful polyfidelity, several women's interactions are merging and receding, smoothly as tides in mother-of-pearl. You are creating an elegant dance with various partners. Ask a good dancer what happens if she throws away a prime consideration like timing.

I have never understood the strange aversion to scoping out one's pleasure for an interval of time, opening up love spaces, and then holding to these dates as firmly as you would a lady in a hot tango. The moist anticipation alone is a swoon. Scheduling one's pleasure is a way of making love with Mother Time. Spontaneity is vastly overrated. The heat in it is actually the novelty involved. Couples fondly remember courtship days, forgetting that each excelled in being a preplanner extraordinaire. You knew the precise hour of arrival and exactly where you were going, probably reserving space in advance. You even knew how soon you would try to glide into home—or let her. One of my best loves was so premeditated that she put a crystal in her vagina to help channel the rhythms of her dates' second chakra. (This San Francisco fetish has been dubbed "the beaver receiver" by comedian Lea DeLaria.)

It is the consciously crafted, scheduled matrix wherein valued "spontaneity" often emerges. Few have ever created classic art who didn't staunchly set aside the hours which incubate that "surprise" illumination, stroke or spin-off. Most excellence involves gentle discipline and tenacity. Someone said art is the act of structuring time; perhaps love is, too. Casual, unannounced break-ins are sexy to some women sometimes, but I notice that these women consciously put themselves in a place, time and mood where "something" may indeed happen. For example, women who have "spontaneous" sex in the restroom of a restaurant didn't break the time barrier and arrive there from outer space. Their hot, discoverable sex had been prepared for hours, if not months before the delicious meal. Many connoisseurs of sensuality agree with the *I Ching:* preparedness is the key. To illustrate: you may keep a blanket in your trunk because you design time around your dates, one of whom may keep a generous pleasure cup she can open to a warm, starry night when you're together at a beach. The only thing purely spontaneous here would be a shooting star.

The more I ask women about spontaneous erotics, the more that spontaneity comes to mean out-of-bed, "out of place" sex, a novel *mise-en-scène.* Most polyfidèles also find that lovers who insist on totally nonstructured time with them rarely expect any such an open season with friends, family or colleagues. With all the fireworks about time conflict, perhaps these lovers are covertly provoking an exclusive? What these women certainly want—and who can blame them—is for you to be constantly available upon their slightest whim. Their free time becomes the tab for you to pick up, an ever-bountiful, ever-welcoming, ever-loving mom. I once thought if I fell in love with women who didn't have regular jobs, perhaps I could get their unconditional attention. What happened was they usually expected me to entertain or heal them sixteen hours a day. Frankly, everybody is a big baby and wants attention when they want it. There is only one way out: time negotiation.

This is one of the most fun and valuable things to negotiate: your love life. It involves flights of fancy and the power of irrationality plus team problem solving, attitude structuring, with personal and group bargaining excitements. Time negotiations are usually a snap at first blush. Love conquers all—in the beginning—and no one is much ruled by clock-time or anything else. Ultimately, the real world intervenes, and you have to juggle the other commitments on hold. In rare instances, lovers work out dependable, flexible routines with a minimum of ruffled feathers and can skip this chapter.

If a lover will simply never negotiate time, she is a solipsism from hell. She likely won't negotiate anything else of importance either. It's clear she runs the fuck. Dealing with time, as polyfidèles have to do early on, is an excellent signal of things to come. Since several women's lives are affected, some sort of routine, however loose, is almost always essential. I am sure there are some personalities who so abhor routine of any kind that their lovers simply develop a tolerance for zero predictability, or have no priorities themselves. I'm not sure what the balance of commitment is here, but if it mutually works, great, you too can skip this chapter.

Sometimes women are leery of schedules—for good reason. Schedules have been rigidly imposed upon us, perverting inner time. Or, the reluctance to commit to any form of scheduling may be: one part fear of failure; one part underdeveloped organizational skills; and one part conflict: is this situation right for me? These are all worthy issues to sit with. I certainly do when I consider any new commitment. It is the nature of commitment, however small, to rearrange the dynamics of life. This can be scary, even when it's going well. We've left the familiar shore.

When very new at all this, I once drew a time map of my great loves. It featured my most demanding mistress, Art, and two very beautiful women, as well as me-myself-and-I needs, like job, spirit and garden time, etc. The whole map is in colors, bright yellow, rose, greens. It is not that I ever "got" anywhere, but the little posted map helped me focus on my inner time and life purposes when I was tempted to be distracted by the usual host of minor interruptions. Sometimes it was okay to change direction, knowing I had a route back and a way planned. I don't fear and resist interruptions so much any more. They are like weeds: a fact of life. Some may become beautiful, permanent landscapes if I find their purpose for me. When interruptions come, I just roll my eyes to my old life/love map. I know within it I have the power to do, delegate or ditch. Each interruption, like each new woman or plant, is an opportunity to make a heart connection—or let go in good will. My loving colors renew my Mother Time connection and my power. One of the lovers saw a copy of my map and tore it up saying, "I can't bear not to see myself on it everywhere." From then on, it was just a matter of time. . .

The actual process of negotiating intimate time is fascinating. It is an arena of life we can actively, cooperatively design, unlike the cookie-cutter conform-time we must usually fit into with school or job. The first person to begin negotiating with is yourself. What exactly do I now want of lover time? What do I need? What are my boundaries? Where is my tolerance? Don't look too far ahead. Perhaps a season is the longest link of destiny we can handle at a time.

Here is an example. Let's say you have various windows of time to open. You want to balance short-term activities with long-range ones like job, quiet time, one lover going on two, and tennis. You want to see new love, Miz Montana, one full night and morning a week, date her sometimes during the week and be in touch by phone. Try for Saturday nights because Saturday morns are best kept clear for tennis, or Tuesday nights because she has Wednesday off. But, in actuality, you only need to intently be with Miz M at least once a month to build an intimate friendship and for you to bond. Otherwise, you can see her hit-and-miss in your schedule that fills up fast, winging it and keeping it casual.

Boundaries? You intend to keep spending Sunday afternoon and night and Monday morning with your lover, Cleveland Sage, whenever she's not on the road. You do walking meditation an hour a day, work Tuesday through Friday, noon to six. You also coach tennis for fun or money, some mornings and Saturdays. In all this, you understand your own energy cycles.

Tolerance? For options, you can juggle and vary Tuesday through Saturday eves and some mornings to Miz Montana's schedule, keeping Sundays for Cleveland, most of Monday nicely floating for yourself. (Of course, even as you call it "thus," it is already changing).

Hopefully, your intended is doing the same sort of review. Just do whatever it takes to clarify and understand her scheduling realities and perceptions, her hopes and needs. Recognize that time may be an even more incendiary discussion than money. You need never agree with all of her ways, but you can respectfully listen and understand. When there is a conflict hot spot, hold your talk to listening ratio low, deep, and slow.

Above all, don't disagree or defend your position during her communication time. Try to eliminate "The Judge." High-control women are somewhat disarmed by lots of friendly questions. Many affectionate whys and what if's often create her own counteroffers. Ask for a fair hearing in return, carefully expressing your desires and feelings as perhaps an inviolate "I" truth, but not The Truth. Then relax. You've both won everything. The most immediate goal of a significant, initial discussion over conflicted time-sharing is mutual understanding, not problem solving. You already have a savory resonance between you, and with such discussion of life priorities you are building a bridge. Congratulate one another on sharing each other's present in joy and respect. Maybe for now, simply drop all contradiction and focus on mutual interests. Here is a fine time for body language in the ever-generous now.

You can get back to a difficult time issue when you are both feeling good and abundant. Reserve undisturbed time, talking about the precise clock-hour schedule last, never first. Come into all this with options for mutual gain; so make no crisp ultimatums at the beginning. The first act is to review all your pleasures, again possibly reenacting them to enliven the proceedings. Remember there is never just one issue—hours. As in real estate negotiation, the sole consideration is never money alone, it's all in the terms. Luckily, you don't need a broker to figure out every term and variable because in love you are not stuck with one contract forever. We get to keep evolving—all the time.

In this, and ongoing discussions down the road, always first affirm mutual delights and confirm understanding, then brainstorm multiple time options. Everything is easier when you agree no plan is forever, but is a living experiment capable of infinite refinement and change—all with due notice, of course. If you still can't come up with a plan that is immediately agreeable, try one of these routes:

1) Take a time-out.

2) Compromise alternatives.

3) Take turns with entirely different schedules.

4) Yield your position—for now—knowing it is respectfully considered and always lives in possibility.

5) Assert your own position after thoroughly and respectfully considering hers, remembering the old sorcerer's rule: if you skin a cat, don't keep it as a house pet;
   or

6) Agree to disagree. Express gratitude for all the sharing you did do, and go your separate times.

The main areas of conflict over time in polyfidelity are lack of clarity, perceived time deprivation, and role fixation. Hopefully, you're refining clarity with every discussion and listening. You are no longer just "hoping for the best," or your loves will crash into each other's time like bumper cars. You have also calculated your actual discretionary time, so you don't fall into the "schedule 'em all" trap.

All long-term lovers need to know each can count on the other, and that each will give the gift of quality time, of full, aware presence. Any professional whose vocation depends on significant, focused personal attention can arrange for it in only one way: special appointments, otherwise it's chaos and short-change. The same is true of caring parents with their children. One would think the gift of special time would be appreciated, yet it is often resented simply because it is limited. Such time resentment is common in monogamy too, but perhaps is more poignant in poly because there is the realization that another lover is receiving precious time too. What we have here is the "wisdom of no escape." It is the human condition to nearly always agitate for more and more of something fine. This is our way: rarely to kiss the joy as it flies, but to clutch it until it bleeds. The neurotic twist comes when you do not taste the delight you do have because your main energy is focused on resisting its end. This anger is usually built on the fear that we cease an activity never to recapture it again. This is essentially true, nothing lasts indefinitely or can be repeated identically. Such is our terrible grief and greatest blessing. As any pleasure that goes on forever would become an abomination, we are given the surcease that every pain, even atrocity, must fade.

When the pleasures run away like wild horses, how does one gracefully let go of the intensity and wave good-bye when duties beckon? Gratitude helps, the balm of appreciation. There is a sweet pain in being lonely for a cherished woman. This is nothing like the bleakness of zero gratification, nor the existential loneliness of a breakup or death. Enjoy the privilege of longing for her mutual ardor. Sometimes a simple, shared acknowledgment helps, a ritualistic, "I'll be back." "I hold you in my heart." Never, ever lose the faith: if the miracle of pleasure happened once, it can happen again.

Sometimes women are hypnotized by a time-hierarchy role fixation, the idea that whoever gets the most clock-time has the highest power or position in the system. Actually, whoever is immediately present has the immensity of personal power and opportunity. What matters is quality presence, since we can only look in one pair of eyes at a time. The fact that I care deeply for others (mother, kids, lovers, friends, animals) does not in itself diminish my care or presence with you. In poly, I don't have to be all things to all lovers, just be what I say I am—householder, muse, passionaria, anchor, etc. I need take only one pledge, "When we are together, I will do my best to be present for you." Of course, this means it's easiest to live in such a manner that nothing keeps jamming my circuits when I see her. I must not allow now to become merely prelude to next.

Whenever you reach an impasse over time, feeling deprived or crowded, first climb alone into the expansive lap of Mother Time herself. Then ask for help wherever you can. Skip the blame game. Time is your problem, your feeling. Your take on events is authentic and understandable, but not necessarily "true." You might inquire of a caring but uninvolved person if they can suggest any ways you may be tripping yourself up. Then simply ask a lover, "What would you do if this were happening to you?" "Can you help me?" You may be surprised how creative and generous people are when they are not guilt-tripped and put on the defensive. Sometimes it is personally valuable to sustain ambiguity about time without fight or flight, as when a lover says something like, "I don't see any way we can be together two nights a week like you want." While you're up in the air, enjoy the view. Observe the whole picture. Perhaps the height of personal power is to be content with what is given.

I am certainly not saying to allow yourself to be manipulated by any lover who is rarely concerned with your best interests or visions. Remember, even well-meaning people feel absolutely no compunction to arrange your schedule to accommodate their wishes. You can always find someone delighted to tell you what to do with your time. For centuries, women have run on men's clocks. Let's not do this to each other. You don't need a love that comes with the kind of time entitlement that exhausts rather than renews you. Develop walk-away power. You always pay top time when you *must* have someone. Necessity never made a good bargain. Look at bored monogamy. Smile and wave farewell if someone does not honor your independent time and those special routines you know harmonize your life. Respect her choices, too, and thank her for what she could enjoy wholeheartedly with you. Understand and be patient with energy cycles, the ebb and flow of Time's cadence. Realize you can say good-bye to a beautiful woman, live your whole life without her, and it will be a loving life.

No matter how smooth the schedule you create with your lovers, its strength is in willow-like flexibility. Most women need assurance that you will be there for them at non-scheduled times if necessary, from celebrations to emergencies like medical problems or bereavement. Every loving schedule has openings for compassion. No realized person would abuse these. I have a friend whose lover stayed with another love a certain day of the week, agreed-to and fine with everyone. But when my friend's mother had a heart attack this same day of the week, her lover refused to come off schedule. I was with my pal; she didn't need everyone around her, but this schedule's rigidity, and its disrespect for vulnerability, helped kill any trust. Be careful the "specter of schedule" does not make a woman feel that she is not precious and special no matter what time it is. There is nothing so strengthening in life as to have a number of relationships you can count on. Absolutely nothing compares in the overall quality of life.

In sum, use a schedule to support the process of polyfidelity, knowing you cannot control, only keep re-ordering things. Stay open to moving from necessarily reactive clock-time to active, receptive Mother Time. Management of time in polyfidelity, as elsewhere, is never possible in any total sense. All you can do is organize your luck. May you and yours, Sonja, live in the world of love's synchronicity... ever and anon.

Clitzzpah

$\mathcal{Q}$uery: I would try polyfidelity in a split second, but I can't find even one lover, much less several. Help!
— *Nora Mance, False Pass, Alaska*

$\mathcal{G}$etting a lover is like getting a job. Unfair as it is, it's easier to get one when you already have one, just as it's easier to get a bank loan when you're already flush. When you have a lover, you are not, and don't come across, as all that needy. Neediness is even deadlier than a sense of entitlement for scaring off prospective lovers. Moreover, when coupled, you seem to have the imprimatur of being chosen and valued, references in order and on the hoof. This doesn't help you, Nora, at the present moment, but it is something to look forward to. It is true: attracting and keeping even one lover is a job, so best approach your quest with all the focus of attaining the career of your dreams. Be careful, though, you may get your wish. In being coupled /tripled/quadrupled rather than single, you just trade one set of problems for another.

Disclaimers ahoy, I wrote one book solely on meeting women and creating relationships, *Lesbian Love Advisor: The Sweet & Savory Arts of Lesbian Courtship.* As few people are born with perfect social pitch as are born with a perfect high C. Would I could tuck the CD-ROM between these sheets. I will instead provide the following revised abstract of *Lesbian Love Advisor's* tips for tops. If this does not work, send me $100.69. I will provide your discerning name and address to each Lesbian who wants to meet someone and also sends me $100.69. Postage and handling included.

Bedding and Wedding Lesbians

Nine times out of ten YOU are going to have to make the first move with a desired woman. Trust me. MAKE THE MOVE or nothing may happen—ever. Women are socialized to wait. Flirting is the social skill women least practice. We are so stiff about *l'amour,* it is a wonder we haven't died of starch. Making the move is therefore called "clitzzpah." Yin is an element of fabulous virtue, but if you want romance, roll into Yang. Do not deign to give rejection a second thought. You cannot die of flirting. In fact, flirting is invigorating, much more so than jogging. Plus you get to rotate your senses at twice the average speed. Great lovers have a rejection list a yard long. I respectfully remind you, however, of the flowery number of miles their lovers make, laid end to end. So, clitzzpah is simple and basic and brave, a form of holy daring. All it takes is normal animal sensitivity and normal animal courage. If your question is really, "How do I find partners without any effort or any risk?" please go on to someone else's book.

O.K. sport, memorize these easy, non-threatening conversational openers: "How are you doing?" "May I join you for a moment?" See, you did it. You can probably even learn them in another language. *"El sabor es lo que cuenta."* All compliments are great openers. So are polite questions. "That's a beautiful pendant. Do you know who made it?" For conversation fuelers, rehearse a couple of positive news items about yourself: "I'm just back from_____." "I'm learning about _____."

Conversation stoppers: gloom 'n doom, preaching, fixed stands, self-boosterism.

Enjoy silence. Sometimes I think speech is the small change of silence. Don't rush to fill all the spark-gaps. Enjoy breathing together. Excitement without breathing is anxiety.

It is not WHAT you say that matters, but that you convey your pleasant, beckoning interest. There is no small talk, only small people. Seventy percent of direct communication is conveyed by body language, never mere words. At first meetings, probably more like ninety percent is facial/body language. This is the intimate apparel aspect in every communication. It is almost universal that every culture uses a come-hither raising of the eyebrows to indicate sensual interest. In slow-mo it goes: brows raised in eye contact, quick (respectful) glance down, and re-connect with eyes and brows—just a few seconds longer than entirely proper. You've just been relayed, waylaid and roundelaid. This is one reason the French are so successful at romance, even if we can't understand all their words. Most Frenchwomen trust and use the *élan vital* of body and face, especially the eyes. It continues to amuse me that my face is not so much my property as everyone else's. We trade faces. This is why "the look" before a kiss can be as important as the kiss itself.

Need I mention—never take bar flirting seriously. But don't forget to get her phone number. This can be smoothly done by giving her your card to get hers. If she responds by saying she doesn't have a card, ask her if you can write her number on one of yours. I have never ordered business cards in my life, but I am never without a "calling card."

The nine-in-ten rule goes for asking out an acquaintance too. Initiate! Again, compliments, compliments, compliments, and opinion-seeking to warm the communication channels. Offer her a book, tape or video you think she might enjoy. Try other non-obligating little tokens of consideration: a bouquet of herbs from your garden for her kitchen, an "extra" theater ticket, flavored coffee beans "just to try." You can hold the flowers and cards for courtship beyond the first date. For the robe of early romance, practice a light, gay touch. "I want you" does not have to translate, "I need you." Want is a relaxed state.

Ask all friends to match-make for you. For wooing, background information on her is priceless. Lesbians love to match-make. You'll do the same for them when they are on the stroll.

Cruise all organizations you have ANY interest in for available Lesbians: those of artists, the trades, computer mavens, Sufis, whatever. In a large city, many of these groups will have a women's or Lesbian wing. Elsewhere, figure at least one-fourth of the women in a group are Lesbian/bisexual or would like to be; most could be. If you like the group's subject focus, you'll have a good time anyway, and may make a friend, if not lover. Plus, you come away more interesting to yourself and others.

If necessary, especially in a small town, start a woman's social group of your own: reading feminist mysteries, an art salon, a professional group, a spirit circle. Again, you'll be enriched whatever happens. A lot may well happen; contacts lead to contacts.

Run an ad in the Personals; this is *much* more efficient than answering one. As well as newspaper personals, there are online chatrooms. (See the chapter "Poyfidelity & Cyberspace.") A woman's taste in letter writing, stationary and cards is more relevatory than standard cyberspace mode. We open *billet doux* like the lid of an enchanted chest. Women have good luck with the specifically Lesbian designed correspondence clubs like *The Wishing Well*, Box 713090, Santee, CA 92972; *New Dawn*, Box 1849, Alexandria, VA 22313; and *Golden Threads*, Box 60475, Northhampton, MA 01060. Be ultra-specific, positive and humorous.* Ads really work, and you get courting practice. Courtship, like any of the contact

---

* Personals Who Played Well in San Francisco:

Troubadour Tryst?
I'm looking for old-fashioned fragrant love, gentle manners, and sex to make the mirror steam. Marriage? Nope. My long-term woman lover and I both enjoy other lovers in honesty—and privacy. No *ménage à trois*. I don't smoke, m & s, drink and drive (no car), but you can recognize me by the rake of my hat, the creme of my dream, and my open heart. I can curry a she-stallion with friendship, lather her with love. Reply Polyfidelity Rising. . .

I Think
Sex is sexier when not mixed-up with sorting the socks, dishes in the sink, who did or didn't do the litter. I'm an independent 44 year-old full of radical opinions, a hard-boiled journalist—with a heart of mush. Who turns me on? Smart, well-slung, sassy women who make their own rules, not mine. I don't care, I even prefer, if you are married, but no back-stairs stuff, duels, or drama. I'm joy-bound. Reply Nellie Bly. . .

Little Old Lady Seeks Same
Can you believe it? I'm into fisting corporate lawyers and playing a twenty-button concertina. You are among the privileged poor, an educated and talented Victoria's Secret and Trader Joe shoplifter, looking for deeper thrills. Monogamy, no. Intimacy, yes. Blue hair, optional. Reply Mother Jones. . .

sports, is a creature of practice. (At a certain demimonde age, it takes practice not to seem practiced.)

The main reason it is hard to find love is that most of us usually wait around for someone to love us. We look *for* love rather than *with* love. We aren't as likely to explore being interested, being caring. Practice by loving yourself with great daring and generosity. Then be open to enjoy, learn, and care about someone else. How rare to respond like a child who is fascinated with the stars, a story, a tide pool—and shows it. Surely, a beautiful woman is no less fascinating and delightful? Expect nothing. Enjoy her. You'll be beaming while most everyone else is anxiously waiting to be loved.

A few observations: You'll throw away love and admiration several times before you learn who is worthy of your powers. Commit to quality, not permanence. Don't expect sex to do the work of love, or love to do the work of sex. If in turmoil, turn to our legendary mistress of polyfidelity, Natalie Barney, whose signature epigram was, "To be coward enough to choose!" Natalie reminds us, "Love, like all religions, has more believers than practitioners."

Lust-Driven Lesberados?

Query: Isn't Lesbian polyfidelity just a dressed-up ploy for getting access to as many women's bodies as possible?

— Anna Mull, Stockton, California

Well, yes. Who hasn't used a dress-up prelude to an undress seduction? But, no, if body count were the goal, we'd simply regress to exclusive heterosexuality. Loads of men are panting for sex. Very few women are available for quantities of hit-and-run sex, unless paid. Due to gender-driven supply and demand, sex work is the only career in which men usually pay female professionals three times the going rate of male professionals. Lesbians, even rich or busy ones, are rarely in the loop buying women's bodies. This is because one can pay for a body, a substance, mechanical techniques, but no amount of money can catalyze warm vibrational streams to flow: exchanging, uniting, transforming. This, Dr. Freud, is what women want, most of the time, especially polyfidèles.

Women spin powerful braids of energy which seek a similar, colorful blend of intimate connection: emotional, physical, intellectual, psychic, inspirited. Our eroticism is psychosomatic energy. We can refuse or release this energy with our genitals, but we also love to run it from other founts, including heart and mind, to enjoy entire biota and soul as a vibrational source and transformer. Lesbians even share a secret sexual code by which connection and exchange is made without physical touch or word. Here... on clitoral dots... I must leave the page...

I return to it to doubt if most women ever experience what men dub a genital sex *drive* to overrun as many bodies as possible. Current male-framed sex theory, or sex "speculation," since it seems to change with every generation, now holds that women's sex drive is powered by our testosterone and related androgens (male hormones). If so, these androgens are produced in the ovaries and adrenal glands in minute quantities, a bare fraction, maybe one-thirtieth, of what is produced by testicles. No wonder our sex energy is something quite different because it is not mainly androgen battery-operated. It is something vastly more solar: intricate, but powerful, diffuse, flowing sensual energy, capable of erosynesthesia.

Many men do act as though sex were a controlling, independent drive, like that for food, air—or power. If this be so for many of them, is it in any way normative for the race as a whole? If fast-food, battery sex is the most popular form of release for some men, next to violence and suicide, do we really want to mimic them? While the female capacity for orgasmic frequency, duration and depth exceeds the male's, few of us are actually driven by the volcanic powers between our legs. Well, if we have a sex drive, at least we have a driver.

We do not strive to blow-out our aroused flow via any means possible: on nameless bodies, protesting spouses, or "let's pretend" sex surrogates, from inflatable dolls to daily pornucopias. Is it true that men can have sex with a venetian blind? We do know that in the insect world, males can copulate despite decapitation. From women, I instead hear gales of laughter or offended disbelief. Yet the male idea that sex is so damn demanding a force explicitly legalizes the horrors of marital rape in many U. S. states. Rape as a prescribed health regimen for our rutting lords? Just because one sex can pop sex on automatic, does not mean males are or indeed should be out-of-control. It simply means arousal happens without much reflection. Women ride the sex tide as intently. To most of us, however, sexuality without the swirling, warm oils of conscious affiliation is a barren wick, mere john-bobbitt twitter.

Let's face it. In human existence, women are not as sexually attracted to men as men are to women. Who does not want to return to the body who first enkindled us? Women literally embody the original love object of creation, so we can be sexually fruitful and sufficient unto ourselves. We are more attracted to our own sensuality and to other women's. The huge fashion industries for women cater to our desire for the female, as does advertising

225

and film goddess worship by women and men. Since all genders share the infant's experience of primordial bonding with the body of a female, women remain magical. This is a reason why women loving together can be fire and ambrosia to the nth degree.

In lieu of driving "force," women who uninhibitedly love the heat, aesthetic and energy of other women's sheer physicality are versatile in experiencing woman *frisson*. We do women's sports or dance. We frequent women's gyms, saunas and sex clubs, attend women's events, classes, festivals and dances. There is now a potluck of scenes and sex parties. We enjoy a Lesbian, rather mixed-media, of arousal.

But even Lesbian-produced erotica and porn (energy and matter?) rarely succeed without aesthetics and ambiance, relationship, intelligence, or emotional color. It has been fascinating to view the Lesbian erotic-aerobics genre, which began to evolve twenty years ago. There has been nothing comparable in the history of media. So far, women's porn and erotica have largely been derivative, colonized by male sex marketing. Stay tuned for astounding revelations. Keep playing, girls, with the full splendor, chaos and danger of hot women's bodies in flashpoint. Let my people come—all over the pleasure map. We are creating the medium where sex becomes art meeting life. We can hopefully erase the curse and grime of dark millennia of shame via the media of Lesbians wet in awe, laughter and love.

But leaving virtual reality, women's greatest social skill may be, yes, actual SEX with each other, enacting the sacrament of joyous interfoldment & caress *Summa Cum Lava*. But a systematic grope of blind lust/fizzle/move-on? Highly unusual, especially for polyfidèles.

Thus, while polyfidelity can certainly be about wet, willing bodies, let's look at what else it is. Relational self-interest for one. Poly is about the jewel of bonding and the treasure of community. It is about learning to create strong, healthy boundaries. Polyfidelity can be about the vision of *Tantra*, or ritual sexual yoga, wherein sexual love may be transformed into a style of worship, where our family of women becomes an incarnation of the divine, our Goddess of Ten Thousand Names. In *Tantra*, one learns to pour the sacred into one another as the ancient temple priestesses did, without shame. Without the earthy passion of sex, much religion has been abstract and fearful. Without the ego-abandonment of spirituality, even Lesbian sex can become as possessive, greedy and mundane as the het habituated form of mechanical masturbation. How the vermilion thread of passion can weave a Sacred Middle Way for you and your lovers is another book—but don't wait. You were born to give at least six lips of service to the Goddess. They are doing what comes naturally.

For this "access" query on your lips, dear Anna, let us consider where access and response to "as many women's bodies" and hearts as possible may lead. In the sweet, wild fields of Eros, what are the fruits enjoyed by a carrier of sexual intimacy? Please remember, I am not suggesting instant sex with every desirable woman, simply asking you to look beyond monogamy for Eros rising. In poly, you gain "a perilous advantage," as Natalie Barney emphasized. For example, your live-in beloved may presently choose celibacy. As monogamist you have the alternatives to mimic her or else break up your household. Take an orgasmic lover too. There are all kinds of vibrancies in relationships. You can love one woman in the cool blue-green waves of the spectrum and another in hot carnation.

For many women, the orgasmic euphoria and exhilaration of attraction often relates to three dynamics: hope, uncertainty, and idealization. Many chaste Boston Marriages (see pages 48-56) are delightfully romantic and sustained in genuine idealization by each partner. But, if crackling passion also depends on hope and uncertainty, the women may have little desire for sex in their atmosphere of warm, daily security. In the good life, daily physical warmth may be the equal of genital sex, who knows? But why choose? It is not "wrong" to find another woman to add the bright spark of uncertainty—to be the barrier, polarity, taboo or danger it takes to lead you on a hot adventure. Another woman may even add that manageable but uncertain edge to rekindle a chaste Boston Marriage into a more tropical one.

This all leads to the realization that orgasms are more the drama of fantasy than of friction. Polyfidèles are often artists, women of great imagination who love having muses to adore. Virginia Woolf's novel *Orlando* is perhaps the longest, most sparkling love letter ever written by a great artist—by a married woman to a married woman. The profound emotional and spiritual side of Eros is legendary in its power to inspire creativity. We are open and receptive, yet utterly daring and tireless to re-create passion as art. Anaïs Nin was another great polyfidèle taking countless lovers of all genders while in and out of marriage. She memorialized them in literature, then turned around to reveal: "To affect my lover's imagination, that is my strongest power."

Many women also find sensuous touch combined with emotional kneading to be their source of replenishment and healing. As poet Audre Lorde sang in *Uses of the Erotic: Erotic as Power*, sensuality is "a longed for bed which I enter gratefully and from which I rise up empowered." Many of us know the sense of wonderous satisfaction and fullness which can accompany lovemaking. This is in contrast to "relieving tension" on another's body, a seeming staple of the male mini-seizure. Relieving tension on someone sounds like pollution. No wonder it's lonely at the top when mind, feeling and psychic energy are censored from the sneeze of the loins. It is the authentic, deep sharing of bodies and life force that works to head off tension and stress in the first place. We don't need to numb streams of vulnerability for the heights of pleasure and joy. Each opening strengthens us to absorb deeper human sensations, even pain.

Speaking of which, don't we need all the succor we can get? Human existence is subject to lifetime mortification of the flesh. It's headaches, back strain, nausea, PMS leading to cramps, fatigue and now carpal tunnel syndrome—is it not blessed when someone wants to present our body with sensual pleasure? Why monogamize this delight to one physical therapist per sufferer? Fucking is one of the simplest forms of yoga when you want to stretch out sweetness and breathe in delight. Kissing uses twenty-nine muscles of the face and increases your cardiovascular rate by 50%. And the tongue—ah! celebrated organ of Chinese medicine. The darting tongue is not only physically adept at the tantalizing, in-and-out, she is reeling poetry in motion as she engages us in verbal foreplay, with prompting asides, orgasmic exclamations. Why limit her eroticism to a one-person audience?

Emerging from a wide and warm erotic field may also give one the triumphant energy to pursue genuine change and social activism without burning out. Polyfidelity is about the pleasure, as well as the sheer power voltage, of Eros among a family of women. There may be something to be said for an army of lovers, but one can sing about a tribe of them. It is difficult for the self-appointed control crews of the world to beat down the happy lover, one who knows her profound powers in bestowing pleasure, who feels pride and dignity in being beloved. Once one has felt the joys of real gratification, it is harder to live on half-rate measures and pie in the sky.

Erotic lovers appreciate, above all, the poignancy of flesh: its fragility and transience, the terrible truth that there is no abiding lover in your embrace, as there is no infinity of earthly resources. Your blissful love is born in the morning, three hundred million cells of her die every hour, and by the longest night our lust is but cosmic air charged with stardust. We learn from a lover's body that it is already too late to settle for less than we deserve, to put off personal gratification in order to take bosses' directives or be satisfied with supplied states of being.

With Eros, we no longer fear the "yes" within. We know that Eros is irrational, chaotic, mysterious, with bodies and imagination slipping inside out, into another, into the Void. Because Eros is such transformative, fluid motion, Eros itself does not panic about returning to the tide of orderly and sensible living. Why then is orderly and sensible living so afraid of Eros? Because the rational self, for all its glory, forgets it can let go and return. In its analyzing, rationality freezes the frame. The erotic self is more likely to juggle excitement and stillpoint into serene release, trusting the powers who care for such things that we can always return to equilibrium.

As death, the ultimate change of state, approaches, a person often celebrates how great or despairs how little, was the love in their lifetime. What life is about becomes clear. Whom did you love and who loved you? It is pathos to make life a business, a trade-off for security or worldly achievements, to never use the gift of the body to go deep, to be absorbed by one's unique heartsongs. Whatever draws one's heart, this is the realm of the erotic, and the spiritual as well. If your heart is drawn by the beauty, the sweet sorrows and creativity of relationships, the laughter and mischief of Eros, why will you wait day after day?

Maybe you haven't been waiting? In the most accurate sense, how eroticized does your life have to be for you to come out as a "poly-fidèle?" Am I polyfidelitous when I don't merely hold hands with someone besides my girlfriend in the movies, but our fingers caress? This type of query came up again and again from women in our poly survey. We began to wonder if a characteristic of eroticism is that it lacks precise edges, indeed moves in lace-like, melding, dissolving patterns to bubble up again in amazing synesthesia. What, in fact, may be said to constitute an erotic encounter between women? Certainly not any definition requiring orifice penetration, which some women can take or leave. Perhaps we can say sex means orgasm takes place? Oh . . . so what constitutes orgasm? It is certainly more than the tired old bell-shaped curve of mechanical arousal, contraction and *la petite mort.* This is a male "big bang" paradigm still clanging around from fifties' sex texts. In contrast, roll around the spherical orgasma-rama of pleasure/release/ecstasy sexologist Gina Ogden creates to represent women's orgasm in *Women Who Love Sex.* It is *la petite satori.*

Or view an erotic Lesbian film classic, like "Entre Nous." There's nary a loud bell or clapper in any of director Diane Kurys' breathtakingly erotic scenes. Remember when the two beautiful French women first meet at the grade school play, in what seems a shower of faerie dust? The attention is electric as they sit, clothes brushing. Their words are soft candles; earrings glint. Honey-blonde Lena (Isabelle Huppert) is royal in blue with hat and veil. Raven Madeleine (Miou-Miou) is the fifties bohemian in short black toreador pants. They suddenly focus on a silky run up Lena's silk stocking. Lena then asks Madeleine in surprise, "Are you bare-legged?" almost as if she were asking "You don't wear a brassiere?" Madeleine replies no, that she is, in fact, wearing . . . lotion, as she caresses her bare leg, smells her hand deliciously and offers her fingertips to Lena. A long look as Lena inhales the fragrance, bringing Madeleine's fingers past her veil. Cut—but not before I feel ripples and waves, leading me . . . where? There are many such scenes, the women framed in a mirror, intensely focused on self as well as each other, then both together, as each applies bright red lipstick across the silvered glass bridge. Later, they verbally caress one another's breasts in reflection. Is sex language?

Then there's the infamous bootleg version where Lena, after a *haute femme* day in her boutique, slips a strap-on dildo under her empire-waist gown to go home to Madeleine, who in moist anticipation dons her crotchless panties, after she has just talked dirty to her very own mother. We see the good girls doing some really bad things that make you realize they have practically forgotten whatever gender—or generation—they are. There is a lot more high drama stirred in, all framed in lush nature, food and fashion fetishism. After some startling character development, more violent menace from the *ancien régime*, our queergrrrls become abundant mentors to Hothead Parisian types in *Les Lesbiennes Vengeresses* and are not shy about moresomes, either.

Well, roll your own and try it on—when is being sexual different from having sex? In film, in our own lives, I suppose it does not matter, unless there is concern about progeny or disease? Or unless you are supposedly monogamous and this creation of extramural eroticism makes you "bad"? Or are you afraid that any acknowl-

edged eroticism may confuse or collapse a friendship? The friend-
ship-complication fear actually comes from any ensuing adoption of
possessiveness, not from the erotic behavior itself. As the song goes:

> *Love is a rose, better not pick it.*
> *Only grows when it's on the vine.*
> *Handful a'thorns, and you know that you've missed it.*
> *Lose your love when you say the word mine.*

Greta Christina, wrote a marvelous essay called "Are We Having
Sex Now Or What?" She makes me wonder if reading is intimacy
between strangers or what? Greta comes around to defining sex
for herself as "If you are turning each other on and you say so and
you keep doing it, then it's sex."[22] Here we have acknowledgment,
consent, reciprocity, and pursuit of pleasure. But then Greta
notices, "Whoa," what about the situation we all recognize where
one person is in full-blown eroticism and the other isn't—not
because of coercion or force—but the cool one is either self-
contained or wandering elsewhere. Is sex happening here?

Or try this one: at the top of a charged evening with a woman,
begin an enticingly explicit, yet subtle-rich, conversation about
what qualifies as being a one-, two-, three- or four-star erotic experience for you. You may have totally different love maps and surprise one another about acts, sensibilities, vibrational pitches,
all the subtlety/acknowledgment aspects. You do not touch or even
see the favorite place she mentions, like the "bubbling well sensa-
tion" just behind the ball of her foot. You never nuzzle and nip her
earlobe, nor graze the angel-down of her neck. But, as you walk
through the leaves and starlight together talking, you feel how the
warm, dry leaves crackled under your back and how the earth
smelled when your first woman lover carefully raked a mountain
of leaves and took you down, whispering of harvest home.

But this evening, with this woman, let's say you touch each other via
waves of sound, vision, aroma, memory, imagination. Did you come?

Don't you play with polyfidelity every day?

Love Addiction?

Query: When I tell my friends that I enjoy being in multiple relationships, they often suggest that I'm a sex addict or a love and romance addict, especially if something goes wrong. During this present bad breakup, I am trying Sex and Love Addicts Anonymous (SLAA) meetings. The beautiful lover I am losing says it is not healthy for me to be unable to sexually commit to one partner alone.

So far, I find SLAA largely for men into flamboyant, illegal sexual compulsions like exhibitionism and child molestation and for women from sex-abuse cycles. I have confessed to setting up theaters of courtship, wild sensual excitements, and sexually intimate friendships. Mainly, I'm happy with my sexuality, which is usually full-bodied, free, and creative. SLAA members suggest I take the abstinence pledge and will help me during "withdrawal." My own best sweetheart, myself, feels bereft, doused in doubt.

— *Selma Soul, Salt Lake City, Utah*

Fiddle-dee-dee, Selma. Why fall from full-bodied freedom into sexual anorexia? Why join some twelve step "Invasion of the Body Snatchers?" Remember you are highly vulnerable to the nostrums of any religious sect like the Twelve Step Program, when you undergo loss, or life changes. An important breakup makes many a Lesbian question her whole identity as a lover, even as a person. This vacuum can be a place where fools and cults rush in. Hold your open space.

Of the twelve step addiction programs, Al-Anon may be more appropriate, less lurid for you than SLAA. In Al-Anon, you may learn about the great suffering and futility of trying to control the behavior, reactions, and feelings of anyone else—your former girlfriend and about five billion others who cannot be ruled by your great ideas. What a relief! Lay your burden down. You are free to go your own way, responsible for your OWN universe of actions and responses.

I tip my hat to Al-Anon for its personal autonomy emphasis, but many people, especially feminists, question the core integrity of twelve step God/He groups which are in flagrant denial regarding the identity of their patrifocal, monotheistic religious tenets. God has always been the inflamed nerve of AA. Perhaps we inebriates of love might relate to a Deeper Power or Inner Power, even Centering Power. A Higher Power (HP) is too separate, lofty, absolutist, and disembodied to love. *Spirituality* may be recognized as one's own changing, personal evolution in awareness. *Religion,* in contrast, always has a fixed, codified dogma and consistent liturgy totally recognizable in any Twelve Step (Lock Step?) Program. It is well-documented that the first hundred men and one woman (suicide) who founded AA took the Twelve Steps whole cloth from the British Christian fundamentalist Oxford Group, a controversial and corrupt gold-mine for its preachers.[23] In order to marshal secular as well as religious support, AA founders tried to mask AA's sin-and-redemption testimonial religiosity. Atheists were even welcome to "fake" the Program! Officials still deny that their external HP is male monotheistic dualism lashed with a frightening dogma of fatalism. "Better to be a self-respecting drunk, than to deny your religion," a friend of mine said.

Why not open steps which address healing the physical body with good nutrition? How about steps to combat the social ills which sustain addiction? The political is more than merely personal except to a status quo organization. Why is there no step to champion free inquiry, only fundamentalist, sexist fifty-year-old "approved" language and literature? Why the shield on debate with no AA cooperation for verified studies regarding AA success/failure? Why nary one step about having fun and celebrating life? Why keep coming back to grovel, grovel, grovel? Why "intimates" whose last names you cannot know due to their ongoing shame? Many people find hospice service to be better "one day at a time" training than meeting after meeting.

Altered-reality aficionados may also muse on how much influence the medical use of belladonna had on founder Bill W.'s famous "spiritual conversion." Why was Bill's delight in megavitamin therapy and LSD censored by the AA establishment? Bill, that's Wilson, unfortunately died of emphysema from lifetime nicotine addiction.

To simplify your quandary, Dear Reader, there is absolutely no such thing as "love addiction." Love is life affirming, generous, powerful, brave, and probably the most nourishing thing on this sad earth. There is no upper limit to love's quaff. If you ever think you've experienced all the love you can imagine, you've only reached your momentary limit, not love's. You can double it, then double that. One of the few intelligent writers on addiction, feminist Charlotte Kasl (*Many Roads, One Journey: Moving Beyond the 12 Steps* and *Women, Sex and Addiction*), notes that saying you are addicted to love is like saying you are addicted to fresh air. This cannot be: there is no depletion, are no harmful side effects. We simply open our hearts and lungs, feel alive. We don't have to measure and control breath or love; we relax, open, and it comes and goes. As we do not breathe too much, we do not love too much, period. A book such as Robin Norwood's *Women Who Love Too Much* should obviously be re-titled *Men Who Hit Too Much*. The former title is not self-help, it is self-blame. It plays on a victim's misplaced remorse, rather than the much-documented plethora of abusive men.

Speaking of relationship addict careerists, one of the most ardent, Anne Wilson Schaef, is, like Robin Norwood, a recovering psychotherapist. (Both have now left conventional therapy dispensation behind.) Anne Wilson Schaef (*Escape From Intimacy: Untangling the Love Addictions—Sex, Romance, Relationships* and many other books) appeared to reveal every nuance of her family and career battles with addiction and relationship dependency.

In focusing on her various husbands' drinking and sexual peccadilloes, Schaef somehow, in all her books and circuit rides, forgot to mention that she took women lovers—as good an errant husband antidote as any. Trouble came when, it seems Dr. Schaef could not keep her expert hands off her women "sex addict" clients, perhaps inspiring her famous *Meditations for Women Who Do Too Much*. Schaef reportedly raffled therapy sessions to subsidize her love nest in beautiful Puget Sound. She, however, generously offered free private sessions to anyone in her therapy groups who was troubled that Anne had sex with group members. Anne Wilson Schaef settled one sex malpractice suit for a quarter of a million dollars.[24] If you want to learn about sex, romance, and love addiction at the knees of a master, on your elbows to Anne Wilson Schaef. As Anne notes in her annual spin-off palliatives to *Meditations for Women Who Do Too Much*, "Truth often comes in strange packages." Too, too strange.

Let us depart the melodramatic, illusionist world of highly-paid recoveroids and move into some homegrown, plain folk observations about sex, romance, and relationship "addiction," since everyone is grabbing the recovery line. They say if you can remember the sixties, you weren't there, but the eighties were one decade-long, reality-soaked Fourth Step. In exploring the inner lip of daemonrum, I also learned *anything* can be a fix: religion, credit cards, work, worry, jogging, a lover, maybe even too much "reality." A woman needs a release valve, no blame. Even the angels stray. There seems, however, to be an optimum value beyond which any "savior" is toxic, anything: oxygen, water, release valves, therapy, self-defense, receptivity, sunlight. As Shaw remarked, "The most intolerable pain is produced by prolonging the keenest pleasure." Humans are biological variables—polyfidèles. Most of us thrive in an equilibrist's middle way between asceticism and excess.

Sex Addiction

Acknowledging said equilibrium, I only imagine there can be too much sex. I feel there is an overwhelm of sex tease, a genre easier to dramatize than fulfillment. I know, however, we can easily dispense with female sex "addiction." Addictions are known as notoriously *quick* fixes, but women, especially Lesbians, are often tantric with time when it comes to pussy *et al.* Nor with most women is there the genital fixation commonly related to sex addiction. Women's entire bodies—plus auras, aurals, and aromas—are eroticized like delicious rainbow vapor trails around our earthly delights. Woman sex is often as exquisitely subtle as the zing of a homeopathic molecule. Genital addiction tends to be so, well, obvious, repetitious, so rapid-fire predictable. A voracious Lesbian in heat is flesh and electric subtle-body, beyond rote control, about as predictable as a she-stallion. That takes care of sex addiction for women, an acquired taste, I suppose, but one few of us acquire.

If you still worry that you love the thrill of the chase, the elegant artifice of courtship, the vortex of hot sex more than most, so what? Sexual minorities have more fun, that's all. A sensible question about multiple romance and "relationship addiction" is to determine whether you have perhaps been blessed with a special personality *trait*. Ask, in contrast, whether you're packing a personality *disorder* undermining your life: are your spirit, work, art, social connections, health, self-respect being endangered? Check how a behavior fits in with the gestalt of the rest of your life. Full-blown addiction is migraine-intense feelings of compulsion and craving. It is behavior repeated despite knowledge of consistently adverse consequences. Is the woo you are pitching usually joyful, creative, and/or fulfilling to you and yours? If the answer is yes, then, hey, you ain't broke and don't fix it.

Here's a handy guide:

> *Sex addicts jump on.*
> *Romance addicts move on.*
> *Relationship addicts hang on.*

Romance Addiction

Well, we've dispensed with female sex addiction unless somehow it's a therapy career path. Let's take romance "addiction" next; it's the most fun. Do you excel in the romance trance, the honeymoon phase, rather than enduring relationship? You are not alone. In fact, you are together in a flowery spring queendom, a fragile bower open to the sky. Romance is a fine state of euphoria if you both know precisely what is going on and delight in romantic excesses and absurdities. Of course, romance may get magnificently out of control, since going beyond your usual ho-hum boundaries is the whole point. Annoying, petty concerns recede as significant and meaningful adventures flow in. Barriers fall to the swirling lyripollen of love. Disarmed, you are open, experimental. The brain's inner apothecary is showering you with its amphetamine sparkle. Those of you who never get into this altered state are probably not mega-synthesizers of PEA. Your cats certainly appreciate how you manage to get home nights to feed them.

Experienced romancers tend to enhance their *élan vital* with potentiators such as nature's bounty or by exploring sensory gratification with ritualistic, long, deep focus. Moreover, billion-dollar industries are available to stoke your every stroke: perfumers, florists, poets and musicians, lingerie, clothing and jewelry designers, elegant bistros and hostelries. Romance, thy name is credit card. After all, romantic love is your pay later, fantasy-partner idealization projected onto a stranger. You are psychologically distanced from her authenticity by your shining image of a make-believe woman. Meanwhile, she is rapturously doing the same thing to you. This is known as the "applause response."

First, you see yourself mirrored approvingly in a woman's eyes. Pleased, you flash back your image of her as being a discerning, sensitive soul. She sees this attractive reflection and flashes an even more delighted view of you back. The applauding images mirror each other mirroring each other like drops of shining dew. What ultimately becomes of this exquisite, fragile illusion only time will tell. It is an entrancing way to begin. People actually transform their ordinary grumpy selves into well-directed dream people, creating true pleasure on earth. Romantic courtship can be the active element in an alchemy that gradually transmutes the dross of selfish love into the gold of giving love. Romance is an inspiration, a muse of love. The Buddhists say the ice of selfish love contains the waters of universal compassion. Romance, of course, is not the only avenue for love. You may be more the commonsensical Jane Austen heroine who "decides" on a partner. But romance holds a glow like fire for some of us, impermanent, yet eternal.

So, how do we plug "romance addict" into this artful circle of pleasure? First of all, I would like to banish the eighties epithet "addiction" being slapped on every common, problematic human behavior: power addiction, work addiction, addiction addiction. Can all human sufferings be packaged into one fat bundle and called "addiction?" Shall we throw every manner of excess into the addiction pot—like Senator Bob Peckerwood of Oregon four-paw-ing dozens of women, then trying to intimidate and blackmail them for speaking up? Senator Bob says blame it all on his "dis-ease." Ditto Mayor Marion Barry of Washington, D.C. His incompetence and corruption are really a "disease" known as fast sex and cocaine. Remember life before the addiction "disease model," when people could be held to standards of decency?

Why not let the term addiction stand for the repeated ingestion of external substances which create morbid body tissue or kill body cells: alcohol, nicotine, petro-chemical toxics, hard street drugs, hard prescription drugs. If you are simply a Lesbian who majors in haymaking first times—well, really two times, the first and the last—I would call you "curious." Or, if you constantly pursue a desirable woman only to discard her for imperfection, I would call you "foolish" and probably "lonely." I would wonder if you have any relationship or any connection involving conflict/resolution and ongoing creativity with anyone? Do you have any extended, biological or interspecies "family"? Any calling? Any matrix of true friendship and love for anything? So what if you don't "couple up" *à la* Noah's Ark during or after the iridescence of romance? As long as you are truly present and support any other creature on a mutual energy loop, romance your nights away with any consent-ing adult you do not betray.

Why do some people judge romance as "wrong" if not pursued for the Great Union of relationship? Romance is bloom; relationship is ripeness. Romance is joyous artifice and play; relationship is rich and dramatic realism. As in the flowering world, each cycle is beautiful and precious in itself. With polyfidelity you can have both. But menstream society is pleasure-phobic and deeply eroto-phobic. There has been a swing to the right from the sexual experimentation of the sixties and seventies. This is why society still wars on queers; despite all stigma, we fuck for pleasure, not from duty or habit. The menstream does sanction canned romance, packaged in material form for sale and designed to reflect the conquest/surrender power model. Quite beyond such props, great romance is really unbridled hedonism, pursuit of altered states, and sensory gratification. It is filled with art and beauty, playful illusion, theater, possibility. Romance is ecstasy in drag.

May we queers be as ardent in defending our right to pleasure as with we are compassionate toward the reality of our pain. While the power structure maintains the queer is a special sort of person, we say that each person is a special sort of queer. Suppose some of us, especially Lesbians, are born with romance as our special art? Natural romancers love to anoint people with faerie dust to bring out their convivial best. They mischievously cut the hinges of our hearts to release a sweet bliss where the vision of unity blossoms. It is called S & S, Spirit and Sensuality. What if our moment together, our vision, is evanescent? Blessings arise, blessings fall. As the geisha sang in "Flowers of Cherry:"

> *It is because they fall*
> *That they are admirable.*
> *What is the good of clinging*
> *Clinging violently to the branches,*
> *Withered on all the branches,*
> *Soiled by the birds?*

The great necromancer/romancer is like the wild cherry tree: she knows how to detach without saying good-bye.

Relationship Addiction

It is not the romancer who would lead us to the clinging "security trap" of the purported relationship addict. If the addiction industry is wrong about the "bliss trap" of the romance addict, what about the "morbid" need to relate? Well, if security is your trap, maybe what you need is a good jolt of romance with its hot juices of transient delight. But, seriously folks, it is true, some people can't seem to buck out of perfectly horrid relationships; they, yes, hang on and on and on. I call this a tragedy more than addiction. People who cannot leave a bad relationship usually have a sense of self beaten to a pulp, followed by self-neglect. Clinging to a poor relationship, however, does not seem to be a major problem with polyfidelitous Lesbians. While we do celebrate good relationship(s), we don't hope a single lover can "save" us like some Higher Power. Our expectations, therefore, tend to be gentle, our dependency short to middling. Our ideal relationship form is to care for, not take care of, to support, not to fix. More likely, it is the mono-relationship which disempowers women, which isolates, which creates the misery of over—and under—functioner. The mono-relationship is the one to engender fears of abandonment, enmeshment, while demanding inordinate time and obsessive attention to "the couple," over the individual. We have seen this couple-cauldron bubbling in a grandiosity of rescue, manipulation, control, all stewing in helplessness with its blame and victimization. Polyfidelity tends to be a lighter buffet, with spices diffused, rather than main-dish heavy.

What about the accusation that polyfidelitous women are actually afraid to be alone? Most of us found out that before we could ever begin to handle several intimacies we needed a strong, loving, self-directed relationship with ourselves. Intimacy is like joy, courage, serenity—you cannot reflect it unless you have created an inner supply for yourself. This means generous self-focus. Most experienced polyfidelitous Lesbians insist that "alone time" be one of the essential practices they build into their lifestyle. Relating intimately with several people can be intense, even disorienting to boundaries and focus. We consciously seek aloneness to ground ourselves, slow down, soften sensations, listen to the heart, and find the breath inside the breath.

So, Dear Questioner, I suggest not accepting the false alarm of addiction for a disease you probably have not got. AA's one-size-fits-all model was probably not designed for you. SLAA's touted love 'n' sex "true partnership" is really monogamy, camouflaged by these two other words. SLAA upholds the traditional patrifocal conservatism that monogamy is the healthy ideal, that celibacy is preferable to promiscuity. SLAA's fearful tales of eternal "disease" may motivate you, but they will not heal you. Fear does not heal. I am glad Twelve Step programs are open to all and are free. I am glad in a world starved for community, they create thousands of little social bomb shelters. Most importantly, they have a well-groomed path to follow if your world is topsy-turvy. In actuality, almost any sane structure would work. "Program" content is irrelevant as long as it holds order and unity, and there is one step that simply says, Let Go. Any so-called steps are a great self-actualizing placebo. There is nothing outside you that will make you happy and well. Which all leads to our sincere, if not sober, corollary: On the world's loftiest throne, you still sit on your own rump. Rumps romp, what can I say?

Unless your journeys as a lover lead you away from self-awareness to physical self-neglect, to emotional as well as ethical blindness, be willing to let this one beautiful lover go her own way. Then you can go yours. Actual addictions or compulsive (*have to*) behaviors keep us afraid, teach us submission, external referencing. They drill a real hangover into the spirit. Is this you? Are your romances props for lagging self-esteem, dying initiative, and the desire to blot out intolerable avoidance/control tensions? Perhaps the primary addiction from which all addictions flow is the addiction to powerlessness fiendishly laced with the addiction to control. While addictions and compulsions are a sign of disharmony in the individual, they most dramatically reflect the tremendous imbalance and disintegration of the social system. It may help that you are actually living a Lesbian polyfidelitous alternative to the ruling social miasma.

May your fields of romance become gardens celebrating how to give without giving away, receive without taking away. May they continue to be abundant lands where you do not perceive vast scarcity with its call for self-denial. May they be wild, benevolent places where you need not deny the weeds of life either. Allow your path to be one of discovery and rebirth, rather than one defined by disease and recovery. Since most everything can be mood-altering to the sensitive soul, consider simplifying your have-to's for a little peace of mind. You may, for example, want to drop any real substance abuse because the life of a profligate needs stores of emotional and physical stamina. Whoever said being a hedonist was easy? So, take a poet's word on the middle way:

> *Better be merry with the fruitful grape*
> *Than sadden after none, or bitter, fruit.*

Desire Discrepancy—Why Not?

Query: I want sensual change, but I don't intend to leave the woman I've loved for twelve years. We share a home, children, economic interests, and most importantly, joyous compatibility, loads of affection and love. My partner, however, has had zero interest in sex for ages (ten years), while I want and miss it. We've gone to three different couple counselors over this one issue. I finally realize that neither of us is likely to change, just as she often plays golf and tennis, and I've never wanted to and never will.

We are at last talking carefully about my taking a lover. My partner agrees—as long as the relationship we've built doesn't destruct over it. We've each created free, separate time in our lives, so I'm hoping a new way will work out. I still don't understand what went wrong, why sex so complicates a perfectly fine relationship in every other way.

— *Tess Driver, Pocatello, Idaho*

Oh, you have left the dismal courtroom for the faerie forest! In moving from realization into acceptance, you can release any judgment of right/wrong sexual frequency. A prosecutor of ghosts may process the why of things forever, but, as my grandmother said, "whys" butter no parsnips. Kneading and re-kneading our how/why past mythologies, in light of the ever-shifting present, monopolizes the precious energy necessary to jump-start creative change and make it work. It is not so hard to know things, but to live what we know. Most therapies provide a passive, serial-form retro-spectacle. Their common delusion is that you make all things better simply by talking about them.

But NOW what? The present, rather extended fact is that the two of you have decidedly different agendas in one area: sex. Another fact, which I wonder if your therapists revealed, is that you two have one of the commonest, most natural dynamics in the world. It is called "desire discrepancy." Why not—you are two different people. Five thousand years of dominator culture has tried to invalidate and dishonor the fact of desire discrepancy. In dominator mode, a couple does sex with the frequency and style of the most powerful partner; any conflict over desire discrepancy is covert. In more equitable partnerships, desire discrepancy can be honestly articulated and negotiated, if not accepted.

Feminists certainly recognize that all personal physical and sexual boundaries are sacrosanct. No one, absolutely no one, has the right to physically touch you anywhere, whether in teasing or in desire or anger. Anyone who does this without permission has what can amount to criminally poor boundary control. They are rank trespassers. Any physical battering, of course, is the one-way ticket out of all Lesbian relationships. This is the only message a batterer understands: one strike and you're out, period. I would also declare continuing verbal strikes for sex, and you're out, too. Whose script are we reading that insists if two lovers move in together, exchange rings, etc., one gets physical entitlement to the other's body upon demand? This assumption is sickeningly menstream. It also leads to the worst haranguing cycle imaginable, fueled by poor impulse control and low self-esteem.

We've all been caught, however, in verbal conflict about sexual frequency, too much or too little. Human nature being what it is, each partner tries to establish her own sexual rhythm as normative. Usually, however, we fall into the male narrative of the essentialist sex "drive," so even Lesbian desire discrepancy prescriptions are aimed at stepping up the flagging libido. Celibate tendencies are as stigmatized in our society as homosexuality, so any contrasexual mode is highly contra-indicated by conventional "experts." Never mind that the celibate cycle or lifestyle can be as loving, as conducive to psychological wholeness as a sexually orgasmic one. Celibacy has its own amazing style of individuation and fulfillment.

But back to the sex wars of the rest of us. First, we may try to negotiate *quid pro quo*, as in: "If you're not feeling sexual right now, will you hold me while I pleasure myself?" Or, we may try to therapize in myriad ways. Is a libido dying due to shame (old Calvinist tapes)? Are we locked in the "role nausea" of control antics? (Who feels sensual being a "critical parent" or "imperfect child" or being relentlessly pursued or constantly begging?) Are old resentments choking romance? (Let go of grudges or you'll never let go in pleasure). Finally, we may try imagination to polish away desire discrepancy. (Romantic getaways, fantasy role-playing, technical innovations, sex paraphernalia . . .)

Any or all of the above may work. Great. Or, (fizzle) they do not. Face it: acres of desire discrepancy stretch into the future. One of you is continuously quite happy just to skip the purported ideal of genital, orgasmic sex. The other is hanging fire. In classic monogamy, this means a tightening Gordian Knot, an intricate problem insoluble on its own terms. One may back away from the Gordian Knot like you, Dear Reader, did because you have other buttons and bows, in fact a primo heart friend of twelve years. In other monogamous cases, a compromise is struck. They get "it" over with as quickly and infrequently as the sexually passionate partner will settle for. So, no one can be wholeheartedly anything, except maybe chronically resentful.

Enter polyfidelity: a fresh, sweet breeze upon the land. The sexually frustrated partner goes a'courting. The more "innercourse" partner focuses her heart energy howsoever she may, unbuffeted by the turbulent weather of sex. Surely, "sexual liberation" also means the freedom to refrain from sex as we know it, just as freedom of expression means the right to express yourself in forms other than words.

This does not mean the original partnership is stripped of romance. The erotic impulse, after all, is not sexual arousal *per se*. Eros is the luminous quality of being related, feeling connected to beauty and meaning, a truly magical state loosely called "interbeing." Eros is being totally alive. People have erotic relationships with the sea, with music, with an idealized friend. Vita Sackville-West, for example, immortalized her erotic "night garden," her white flowers lovingly cultivated to bathe in moonlight. Eros is the ability to pay attention, to take it "all" in. You drink the sun flecking gold into the hazel of your beloved's eyes, how she tosses her hair in anticipation, its fragrance, the way her voice deepens in awe, how she opens her hands when listening. Note most long-lived Boston Marriages are highly eroticized, sweet with intimacies, tenderness, romantic tokens, and the little caterings a lover performs. Why continuously label a relationship in terms of either/or, friend/lover? Why not consider intimates as women you eroticize for whom they are, not wrench them into one camp or another? Try the carousel of romantic friend, sport-sex buddy, ecstasy traveler, intellect teaser—moving, changing with your rhythms. In India, there are ninety-six words for love. May a woman not have at least a dozen forms of lover?

One last thought with my good wishes. Once you both step out of the long polarized roles, sexual/non-sexual, anything may happen. You may be quite surprised that your seemingly more chaste partner goes a'courting herself. Parity, right? Her mode may be similar to many women I interviewed: she wants her home and hearth love to be affectionate, but serene. For passionate sexual arousal, she desires uncertainty, barriers, even danger. This is why first-time sex in new relationships is so exciting. It is laced with doubt, with the unpredictable. Some of us go as far to seek the dangerous, the taboo, or the most highly differentiated, strange exotica we can uncover. Unlike women who cannot even begin to enjoy sex ecstatically or let go with a new lover until there is long familiarity and intimacy, the *liaison dangereuse* sisters swing on the question mark. Polyfidelity, as a radical, innovative frontier, itself is energized, sexualized by uncertainty. How will open relationships change us? What will new women introduce?

So, dear Tess, you are co-creating a new lifestyle with your trusted love, something both secure and exciting. Now you approach true sexual liberation: to take sex or leave it. Keep in mind this is only an experiment, everything on a trial basis, but now sans the sex frequency judge and jury. "Go easy," as Gertrude Stein said, "and if you can't go easy, go as easy as you can."

Your greatest refuge will be friendship and laughter.

Polyfidelity and
Sexually Transmitted Diseases

*Q*uery: When my lover and I told our couple counselor that we are both interested in experimenting with polyfidelity, she was aghast. She said that in today's "viral climate" poly would be dangerous. Is a polyfidelitous Lesbian at high risk for AIDS?

— *Ada Lemma, Boston, Massachusetts*

*N*ot unless she mainlines drugs or semen, too. The AIDS virus is overwhelmingly blood and semen borne, remember? Both these special fluids are designed to keep living cells alive. Then, for contagion, the infected fluid must somehow invade your bloodstream directly. I heartily wish we could put a latex barrier on this type of alarmist aural intercourse, especially since professional caregivers should know better. Around AIDS, gay men got condom sense, while it seems that Lesbians could use a lick of common sense. Are we casualties of post-feminism's "Keep your bra. Burn your brain." Why can't every intelligent Lesbian distinguish between these two contrasting, yet equal facts:

A. *Due to "crossover" activities, Lesbians and bisexual women are contracting AIDS via blood and semen (sharing needles; sex with HIV positive men). This fact is tragically documented by women whose struggle we need to share.[25] It exists side by side with the obvious reality that*

B. *The actual transmission of the AIDS virus as a result of the typical woman-to-woman sexual practices of exchanging vaginal fluids, saliva and touch is an unrealized fear not convincingly documented in fifteen years of AIDS study.*

It is not what you call yourself on the sexual spectrum, from Vanilla Vestal to Dyke Daddy, but what you *do* that spreads AIDS. If you get *blood* or *semen* inside your body from an AIDS carrier, proven statistics and common observation reveal that you may be off to eternity earlier than planned. Even the blessed state of Lesbianism does not confer immortality to one involved in any high-risk situation with blood or semen. Many of us are, or know, self-identified Lesbians who occasionally do have intercourse with men. Here, we must observe every smart sex practice, since efficiency of transmission, male to female, is about twenty times higher than female to male.[26] This is why most U. S. sex workers insist on condoms, why it's a delusion to scapegoat them as prime carriers. Many of us also are, or know, Lesbians who, by way of IV drug use and contaminated needles, can shoot AIDS virus directly into the blood stream. Very rough sex (extreme whipping, piercing, cutting, lots of bloodletting) also may allow one person's contaminated blood to enter another's.

In dramatic contrast, woman-to-woman sensual/genital acts, *per se*, our kissing, caressing, tribadism, fingers, and superficial, diffused spread of vaginal fluids, rarely include the commingling of bloods or contaminated needles. It's for sure none of them include semen! The AIDS virus is a fragile one, dying easily in the air within ten or twenty seconds. Yes, the AIDS virus has been found in vaginal and cervical secretions, but in insignificant density compared to blood or semen. The amount of virus in vaginal fluids seems to be dependent on the presence of other infections and open sores here, which provoke discharge of white blood cells—the vehicle of the AIDS virus. It is now believed that in an ecologically healthy vagina, our natural lactobacillus acidophilus and other bacteria may in fact be toxic to the AIDS virus. These useful vaginal flora can be unfortunately absent due to various infections, poor nutrition, hormonal imbalances, etc.

With our typical sex practices at low risk, the Lesbian community has gratefully been spared wide contagion. Anal sex, with whisper-thin membranes involved, as well as rimming, should of course be protected with kit and caboodles of cots, condoms, and lube. We may as well do the same for menstrual shows, although theoretical menses dangers, unlike anal sex, have been neither observed nor documented.

Even though there is no clear evidence that a Lesbian's usual low risk sex behaviors can spread AIDS, Lesbian AIDS alarmists declare they can. I guess this humbug means many of us have AIDS, don't know it and don't show it, the Incubators Eternal. (The average symptom appearance is four years.) May all other populations be as benignly abducted by the AIDS virus. Hold a workshop on Lesbians and sex. It's SRO. Try holding a workshop on Lesbians and AIDS. No one shows up but AIDS professionals. In the sexy Lesbian film "Go Fish," for one instant a safe sex packet is flashed on the screen. The audience laughs. During the key sex scene, replayed in multiple versions, there is not a whisper of latex. No one cares. The hilarity of the seduction scene turns on safe sex all right, our beloved ritual of nail clipping. Nor is safe sex deigned a whisper in *any* mass distributed Lesbian film: the sassy, mocking "Bar Girls," "The Incredibly True Adventure of Two Girls in Love," "When Night is Falling," "Costa Brava," or our tale of rollicking polyfidelity, "French Twist."

Alarmists say AIDS research statistics have heretofore ignored the delicious technicalities of woman-to-woman sex, as though Lesbianism did not exist. They are quite right about the government's dodo bird statisticians. (No, fellas, "intercourse" does not equal "sex," unless you have tunnel vision, nor did the CDC definition of a Lesbian, "a woman who has not had sex with a man since 1977," take a prize for precision.) We do need to fight for the sexual representation of Lesbianism in all demographics, principally health studies, especially since LESBIAN SEX LOOKS MORE AND MORE LIKE SAFE SEX. Say this loud and clear to Ms. Middle America. May I also remind them of the eleven studies which show the condom average failure rate to be 31%.[27] Is the statistical blank on Lesbian love just dumb—or fear of recruitment material?

At least change may be coming. Hark the City and County of San Francisco being the first official U. S. agency to collect specifically Lesbian AIDS statistics.[28] In October, 1993, the AIDS office of the San Francisco Department of Public Health, with federal CDC funding, released two studies surveying around 1,000 relatively well-educated Lesbians and bisexual women in the Bay Area.[29] Among the predictable results: zero evidence to suggest woman-to-woman HIV transmission. "Woman-to-woman transmission for HIV was clearly not evidenced in the study," reported Melissa Jones, project coordinator, who was joined by fellow researchers in announcing woman-to-woman sex is not a primary, volatile infection transmission zone.[30]

The unpredicted, alarming study results were that 22% of the self-defined Lesbians surveyed have largely unprotected (!) oral, vaginal and anal sex with straight and gay men and that many who use IV drugs do share needles. Other studies report sex with men by 30-40% of self-identified Lesbians.[31] Every woman who tested HIV+ in the San Francisco studies engaged in sex with men or used injection drugs, no matter what they call themselves. So much for "identity politics" and the magic of label protection. The San Francisco studies show that these Lesbian and bisexual women—all playing with the vectors of blood and semen—have three times the estimated HIV+ incidence of the female population at large, making them a very high risk group, about where gay men were in the eighties.

So for poly women with HIV+ and new lovers, here are simple, realistic sex guidelines to memorize.

Unsafe Sex Practices with HIV+ People and Sero-Status & STD Unknowns

1. Unprotected penile penetration of anus.

2. Unprotected penile penetration of vagina.

3. Sharing drug works such as needles.

4. Penetration with anything (fingers, sex toys) that has not been cleansed or condomized since its last use.

5. Rimming (analingus) without a latex barrier.

6. Fellatio without a condom.

7. Transfusing menstrual blood directly into your bloodstream, bypassing saliva and digestive enzymes which tend to neutralize HIV. Menstrual (vampire vamp?) blood danger is only theoretical as of this writing.

8. Commingling blood lines as via lesion-to-lesion contact. (That's "lesion-to-lesion," not "Lesbian-to-Lesbian" contact.)

9. Not looking before you lick.

I often ask myself how such Lesbian alarmism rose to charge us to use latex for everything but a dry kiss? Are we a people with no quality of life concerns? Why are we confusing the deadly severity of AIDS with its contagion? Well, someone gets money to produce those dam brochures about Lesbian AIDS, sell woman juice impedimenta, make safe 'n' sexy videos. AIDS, like "addiction," has become a large commercial complex. There are groups and professionals with a vested interest in AIDS seeming an even wider problem than it is. One entrepreneurial Bay Area therapist charged Lesbian audiences $10 a head to watch a baby dyke go down on her with a dental dam, that safety patch of illusion. I saw the damn thing slip. Double-wrapping her dildoes was not titillating, of course, but "educational." This social scientist never asked us how come not one of our ten+ former lovers with a past had transmitted AIDS to us, how come none of our friends or their ten+ lovers and their friends, in fact nobody in our 10,000 acquaintance pool that night of the performance had tested HIV positive? Transmission, transmission, where's the transmission? How about one single commercial, academic or government study from the AIDS industrial complex to prove that dental dams for saliva provide an effective barrier for the minute HIV? How about

ONE BIG REALITY CHECK based on your independent powers of observation and deduction?

Pestilence and disease capture the public imagination, inchoate terror sells. Fear is a virus too. As epidemiologist Susan Chu emphasized, "You are not doing a public health service by telling women that being sexual with women is high risk. Making up risks that don't exist is completely irresponsible... If female-to-female transmission were common, there would be lots of reports. There aren't."[32] Or listen to Sarah Schulman, writer, AIDS activist and a founder of the Lesbian Avengers: "What do they mean by woman-to-woman transmission? I travel all over America and meet thousands of Lesbians of every geographic location, class, race, and I have never met a woman who told me she got HIV from another woman. I know about six Lesbians who've died of AIDS that they contacted from IV drug use, and although they weren't practicing safer sex, their lovers did not get the virus from them. There are cases of women who've got syphilis from their HIV+ lovers, but not HIV. So anecdotally, it appears that HIV is not sexually transmitted between women."[33]

Could it be that some Lesbians want back into the coed gay community, to appear as endangered as men: Mrs. Homosexual? Can there really be what Elinor Burkett calls "Lesbian AIDS envy" in her book *The Gravest Show on Earth?* More certainly, we know that reactionary, professional fulminators from Jesse Helms to the Pope use the AIDS tragedy as a cover for pushing their repressive agendas. These include chastity and monogamy for women and strict controls against women's sexual spontaneity and power-packed lust. Refuse to be afraid of delicious cunt juice. Lap it up! Be afraid of semen and blood and pus and ignorant fanatics. Our dangers are infected men and intravenous drugs, *not each other.*

Perhaps the main reason for safe sex talk (and it's mainly talk) is that we get a chance to share revelations about Lesbian S-E-X, what in heavens we're doing down there. Women are socialized to keep sex secret. Gay men, after all, have a simple, precise menu of thrills, which everybody knows about by now, thanks to the Senator Sam vs. Queer Warriors charade in the U. S. Senate. But we didn't hear about Lesbian locker-room lust. One reason for the fascination with s/m is that practitioners actually discuss—in great detail—exactly what they do and fantasize. It took an epidemic for Lesbians to feel justified, even duty-bound, to discuss past and present sexual narratives, to openly describe our different shades of sexuality and desire. A Lesbian is so multiplex-sex, even a Lesbian doesn't necessarily know what a Lesbian does. So, let's keep up the high-touch, low-down talk. It's so, well, sexy.

But, of course, talk is cheap. People lie. Only the Goddess really knows a pretty girl's past. To alleviate anxiety, you can take AIDS tests, one test at the beginning of a six-month period and a second at the end. Two are necessary because the antibody the test is looking for, which indicates you have been exposed to HIV, may take up to six months for the body to manufacture. During the six months, practice all our Lesbian myriad no-risk sensualities *not* listed in the "Unsafe Practices" above.

Now, Careful Questioner, beyond your AIDS query, to be a real health responsible poly, I must move into other mouth watering table talk such as herpes and hangnails, chapped skin and chancres. A realistic concern for the polyfidelitous woman is the transmission of other STDs: sexually transmitted venereal diseases—syphilis, gonorrhea, hepatitis B, chlamydia, etc. Know, first of all, that every STD is largely preventable with knowledge and common sense. Their incidence goes way up with poor sanitation; plummets with proper hygiene. Secondly, heterosexual intercourse is much more risky for STDs, with the penis as the disease and trauma vector again. In the total population, the Lesbian STD rate is 5%; het STD rate is 16.9%.[34] But, hot and reassuring as woman-to-woman sex may be, if you are a polyfidèle, you are probably going to play more, so play smarter.

Use your sense of sight, smell, and touch to check for discharge or sores in yourself and your partners. Don't share the same sex toys without washing them between acts or use a condom on them before switching. For anything you do in your lover's sweet ass, from rimming to finger waving to fisting, use latex protection, gloves or finger cots. Cots are little condomettes for just one finger. Goodbye to worry about rough nails, minor cuts, hangnails. Use water-based lubrication jellies to make penetration a sleek, satiny annointment of passion. Rimmers, get the hepatitus A and B vaccines.

Rimming is stimulating your lover's wildly sensitive nerve endings at anal entry with your tongue. Use latex squares or double strength plastic wrap. The colored see-through wrap at Christmas is festive, but is the dye hygienically incorrect? Try not to use microwave wrap, the pores are probably too big; or off-brands, they tend to tear more easily. You can always choose Glad Wrap for its name and because it is the only wrap ever tested for virus control. It blocked herpes. Latex gloves are absolutely essential for fisting, the predilection for putting one's entire hand into a lover's vagina or anus. "As close as I come to the experience of having a baby," a friend remarked. She also counseled, "Take off your watch, or it'll be taken off for you." Whatever your thrill, remember the lower intestine is, for good reason, a teeming Microbe City. Always use cots or gloves and throw them away. This way, you will not be passing along hepatitis, venereal disease, or parasites, problems for the adventurous long before AIDS.

In short, the polyfidelitous woman is certainly no more a walking incubator of dread disease than the chaste. Connecting triads or quads of lovers may occasionally pass around the same cold, as all families, offices, schools, and restaurants share a germ pool, but we don't give *them* up. Regarding health, worry instead about air pollution, crashing cars, junk food. With one woman dying of breast cancer every twelve minutes, maybe the sweetest, safest and smartest sex practice of them all is to examine your true lovers' breasts at least once a month in circles of precious attention.

Alert affection is great protection. And always stay tuned for new information.[35] Latex won't save you. Knowledge will.

Stud Muffins: Diet Desiderata

*Q*uery: I'm not such a young buck anymore. Doesn't polyfideli-ty take a lot of sheer physical stamina?

— *Anita Fixx, Montreal, Quebec*

*N*o. It is physically more a question of keeping your nails short and your center of gravity low. Just take a couple of vita-mins, a low-fat *latté* and call me in the morning if there are any problems. I must admit there may be a physical problem in poly if you don't walk alone somewhere twenty minutes a day, and if you don't keep a store of excellent breakfast or brunch food around for you and *les amies*. It is unseemly to be out of coffee, cream, tea or juice when you wake to the wondrous hum of a well-tuned lover.

This leads us to the delicious physical stamina secret of many long-term affairs: the lovers like to eat together. Those of us without a nesting instinct are not without our nurturing one. "Eating out" has succulent meaning among Lesbians, but eating in is savory as well as sustaining early in the morning. Low blood sugar lowers the libido and turns trifles into travails. In triangles, there do tend to be trifles to attend to. Master the quick-fix breakfast if you spend lots of time rolling around before work. Surely you can keep dry cereal, dried fruit, soy milk (shelf life, years), and frozen buns around even if you don't indulge in breakfast yourself?

On leisure mornings, there is great flourish in serving home-baked muffins or "a special" omelette. The muffins are a snap. Here is a dry mix to toss together right now and store for the morning's after-love glow. "Stud Muffins" have protein and are loaded with vitamin B for the nerves. Simply rise up and add liquid to this mix after your lover has kissed you into the dawn.

Stud Muffin Supreme Mix

5 cups white flour and 5 cups whole wheat flour—or any 10 cup flour/grain combination you like: rye, buckwheat, rice, soy flour or cornmeal. (Just ¼ cup of soy flour shoots up protein.) Corn meal muffins can take wild seasonings like chile powder, oregano or marjoram, even salsa. Some women like a 2:1 flour/grain mix. Grains such as oats, rye flakes, bran, polenta, blue corn, and left-over cooked rice are fine.

½ cup good-tasting yeast	2 cups instant milk powder
½ cup wheat germ	¼ cup sugar
½ cup baking powder	1 ½ cups margarine

Combine all dry ingredients, mix well, and cut in the margarine until it is the consistency of corn meal. Store in the refrigerator, tightly covered. Makes four pounds of dry mix.

To make one dozen Stud Muffins, preheat oven to 375 degrees. Mix together one beaten egg, one cup of water or juice (sweetens), and two tablespoons of sugar or any sweetner you like: ½ cup honey, molasses, maple syrup, barley malt, marmalade. Combine with three cups of dry mix. You can now add frozen or dried fruit (cranberries are superb), nuts, poppy seeds, roasted sesame or sun-flower seeds, grated carrot, apple, zucchini, mashed banana, or cheese—along with any arrow from your quiver. For adventurous tastes, use teaspoons of vanilla, cinnamon or ginger; tablespoons of grated orange or lemon rind. All are said to be compassion aphrodesiacs.

Spoon into oiled muffin tin, ⅔ full, and bake at 375 degrees for twenty minutes. Name a winning formula after your lady. Send her the recipe with an invitation if you ever need to thaw a tiff.

L'Omelette Ardenntaise

A way with an omelette can become your signature, especially since eggs are revered in aphrodisia. Omelettes are excellent because you can vary them infinitely after you master the basic flick of the wrist. They are impressive, good for breakfast/lunch/dinner, fast, handsome, good for you, and morally sound if made from the eggs of happy, free-running chickens raised by Wiccan virgins. If you eschew factory eggs from supermarket chains and pay a bit more for farm eggs from natural food stores, you are investing in yourself, your beloved, and the right of all creatures to cavort.

A fine omelette, like a fine romance, is dependent on high heat and focused attention. An omelette pan understands this and its investment will repay you the rest of your love life. A seasoned omelette pan never needs washing, just wiping, and the omelettes rarely stick. A problem here is that omelette pans, like people, are rarely monogamous. The very first time I arduously seasoned mine, one lover melted chocolate in it. But onward.

Let the eggs stand in their cosmic round packaging for an hour at room temperature (*à chambre*). Cold eggs do not cook evenly or fast enough. You can think of something to do while they peak, like go back to bed.

For each omelette, beat three eggs. The more you beat the eggs, the lighter the omelette. You can create an almost soufflé-like creature by beating the whites separately before folding them into the yolks. Different lovers have decidedly different preferences.

Put one tablespoon of butter in a hot, ready-to-sizzle seven-inch skillet or omelette pan. The pan is ready when a water drop dances on the surface. Let the butter foam, not brown. The whole "trick," as they gaily say in *Cosmo*, is to cook an omelette quickly because eggs toughen if exposed to prolonged heat.

When the foam subsides, pour in the eggs, swirling the pan to coat. Again note, omelettes should be made fast, fast, fast. Stir eggs in a circular motion and shake pan until set. Pour any liquid egg over the outside egg edges to cook. Flatten large bubbles.

When set, yet creamy, add three-fourths to one cup of filling *(see below)* to half the omelette surface, saving a bit to put on the top for local color, unless you have fresh herbs. Start rolling the omelette out with a spatula or fork; tilt the pan forward and let the creation flop onto a heated plate. Put the plate in a 200 degree oven while you do the other omelette. As in politics, serve from the left, remove from the right.

If an omelette sticks and must be served *au scramble*, never apologize. The great fault in cooking is fussy apologizing. Put a flower on *au scramble*, a kiss on her lips, and say 'tis all a morn of delicious dishevelment.

Omelette fillings can be as eclectic as your imagination. In common use are cheese; any *sautéed* vegetable like green and red peppers, mushrooms, sweet onions; or roasted seeds and nuts, etc. A good rule is to mix the cheeky (like salsa) with the impractical (water chestnuts) with the inspired (fresh mint). May you always have one ingredient too many. Save it for your next home-cookin' woman.

The Wealthy Philanderopist

Query: Running around with all these women, dating and romancing, doesn't it take a lot of money to be polyfidelitous?
— *Iona Sawbuck, Sausalito, California*

Like everything else in the world, polyfidelity is, yes, easier with money. It is true, of course, that the chief value of money is that the world overvalues it. But who can deny that money is the difference between living on the slopes of a volcano or being safe in your Sausalito sea-perfumed garden? George Bernard Shaw remarked that the Seven Deadly Sins are food, clothing, fuel, rent, taxes, respectability and children. Nothing can lift these seven millstones from humanity's neck except adequate finances. Only then, can the spirit soar. So Shaw continued, "Don't waste time on Social Questions. What is the matter with the poor is Poverty. What is the matter with the rich is Uselessness."

Now let me ask you this: Who owns your heart? Is she in a trust fund, growth stocks, active in mutuals? If none of the above, I can send you my amazing 30-day "Buy Yourself Back Formula." Reacquire your high intrinsic self-worth in a program guaranteed to transform buyological urges to purely primordial ones, eliminate craving in dangerous advertising zones, and generally get you off your assets. Exercises in due diligence and passionate profits provided. We begin with plastic surgery, deftly slicing the credit cards from your wallet forever. You next take a fearless personal inventory, giving new lovers all items you do not use at least once each six months. Deep secrets of Dowism will be revealed, such as the mantra, "Do Whom You Love, The Money Will Follow," along with other techniques for fiscal fitness.

Seriously folks, polyfidelity is not built around consumer fetishes at all. As a form of radical intimacy, poly focuses on the great commonwealth of love, rather than love as commodity, one to be competed for in an economy of scarcity. It is, of course, logical that our

261

consumerist culture usually treats love precisely as a commodity. Certainly sex is a typical medium of exchange in emotional territory. How often do we sell expressions of love for acceptable behaviors such as exclusive sexual possession, security, or flattery?

See a cycle of this love-economy crash when the lover-bookkeeper feels cheated and then spiral into an upturn when her cupidity finds a more promising product. Watch eyes appraise as much as they adore. See an inflated image initially outperform a previous bond, only to plummet when its ninety-day warranty has elapsed. Watch the love-economy create sexual specializations to make certain commodities scarce and drive up prices: idealize elaborate, contrived femininity and stud bull masculinity, fetishize silicone and leather. Be coerced into buying love-economy products to make you physically and culturally more desirable, according to harsh advertising standards and the highly conditioned trick of "engineered social consensus." If the sex act is no longer completely novel to you, allow costly ambiance and mood-setting to become more and more important. Note a broken heart can be almost a pleasant complaint if you have a comfortable income. Thus relationships cost between a little and a lot, cash usually being spent on the same level as its availability.

I wish I could say the hot women of polyfidelity escape the need for cold cash. One thing polyfidèles may definitely want to rent is privacy. Since both women are often part of a live-in couple who keep their home clear of assignations, a charming little bistro adjoining a romantic little hotel are real assets to be able to afford. I don't care for money actually, but here it quiets my nerves. One way to economize on privacy is to ask friends for house-sitting and vacant summer places. As Truman Capote said, "It pays to hang out with rich people." Note he did not say "rich lovers," although we are not against these either. Just be careful of the small minds which often accompany large fortunes. Also, some cities have amazing "Entertainment" coupon books which offer great lodgings at half price for as many times as you want to use them. I sometimes stay in a $60-per-room elegant cobblestone hotel in Santa

Rosa's old town for the book's $30 price, split two ways for only $15 each. We can't always afford to eat dinner out, but the hotel's all-you-can-eat guest brunch is $3.50 each.

For hotels which rent by the hour, check the local sex paper or swingers' mag in many large cities for advertising hotels. Or, phone a hotel/motel and ask about rates for "a business client who is occasionally in town for the day and needs a place to shower and change." Some quite upscale hosteleries who don't want a "hot sheet" rep offer short term rentals. So do some Lesbian b&bs. Don't forget hot tub establishments have cedar "suites" for water nymphs, complete with fluffy towels and mood music.

I suppose it is true that you may, as a poly, buy multiple birthday, Valentine and holiday gifts, but then you receive more, too, especially if you make your presents getaway treats. Or, in lieu of any money spent, offer to be your lady's "love slave" for the day. There are always free-for-the-taking riches, like nature's bounty and museum cultural treasures. You can make it your quest to find the most romantic park bench in town. In San Francisco, we are fortunate to have a five-way tie between the Rhododendron Dell (secret nooks), Marina Green (sea-swept), Strybing Arboretum (florid), Seacliff Park (moonprint in ocean), and Alta Plaza (mansions in sky). Most agree that the dark, circular room of the Steinhart Acquarium is the deepest, most primordial, florescent make-out zone of all.

Another adventure is to smooch while riding the elegant elevators of lovely hotels. Glass ones have amazing views. In San Francisco, some elevators come in paneling lit by chandeliers. Be sure to nod and smile at all the hotel guests and workers. Watch tourists' eyes pop when you intimate that any fem types are drag queens.

Always be alert to saving on necessities, so as to afford the luxuries. This practice ratifies Jenny Jerome Churchill's observation that, "We owe something to extravagance, for thrift and adventure seldom go hand in hand." A friend of mine, whose ruling planet is expansive Jupiter, sums it up, "In poly, you may get twice the hassles, but the pleasures are compounded."

As it helps in revaluing time, polyfidelity also opens the way to an altered state of financial consciousness. Poly provides large "windows of wealth," which are far different creatures than dollars. This is because poly not only accepts, but exemplifies the fact that human beings, at our core, are striving to create the opportunity *to exchange something*, be it goods or services or love. Zen master Suzuki Roshi said, "When you exchange things, it means to purify things." Money makes exchange easier, but he noted, "only when we pay with respect can we purify our lives. Money purifies our world. It is not something dirty. It is very pure. If money is going slowly all over our society, then our society is wealthy." Surely a civilized country depends on the good circulation of its money just as an animal depends on the circulation of its blood. Such health in wealth is called socialism. So, true wealth is really the ability to exchange, to invest, and to get the credit you deserve. We think of economics as statistics, but economics is really myriad interactions. As Gertrude Stein pointed out, "Money is a flower." Let us put the *eco* back in economy.

Now look at your greatest resource, your precious human body, as the Buddhists celebrate it: "so free and well-favored, so difficult to obtain, so easy to lose..." Like money, we can park the body, save it, invest it, risk it, protect it, enjoy it. If you park the body, say in front of tv, or save it for Ms. Perfect and The Ultimate Relationship, your life is but a rehearsal, when it could be a magnificent adventure. If you invite your body into relationship, allowing for a bit of protection and some heart risk, you can also enjoy it. As Emily Dickinson said, "My friends are my estate." The three greatest investments in life are your health, your special talent, and your family of intimates. Each meets the five standards of true wealth: all are sustainable, useful, beautiful, renewable, and pleasurable.

So, join polyfidelity's "underground economy." When you don't have money, you can invent your own. You may have thought the underground economy was only drugs and graft. The underground economy's other realm thrives with small service and retail businesses which exchange resources, information, contacts, power, influence, skills, and security. It also rejoices with happy lover networks sharing pleasure and personal riches like caring, wisdom and beauty. Our basic metafiscal truth: the more friends and lovers you have, the less money you need.

I offer one caveat in this glorious ticket to abundance via polyfidelity. As far as cold cash and hot women, it is better to give than to loan and it costs about the same.

Kiss a lover's navel every day and may all good fortune be yours!

The Kids & Polyfidelity

Query: I can't even explain monogamy to my children, how in the world do I talk about polyfidelity?
— *Mamma Reese, Baltimore, Maryland*

In relationships (poly or mono), let's face it—the children most often involved are the principals. This is why, although I am not a biological parent, I have ideas on how to deal with real kids, but most of this chapter focuses on interviews with poly moms, my beloved "momazons." It seems that if children are under three feet tall, you do not need to go into great logical, moral and philosophical explanations of polyfidelity. Don't bother to equip yourself with brilliant defenses, apologia and stunning ripostes, capped with hypotheses and verifications. Just make your children feel their own world is safe, predictable and happy. You know, of course, that amorous secrets from children are only an illusion. So, stand up for what you believe in: love in its myriad forms and branchings, including the current family tree.

Choose your words carefully. Since polyfidelity involves sensuality and sex, a lot seems to depend on the age of the children. You can talk openly with most teenagers, in less detail with tots. Avoid any discussion where the child thinks they must take sides or choose between any of your partners or lovers. This is, after all, not a divorce, but an opening of the circle to more "relatives." Emphasize that in the family's new form, loyalty oaths to one versus another are never part of the process. It is a great teaching that loyalty can be shared, one most adults don't even learn.

What kids of all ages really want to know is how any new people are actually going to affect their lives. If they perceive women are "taking you away," they are going to react with some anger or hostility. Here, zero in on the reassurance, forget logic, pour on munificent reassurance that you are certainly going to honor your special times with them and with all your family. You want the child to understand that although a new person may bring changes into your lives, there is no loss of family. You are not abandoning them or any parent they know and love. Be prepared to go over and over the details of how you think polyfidelity will affect their day-to-day life. You have to be creative to point out what's in it for them when an evening they spent snuggling with Mom is now shared or spent alone. State your intentions and commitments for the present and future, don't rehash the past. Children always deserve to know as well in advance as possible whom they will be with on weekends, who will take them places, in short, who will be their responsible(s). They are not boxcars to be shuttled about between stations.

There is no magic remedy for dislocations and hurt feelings as the family expands and contracts. Most interviewees, however, said the most important thing is to get all the feelings out in the open, then to work at being respectful of one another as bad moods come up. For older children, acknowledge that everyone has a right to their goals. The next step is to clear up which goals are really in conflict and to establish that if one person always gets everything they want, other people may get hurt, be angry and withdraw. The final step is to work out a system where everyone gets what is absolutely essential, even though it can mean everyone has to give something up. Reconciling conflicting interests rarely sets things right once and for all, so the relational beat goes on, just like it will for everybody throughout life.

I began to see each blended family I spoke with as a small, self-contained unit of government, complete with rights, obligations and trade-offs for what is "yours" and "mine" and "ours." Especially in the shifting world of adult alliances, women spoke of structure as being really necessary for the household. I heard brilliant social contracts developed to flourish a while, then give way to refinements. Families held the possibilities of classic tragedy or sophisticated situation comedies. I saw dogged, boring, hang-in-there, go slow patience opening into profound affection and life-bonding. I asked polyfidelitous women and their families to share stories and advice. I'll begin with two longer interviews and close with a roundup of assorted ideas.

Anne: "There are no monogamous mothers."

I have always loved kids and can't have any of my own since a botched illegal abortion in the sixties when I was a kid myself. I am lovers with two different mothers who each have different households of two children each. Both mothers told me they can accept my having other lovers since a woman with children has to divide up her love time, too. I must be able to share the loving cup with a woman who loves her children as much as she does me and who usually puts the children first. As one of my lovers said, "There are no monogamous mothers." Both of them say that they had a hard time finding lovers because many people simply can't accept the competition for time, affection and space that the children create. Children on the scene are great training for poly and *vice versa.*

No, we don't blend the two families. This way I'm like a roving ambassador of love, not a tightrope walker in an emotional circus.

We've had different systems, but now I usually alternate one weeknight with one lover, that weekend with the other. The families get used to me "Wednesdays or weekends"; we just put it on our calendars.

One of my favorite things is when one set of kids comes to my home for the weekend. Each of the four kids has their own special drawer in a big bureau as well as a shelf. I like seeing a whole cup of toothbrushes, while having the bathroom to myself most of the week. Even when their mother hasn't been able to come over— sometimes one has had to travel; sometimes we've been grumpy with one another and need a break—the kids come over if they want. When we're alone, the kids often use the "But mom lets me —" ploy. I replay a version of "I know. We disagree about that. My living space thrives on a different ecology. I really want you here, especially to enjoy the hot tub or whatever, but the rules here are just different, that's all."

I've had to be on the alert to figure out my own way because the authority, the executive system of each family I'm involved with is different. Each one has its own personality, like each lover does. It's fascinating. I suppose family styles usually run from authoritarian to democratic to permissive. One lover's family is more on the authoritarian model, mainly a wise, benevolent dictatorship. The other is democratic in that the children's wishes are totally process-ed and considered, then in tight calls the mother's word is final. I've also been involved in extremely permissive families where there is so much wheedling and wildcatting, I never get much consideration as a lover. Civil behavior is reasonable to expect, while acknowledging a child's feelings. Without it, I'm gone.

I think the best role for me to assume with the kids is that of "caring friend," which is no small feat. I am clear with the mothers that I am not automatically to be used as a babysitter, entertainer, cook or cus-todian, although as a friend I may accept these functions when agreeable. To try to become a caring friend of children, I've learned to move very slowly, with no assumptions of instant intimacy just because I'm crazy about the mother. Anyone who tries to move fast into some sort of co-parenting, nurturing or disciplinary role invites disaster. These functions need to be clearly set by the mother as the relationship commitment grows. I wouldn't hand my kids over to the standards of just any lover who comes through the door.

Even though things have been fully explored and settled with the mother, the kids can be hostile, passively resistant, or at best, indif-ferent. Never go in with the fantasy, "If I work hard enough at it, the kids will love me." After three years, one boy hardly ever wel-comes me. I just have to accept his painful feelings with open curios-ity. For a while, I didn't accept his behavior, though. I simply left the room, but not the house. Recently I asked him, "What if you had to say one truthful, positive thing about me?" He paused a long time. Finally he said, "You never make promises you don't deliver." Then it was clam up. This observation relaxed and pleased me more than any easy good time because it was something I had always wanted desperately as a child. He'd made it mine to give.

Emily and Dorothy *et al.*

Emily: We moved into this huge old farmhouse together because we were both single moms, and I had always had a crush on sup-posedly straight Dorothy. She has two sons and I have three daughters. We became lovers before the first month was out. I believe this helped the family to make a smoother blend, even though everyone had a lot of adjusting to do, with the usual kinship rivalry. Our passionate love gave us a lot of staying power during the early years when it was hard to make ends meet and one of the children also had a bad accident.

Dorothy: A couple of years ago we each took outside lovers. It fortunately happened around the same time, when most of the kids were in high school and more independent. Our friends were absolutely shocked. They think of us as two stable Earth moms, not party girls on the loose. And the kids wanted to hear over and over, "Emily and you all have a special, ongoing place in my heart, a place that will always be here, and nothing will change it."

Emily: (Laughing) Hot spots? You mean besides our erogenous zones? Well, one of my daughters and Dorothy's son created a romantic bond with one another, after years of competition and terrible bickering! This has usually been a rather taboo-breaking household, but I freaked out. We went to a family therapist who theorized that the kids were acting out our romance-is-in-the-air tension at home, plus it's a terrific bid for attention and affection. And, after all, adolescence is adolescence.

Dorothy: Not to mention the fact that we'd been pushing them to love each other for years! I figured, so why go into shock? It's not incest with step-siblings. All we can do is explain the facts of life and condom sense to them, with lots of room for repetition and feedback. I was mainly surprised because I figured they were heartily bored with each other, but I guess some mystery, real affection and alliance asserted itself. I certainly made it clear that I'm off duty for any grandchildren in this family until I'm at least seventy or so.

Emily: We sort of desexualized the common space areas and reestablished a mild dress code. While remaining physically affectionate, we made it abundantly clear that we were to be informed if anyone ever touched or fondled anyone in a manner they found offensive. I would hate it if my daughters didn't feel total physical protection and privacy in their own home. I started singing the old women's liberation song, "My Body's Nobody's Body but Mine."

Dorothy: We also tried to clarify that fantasies were okay, but nothing to necessarily act upon at all. This caused the kids to question us about polyfidelity. Meanwhile our idea of encouraging their romance and friendship networks outside the home sort of reflected our own "outreach."

What do our lovers think? Well, I lost mine after about a year. She said she couldn't deal with the "Home Team" and "Visitors" feeling. Working out the complexities of holidays is a challenge, and I always wanted us to be with the kids and Emily. I even think the kids spotted a weak relationship and sometimes tried to undermine or at least test it. Yet, Emily's lover actually likes the kids and farm so much she has done family-care for the "Lavender Hill Mob" while Emily and I take off for a long weekend!

Emily: My lover calls being here "living in step." She's a botanist and will take each child and a friend all over the county. Lovers usually take lots more ongoing interest in your children than most friends do. She has, in turn, introduced them to her political circles, so the kids are seeing new sets of values, power strategies, even aesthetics.

Dorothy: I gave up the fantasy of "one perfect relationship" and just "one big happy family." Now I'm enjoying the thought of an extended community as less intense, more variable, just as enfolding.

Observations from Other Families

It seems, whatever you do there is bound, to be some tension being in a family that breaks cultural barriers. There are no easy answers in trying to meet your children's needs along with your own. Select lovers who can be open to this difficulty and work with you. When you find one, hold on; they're scarce. They have to really like children and understand you will often put your children's needs above personal relationships, like men have always done with careers. Neither lovers nor children are wise and wonderful all of the time, and you can't expect yourself to be either. If you're lucky, your children may understand that as a mother can love more than one child, she can love more than one woman. Polyfidelitous women may be the ones more likely to understand the dynamics of my shared heart.

Being lovers with women outside my home makes me more cheerful in it.

☙

Don't use children inappropriately as romance confidants. They are not your adult best friend or counselor, and may simply not know what to do with loaded information. Watch the gossip too. The kids may boomerang it from one love to another. Ditto expounding on the errors of others.

☙

Many children are very judgmental—just like their moms, I guess. Expect critical opinions, even dead-ringer impersonations of you and your lovers. My children went from being puritanically indignant toward polyfidelity to the most relentless teasing. Now we just kid around a lot; they see I try to be a good sport, to smile at their foibles, too. Always have kids that know how to laugh, eat and sleep—Saint Teresa said this about attracting novices. I think laughter is often the shortest distance between kids and adults.

☙

Never approach polyfidelity to children as though it holds even a hint of moral impropriety. Poly offends prejudice, not ethics. No one, after all, is cheating anyone. My kids tend to be possessive, and wonder when someone is sharing, if everyone knows what is going on and how much. I swear, kids learn somewhere we are supposed to be jealous. The impression to communicate, I think, is that, "We can all handle the situation and want to help each other." Keep a hopeful attitude. The kids may reflect yours. Then again, the kids may hate particular lovers. It's agonizing if you put your needs first. It's agonizing if you don't.

❀

I don't assume any lover's kids will like me, just as I hit it off with some people and not with others. But as far as people go, I usually like kids the best. My heart really aches that a quarter of the kids in this richest country in the world live below even what the census calls poverty. Polyfidelity often leads to sharing resources. I buy toys and clothes that cycle and recycle. When kids ask, or sort of test me, as to what my role is, I say, "I'm one of your mom's buddies." "Oh yeah," this little guy once says, "you mean fuck-buddy." So, I coined the word "step buddy," like a "step-love," you know, not a live-in. The Steps, the kids call us real pleasantly.

❀

"It's not fair! Everyone else's single mom cares for her first!" Children learn (guess where?) that if you feel guilty, you'll give in. On the other issues I sometimes do, but with polyfidelity or Lesbianism, I just stay with my own standards, and the kids sometimes learn to accept them or at least keep breathing. I can't tell you how I've learned to feign calm, cheerful, unruffled indifference to critical remarks. It usually gets us through.

❀

Kids say, "Mamma's other girlfriend does this and brings me that." Don't get hurt or let yourself be manipulated. Hold your own style, as long as you're polite. Life is a co-op of real different beings, and kids learn this. I don't want kids to have to watch themselves with me, but I sure protect myself from them sometimes.

❀

My kids like that I have simultaneous partners to teach them everything from chess to skiing, especially since I hate both. Now one of these lovers finally has one kid or another to constantly go with her to the Winchester Mystery House—she's doing a book on Sarah Winchester—and everyone is happy.

❀

Clear boundaries for different lovers' areas of authority need to be set in frank, open discussions—include the kids somehow in the process. Like I can help the kids with computer stuff, but Joanne and Cindy set their curfew. I once totally hated being an authority figure with the kids when no parent was around—since my father shouted at everyone's child within a block's hearing distance—so I never used to say "no," rationalizing that the children were not mine. But that's a technicality, all kids are ours, including us, and now I'm learning how to act as a part-time parent and show the kids my standards of behavior. Be sure to discuss who's the final arbiter of what, though—and keep a united front. A united front doesn't mean all adults must agree on everything, but they need to know about and support one another's decisions.

꩜

I used to worry about what my kids would say about polyfidelity in public, like our being bisexual with the poly variations. Then I realized that polyfidelity rarely comes up with teachers or casual acquaintances or strangers, by name, anyway, it's still too radical a form. Usually, just being bisexual takes all the heat. So I let sleeping dogs, and multi-gender lovers, lie, especially when it comes to people I'm not even going to know in a year. The kids are pretty savvy about this, but they talk about poly with best friends and can get hurt by any negative opinions. Then again, sometimes their friends tell them they wish they had more, different parents around and to visit. I guess polyfidelity is like any other cultural intolerance in a bigoted world, you have to help your kids with it, be proud—and pray.

꩜

I mostly like my mom's having a bunch of lover friends. Some of them I even like to live with awhile, some I just play off—one against the other. I do feel it's trouble to censor my conversation sometimes, "editing" my mother calls it, to keep the peace. Her friends I like to be with most are not dramatic, they seem to care what's up with me too. Is she a well-behaved grownup or what, that is my question.

꩜

A Shrink to Fit: The Polyfidèle Meets the Psychotherapist

Query: I have loved my partner for years, yet new loves spring up like wildflowers. I know I'll never pave over my desire and decided to stop trying. So we went to a highly recommended couple-counselor. She said upon our arrival that she would work with us only if I gave up my other lover for at least the first four weeks of intensive therapy. She said the other woman can wait, that we are the ones putting time and money into therapy. "If you're still carrying on," she told me, "we'll waste our focus on putting out current brush fires. Clear the decks to give your relationship a chance for me to help you." I was flabbergasted. My partner thought this was no-nonsense "tough love." What do you think?

— *Norma Lee, Omaha, Nebraska*

Sounds like a tough bird to me. I would have sent this therapist a frozen turkey to cuddle up with instead of a fee for service. Cold turkey may work for substance abuse, but her value judgment is screaming here: non-tolerance for nonmonogamy which she considers a form of abuse, plus the dictum that "I'll bring you along my way to my way." A skilled therapist, like any good teacher or healer, helps you learn how to find your *own* best answers. How dare a stranger present you with her totally subjective code of behavior? Just because a professional is highly recommended, it does not mean that she is equally good with all types of people with all types of problems. You would not go to a tax lawyer for copyright law or to a home realtor to sell a racetrack. I doubt this counselor has ever trod the path of honest polyfidelity. Worse, she suffers from the lack of adventure and the failure of imagination to accompany you. She has issues here, herself, and her own agenda.

Aside from this therapist's assumption that she can and should heavily direct you into placidity, out of mania, her stratagem lacks good judgment. Cold turkey intervention, while a common professional protocol, usually backfires between two women lovers. It was designed for the adulterous male whose outside physical relationships are often of marginal emotional value to him and can easily be dropped to clear the decks for a temporarily less complex scenario. Lesbians who try separation usually end up with an even more powerful bond between polyfidèle and odd woman. Out of sight does not necessarily mean out of mind. Often, absence does make the heart grow fonder. Any odd woman who ostensibly goes along appears noble, even large-spirited. Isn't this the proof she does not want to upset the couple? The spouse, meanwhile, is likely to come across as faultfinding, needy, angry, and prohibitive. After a month or so of "doing time," the separated couple is usually even hotter for one another. Absence in love is as wind is to fire. It extinguishes the small, enkindles the great.

A fact is that many therapists are not pioneering spirits in personal, social and spiritual consciousness. Look at their own personal life wreckages. How often is the doctor not also a patient? Therapists are usually trained in a rigorous establishment modality to help us adapt to the herd or hive, to cop to whatever the current "collective hunch" about reality may be. Presently the Myth of the Romantic Marriage reigns. Somehow an ideal companion should also be a sex siren, so we aspire to become a security/excitement model all in one. Psychotherapy's second operative myth is that lover adaptability is better than autonomy. Thus, psychotherapists act as agents of social control, in this case for monogamy. R.D. Laing, Thomas Szasz and Ivan Illich noted therapy's entrenchment function years ago. There is a tide of agreement in the nineties, often by therapists themselves.[36]

Psychotherapy typically presents a personal explanation for a problem rather than a political power analysis of the situation. Institutional, structural, and economic oppressions are thus individualized and privatized. The language of politics is translated into the language of psychological health and sickness. Look at therapists' shiny word "empower." Actual power means the strength to prevent violence, to stand up and be reckoned with, to define our own experiences in our own terms. It is authentic power in comparison to empowerment by affirmation. Power is the power to *do*, actual movement for social change in contrast to "the revolution within."

Notice it was not probing family therapists who discovered epidemic wife-beating and child abuse by men. They, in fact, covered up abuse ("fantasy") until it became a profitable wave, unleashed by the massive political uprising of its survivors. Ditto, therapy's timidity in relation to almost every other transforming awareness of our century: feminism, age, race, class, homosexuality, etc. Some argue that therapy effectively depoliticizes and sells heavily medicated, bland politics back to us for fancy prices (abuse, addiction, etc.). Common therapy often labels existential suffering as "abuse." Why let someone pick your pocket, then charge you for your wallet?

Instead of feminism's "the personal is political," shrink-think tends to make the personal psychological or neurological, and usually historical. Most memory, however, is a form of fiction. We "versionize." Fantasy is part of reality. The radical feminist question is therefore, "What/who is actually abusing me right now?" Neo-Freudian psychoanalysis is probably the most ludicrous, pessimistic sink of all therapy forms. To fully accept the idea of unconscious motivational control is to cease to be human.

Even more dangerous than therapists dispensing conformist placebos, which hopefully do no permanent biological harm, are the psychiatrists dispensing heavy, toxic drugs as cure-alls. These people could pasture all us polyfidèles out to prozac, to effectively muffle our sexual desire along with the anguish and joy inherent in all life. If the brain is like a primordial, wild forest, then psychiatry may be like commercial forestry, clear-cutting brains to shore up insane superstructures.

Before you ever walk in a counselor's door, ask her if she patholo-gizes or morally judges polyfidelity. That's "committed non-monogamy without cheating," to her, if she's been sitting out the nineties. An entire professional psychologic literature is based on the value judgement that the extra-dyadic liaison is "bad." This, of course, reflects the uncertainty and anxiety of the professionals themselves, many of whom are cheaters or would like to be. They are entrapped in an outworn ethical system and the moral shibbo-leths of convention. Regarding monogamy, therapy statements and practices are wide open to challenges of validity and accuracy.

Ask a prospective therapist if she believes passion is an emotion or a way of life. Ask her if she has experience to help you create this innovative, committed lifestyle, to forge bridges and boundaries, to open communication, to mediate fair fighting. Here, it is entirely appropriate to ask if she herself has affairs and multiple partners. Ask her questions from the survey at the end of this book. Would you hire a mechanic who has never driven on the highway? If it is a factor, ask her how she treats any conflict around desire discrep-ancy. Is her best shot to ply the flagging libido with sexy gimmicks rather than to support a variety of partners? Does she pathologize loving celibacy between partners? Be clear yourself whether refin-ing a philosophy of polyfidelity and its skilled behaviors is your main priority. Or do you wish to move into some vast exhumation of parent, sibling and lover histories? We seem to forget we were built to forget.

I would not go so far as some within the profession and assert that most therapists are untreated co-dependents and wounded healers. It does seem, however, that many therapists are people with high, yet tightly bridled, affiliative needs. They seek out the expression of another's intimate secrets, partake in reliving the other's life. There is usually emotional as well as financial "feeding." Yet the therapist must refuse the role of peer, always retaining the safety and control of being one up, the "sane" one. She can propose new scenarios, yet never be present to feel the fallout. In any event, a client can be terminated at any time. Or, if change is never forthcoming, as a client's boring rehash rolls on and on, the therapist can nod to the rhythm of a dollar-a-minute-plus with no pain at all. It is easy to fall into a rapport with a skillful emotions expert who encourages you to open up, even makes you feel exciting and important for doing so. This is somebody with status you can count on for full attention, with none of the burdens of reciprocity, as long as the insurance pays or the money holds. Your own prosthetic friend.

I've met several women who feel their lover's therapist is comparable to any mistress in a polyfidelitous system. As noted previously, a vast amount of quality time, focused and attentive, is regularly spent together in confidence. A woman prepares for "her hour" with attention to personal detail and appearance. Money is spent lavishly. Secret little compacts are arranged. There are swooning peaks and valleys during the visit. Some women delight in the distinctive, non-interchangeable roles, or charge the atmosphere with a little pretend role-playing. The client's "masks" are as carefully removed as outer garments. Intimacies are wrestled with. The client may feel as courageous and as vulnerable as a lover who risks exposing her authentic self, her fears and imperfections, her deepest hopes, creativity and dreams. In reality, there is no exchange of body or spirit; in fact, little mutuality at all. Nor is there ever true equality of power in a relationship when you are required to tell any person more about yourself than they will ever reveal about themselves. But as the risk of vulnerability is all one-sided, even this risk can be canceled as easily as an appointment. Click! Therapy is a form of "virtual polyfidelity," with money as the remote.

Some take lovers, some take therapists, who can say which is best? Some take both as when a paid therapist becomes a client's physical lover, too. But this is a book on polyfidelity, not poly-perfidy. Otherwise, I would advise you, if physically compromised, to collect evidence and charge such a therapist blackmail rates yourself. Be also warned that you usually have to play monogamist to your dashing therapist. She will emphatically discourage you from popping around to her Jungian sandbox on Mondays, then to the hyp-

nosis madam on Wednesdays, and on to the exotic Morita therapist on Fridays. Most treatments, alas, like most theologies, are
monogamously closed systems.

Old pluralist that I am, I still say "go gestalt" if it helps. Do consider a therapist's character, however, over her method or orientation. Find someone who is not so biased and directive (or blasé)
that you have no support for living up to your iconoclasms. Never
choose a professional anybody who is not a friend of your passions
and vision. I do know there are therapists who can help remove the
isolation, secrecy and stigma surrounding polyfidelity, since many
couples feel they must hide poly behavior from prejudiced friends
and colleagues. Many well-meaning, but fear-driven, best friends
will swear nothing works but the monogamy quarantine. You may
need outside creativity. A good counselor can also help you keep
negotiations open, so you don't abort a perfectly good relationship
in poly panic or discouragement. It is wise, before you go to counseling, to be as clear with yourself as possible on which style of
polyfidelity you want to live: a singles or couples orientation? Be
especially honest about whether your "polyfidelity" is, in fact, a
handy transition out of a current relationship into another round of
serial polygyny.

Besides therapists, consider spiritual workers of the more progressive religions as possible counsel. An amazing number are poly
themselves or understand its dynamics very well. Such utopians
are producing the anthology, *The New Polygamy: The Polyamorous
Lifestyle as a New Spiritual Path*. The general personality type found
to prefer polyfidelity often parallels that of many spiritual workers:
heartful, mindful seeker. Most spiritual workers answered my survey positively. You may be uncomfortable with psychotherapy's
reliance on a dualistic, individualistic view of the world, in which
we look at our personal history in relation to others and external
factors. This personal past has no reality other than what our
thinking tells us about it, so how do we ever escape the dysfunctional loop? Psychotherapy tells us the self needs to be *fixed*, the
customer is always wrong. In contrast, a spiritual awareness sug-

gests that the self deserves to be *known*. We can use questioning, solitude, service, and the lifelong development of compassion and joy, as the self experiences its great interdependent connection with all living beings. It is the known self/soul which can interiorize community, a psychic field absorbing duality while watching it rise and dissolve. Such "intimacy" often leads to a life of service, of helping to change the world. This contrasts with the bleak, endless process of perfecting ones ego via "self-help" therapies.

Again, check out your initial rapport and purpose with a spiritual counselor so as not to waste your time. At least their monetary fee is kinder than the secular set, but the price of admission may be your ordinary mind. Alas, some spiritual teachers will still emphasize the pain and suffering of any uninvolved spouse and the immaturity of the polyfidèle. Meanwhile, we know how populous the hypocritical community of religious philanderers is, from Paul Tillich and Krishnamurdi to the legion of smarmy tv evangelists.

So, good wishes in the therapy bazaar, Sweet Seeker. Never allow the soft police or the white shirts to label you a security risk. We are all dancing with the dark on both sides of the rainbow couch. I, for one, have always loved a second, even poly, opinion on it all.

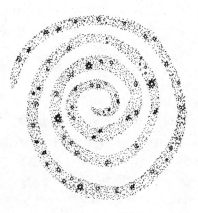

The Guilt and Shame Racket

*Q*uery: Just being in multiple relationships, I don't feel remorse since there isn't any deceit or betrayal. Yet, I often feel guilty when doing something that we even agreed upon, like my taking off to see another woman. If my live-in lover is around to see and hear me, I can feel guilty just singing in the shower, making ready for a trip. Also, I feel guilty admitting to anyone I'm involved with how much pleasure I have with someone else. I edit, edit, edit, and feel guilty for this, too. Then there's being ashamed when I do feel possessive or like angrily criticizing my partners' polyfidèle ways. Sometimes I think of myself as One Big Pope. Now, I feel guilty for feeling guilty! Where does this come from?

— *Cody Pendant, Hazelton, Minnesota*

*I*n today's climate of coarsened conscience—the "no-fault" toxic spill, the S&L slash and loot, the politico who smokes but doesn't inhale or gets an adulterous massage, but doesn't come—well, it is almost refreshing to receive your letter, *mea culpa*. I am back in Madam de Staël's world: "The voice of conscience is so delicate that it is easy to stifle it; but it is also so clear that it is impossible to mistake it."

Right Speech

First of all, I cannot imagine that you sing your other lover's praises in the shower at the top of your lungs. If so, switch to whistling. While it is important to respect a live-in lover's mood, especially if it is a solemn one, you are, I hope, not a chameleon, whose survival depends on reflecting it back. Moving on with your schedule in a soft, amiable and purposeful way seems due consideration for another's feelings. Likewise, any glitch in your outside pleasure pursuits should not be considered as your uninvolved partner's problem, either.

When it comes to actually discussing the rendezvous of one lover with another, right speech* rarely errs when it is composed mainly of silence. Alas, Americans seem to perform within a virtual confession booth. We engage a world of paid confessors ranging from the priesthood of therapist and church to the 900-number speakeasies. We have Twelve Step confessionals for every specialized pursuit of perdition. A vast spectrum of radio and tv airwaves, as well as the Internet, are dedicated to foaming rivers of self-exposure. People prattle confidences to strangers at parties and bus stops as though silence were not balm but toxin. There is so much talk going on, I wonder who is left to do right listening? Before you carry on, whirling juicy stories of your own to one and all, remember there is no such thing as "free speech." Whatever you say creates consequences, from micro to major. With one frivolity or one harsh world of malice, you can raise hell in the ten directions. With a loving word, you can open hearts and lodestars.

With so many people feeling the need to speak up, there are unfortunately no clear-cut, absolutist rules for declaring matters of the heart to those not directly involved. Why not just follow the suggestion embedded in right speech to carefully examine your actual motive whether telling all or "editing?" If the motive in telling is selfish, such as ego-gratification, jealousy provocation or attention, back off. If the motive for truthful, but well-pruned, speech is kindness or honest privacy, don't beat yourself up, take a little credit.

One lover may indeed pointedly ask you for information regarding your other relationship(s). Women do not often directly ask for information they are not ready to hear and deal with. This does not mean they are asking for a welter of detail, theory or

---

* Right Speech is so valued in the Buddhist canon that it is one of the key elements of the Eightfold Path of the Great Middle Way. The qualities of right speech also comprise a full four of the ten cardinal Buddhist Precepts. Right speech is not "right" in contrast to "wrong," but right in the sense of whole, healthy, or even just right in holding to the Middle Way. Right Speech is, above all, conscious, helping to prevent one from falling off the extreme edges of needless or of conterfeit words.

even conclusions. Questions may be in the realm of "Do you have a really good time with XX?" "Do you love XX very much?" This type of emotional big-game fishing is not usually asked to obtain myriad facts on file, which no one is obligated to reveal for reasons of privacy and confidentiality. Rather, your lover is likely running a completely essential security check. She needs a clear compass reading to understand her position, to align her energy. More especially, we all need reassurance. You might answer the above two questions with a truthful "Yes," if this be the case, while importantly keeping all the other realities current too. "Yes, I usually do have good times with XX, and I'm also really looking forward to this dinner and evening with you." Bouquets. Bouquets. Or, "Yes, I do love XX, and I love you so much I think I'm the luckiest woman on earth to be with you." Bouquets. Bouquets. The point of right speech is not glibly to discount a valid question, but to find out what the actual issues are and try to address these kindly. It is not only the words we say, but the way we say them. As Cate Gable put it:

> *Right Speech*
>
> *The tongue just right*
> *the lips just right*
> *the breath just right*
> *the heart just right*

O beata culpa, consider yourself to be a "just right" perfectly imperfect lover like the rest of us, the Velveteen Rabbit if not the Venus of Polyfidelity. To love yourself even when you are perhaps much less than you could be gives you the right to imperfect lovers—like us. This is a profound relief because all relationships are imperfect at best, ruinous at worst. You do not need to feel shame for every conflicting feeling that coexists around your lovers. Shame is not our core, love is.

Guilt

A fact of human relations, not just polyfidelity, is that when you choose to spend exclusive time with someone, another friend may—momentarily—feel left out and hurt. If you witness their hurt or anger, feelings of shame and guilt are not called for. Compassion is. Shame, on the other hand, is the perception that we are imperfect, unfinished, especially in the sight of others. Surely your standard of perfection does not include the omnipotent quality of "fixing" another person's moods and emotions? Training our own moods is the challenge of a lifetime and our only possible arena of action. Drop shame. Guilt, often shame's companion, is not accurate for what is happening here either. Guilt is the alarm system which goes off when we have transgressed a substantive internalized ethical standard. Guilt is an ethical guide, one of the Major Arcana. To speak of guilt in terms of indulging a piece of chocolate cake is a wretched trivialization, as is your contrition for singing if someone else chooses to mope. But, as Erica Jong said, "Show me a woman who doesn't feel guilt, and I'll show you a man."

Anthropologists have designated various cultures as predominantly "shame" or "guilt" cultures. Shame and guilt are among the most powerful forces societies use to induce self-control. Non-Judeo-Christian societies tend to use shame, fear of public scorn. Such peoples worry, say, about being caught cheating at trade. Otherwise, cheating is simply clever or "sharp" practice. In contrast, theocratic-leaning, especially monotheist omnipotent cultures, rely on guilt to enforce behavior. With every power of persuasion, especially fear, they inculcate a tiny, yet invincible, rule keeper inside our skull. This internalized police officer is called "conscience." If we don't follow certain arbitrary rules of conduct and belief, the little ruler torments and flogs us.

Guilt may be worthwhile, albeit painful, if it lasts longer than five minutes and creates actual change. It can be an exit point from folly. On the beach of consciousness, guilt is interesting to comb through because it fleshes out personal ideals and opens up the intricate moral dimensions of restraint and liberty. Guilt can be so powerful that it freezes one, or it can open us to deeper response and knowledge of the heart. Guilt's immobilization or action usually reflects the extent of one's self-absorption. When the Ancient Mariner's heart could selflessly open to blessing and love for all creatures, then "The Albatross slid off, and sank/ Like lead into the sea." Guilt becomes actual good when it follows the cycle of remorse, renunciation, resolution and reconciliation.

As far as polyfidelity goes, the foremost dimension of guilt has been plumbed as soon as one decides she will no longer lie about love in order to appear to fit in with the myth of monogamy. This commitment to truth and honor is such a marvelously challenging and rewarding vow, it alone could take up a whole book, but see the truth telling chapters herein, plus the plots of all the great adultery masterpieces. One warning: Stay away from guilty women in polyfidelity even if you are not the deceitful one. When their guilt washes in, they can be at their absolute worst: uncomfortable, angry, fearful. Mistaking the source, the guilty party often lashes out at the ones they love most. Or, the guilt-ridden one passively distances herself from her partners. Usually, unreconciled guilt inexorably moves toward its other release: punishment. To gain the "satisfaction" of punishment, a guilty person may try to take you to the whipping post. The Sadeian type is famous for this.

Another warning: Avoid high dudgeon yourself, bearing the heavy robes of judge and prosecutor. Don't mine another's lapses, such as your lover being a poor sport, condemning not only her actions, but her person. Let her exercise her right to be miserable. It's fine to make your views clear. Why bludgeon? Use a prism, reflecting the complex light of myriad causes and conditions. Marianne Moore wrote:

> *What is our innocence*
> *what is our guilt?*
> *All are*
> *naked, none is safe.*

Human creatures do seem to hold both conditional and unconditional love. Courtship often begins with unconditional love, the non-judgmental, hopeful love which says, "You do not have to be worthy. Just be." Unconditional love usually swirls into its complement, the stark "conditional." Conditional love holds that love received should be love merited. It considers dimensions of responsibility and obligations created for any damages inflicted. Both forms of love are good working together, much as justice and mercy do. The Holy-One-Blessed-Be said, "If I create a world with only mercy in it, errors will multiply. If I create one with only justice, how can it stand? Therefore, I create a world with both mercy and justice. Let it thus go on." When arrows dipped in judgment start flying, shift back to the ground of unconditional love for a moment. Unconditional love is highly creative. It sees the good, opens the tiniest, most fragile flower. Stormy elements begin to pearl and soften in the light of appreciation.

At all costs, avoid shaming your lovers. Shame is the monster behind control. We shame others to avoid shame ourselves. We employ the blades of blame, judgement, expectation, discounting and ridicule. If you are not perfect, you will find yourself using the above quite regularly. To repair such ongoing shameful behavior, memorize and use these two awesome words, "Forgive me." To forgive is to cease to cherish displeasure in ourselves or others. It is to let go of *my* version of a story wherein I depict myself as victim. In saying "Forgive me," add a sprig of restitution to clarify your life-affirming libation, and take a sip for yourself.

"I dreamed there was a beehive here, inside my heart, and the golden bees were making white combs and sweet honey from all my past failures." — *Antonio Machado*

Shame

Whereas guilt feelings seem to be self-generated from one's own personal code or manufactured one, shame is often linked to the heavy judgments we perceive in other's eyes, the vigilant "They." Who *are* these people? What are *their* credentials? They may deem that we have the wrong body, wretched manners, stupid responses, inadequate resources, lives too long, goals unrealized, not enough (*you fill in*). Shame seems beyond one's control, yet insidiously one's fault. Why can't you be in many arms at once, polyfidèle, and please every woman all the time? Shame is a truncated sense of pride. We fall short of the most impersonal, irrelevant expectations and feel bad. I do not mean "badly," but ontologically "bad." This is not functional, but neurotic self-hatred, ultimately the cruelest of all behaviors and perhaps the leading cause of every meanness. It is Pascal's hateful self, "*Le moi est haïssable,*"* a far cry from simply recognizing that connections are still lacking, functions underdeveloped. Of all infirmities, most savage is to despise our being.

So it goes. We can never have enough time, wisdom, charm or money to achieve perfect acceptance by all lovers all the time. In fact, we occasionally, purposefully, do the very worst, not the very best we can. Sometimes feeling badly about this is enough. Constructive amendment is always an antidote, so is loving more. Let's say you do erase your shame tapes. You do honor your many selves. Never fear. There is no call for smugness. All perfection is ephemeral. Giant cartels of tabloid print and tv exist solely to chronicle how low citizen, as well as mighty, have "fallen." There are always vast new frontiers of shame for talk show commoner and superstar, especially the beautiful woman who puts on weight and the man who can't get off whatever counts. Oprah and Jane, Jenny and Jerry represent the growth industry of shame, one totally recession proof. As there is no way to abolish imperfection, there is probably no way to abolish shame as a recurring pain to be healed.

Polyfidelity very rarely receives affirmation in our society. We, in fact, are usually treated as shameful beings to even consider such a venture, not to mention live it openly. So if we even try polyfidelity, we are likely to vault into a perfectionist mode to stave off further criticism and shame. Consider, however, that there are thousands of articles, books and performance pieces on the care and feeding of the faulty monogamist, an orotund army of couple-

* "The self is detestable."

288

counselors, a matrix of supportive family and friends. Who of our newly born generation of Lesbian relationship pioneers can spring full-blown as the perfect Venus of Polyfidelity? Should she indeed arise, she probably would not have enough (*you fill in*) to fit the proper media frame to tell us about it.

Women run into a similar shooting range as feminists. We seem to be on a track of either Superwoman or failure. To hold the visionary feminist ideal for personal change which embraces transforming the world from needless suffering is, in itself, wondrously fine. It by no means follows, however, that we effortlessly attain magnificent, perfect behavior in word, thought and deed without daily practice, daily blunders to learn by.

Remember all shame is tied to the terror of being rejected and deserted. "If they know my secrets, they will surely leave me." In argument, or hit with "secret" angry tensions, stop and breathe. For one blessed moment, accept the essence of your shining original face, your core acceptability. In this momentous realization, grace conquers shame and reconciliation bridges gulfs of estrangement. Nothing is asked for but acceptance. Well, maybe laughter. If someone could teach us to laugh at our failures, perhaps we could easily learn everything else. Imperfections would not be lonely liabilities, but bright leaves of natural growth. As Shakespeare smiled, "Most become much more the better/For being a little bad."

The Open Robe of Compassion

Polyfidelity as a style also has great shame possibilities in that you have more intimates to relate with, thus more opportunities to expose your imperfections. For a vanity of bonfires, think of all the shames to rake: shames of omission and commission, venal shames and mortifying shames. To decrease the heat, try dropping the vanity of ego, the obsessive preoccupation with self-esteem and what "should" be. The *maladie du moi* fades considerably. The *maladie* of heavy self-assessment usually leaves one feeling soiled, fatigued. Petty shames layer one upon the other, collecting like old kitchen grease. When the ancient taped verdicts roll on and on from people and times long past, gently switch into the post self-hate mode. Here the voices of compassion replace mean-spirited jingles with a new theme: "I am adequate to my life. I am not here to become an acceptable woman, I am here to become the person I am." Any tapes not speaking compassion to you have nothing to tell you. Compassion is not always soothing, but it is not the squawk of the conditioned mind. It comes from one's own heart of shared connectedness.

As Virginia Woolf wrote, "We need to adopt an attitude of sympathy toward one another, given that life for all of us is arduous, difficult, and a perpetual struggle. Compassion should displace analysis and ideology." Thus, compassion does not analyze a lover's suffering, her attachments or "setting sun vision."* It does not reject or become bound by pain. Compassion's essence is non-complicity and non-harming. It does not lash out or use rootless words to try to prevent attack. Compassion speaks softly or not at all in words. "I have no sword. I make absence of ego my sword." Compassion understands that "faults" are the living cracks where a person can grow. My friend who keeps snakes told me that a snake's eyes go white, frozen and blind before molting. Be patient. Your eyebrows won't fall off before your lover lets go of her bad mood.

Compassion acknowledges one's own weakness and attachments, our own dark as well as shining side. They say the realized mind is quiet and deals with things as they are, such as someone being angry at us. The ghost mind is noisy and deals with its own creations. Acknowledge your lover's pain, don't make some of your own. Compassion is the affinity which does not dwell on "you" against "me." Forget the ego and good teaching is all around. Saving all beings is saving them in your own mind—along with the vow, "I will be satisfied with myself."

No false guilt.
No false shame.

---

* The Tibetan Shambhala tradition speaks of a "setting sun vision," which fixates on misery and denigrates human dignity. A setting sun vision feeds on bathos and snubs the calm heart for an embroiled mind.

polyfidelity: cyberspace

$\mathcal{Q}$uery: My new girlfriend is not only a babe, but one of the sweetest, most imaginative people I know. She told me when we met, however, that she usually has around six girlfriends, who are hundreds, even thousands of miles away "on the Net." I thought, so what—besides her phone lines being damn busy and occasional sleepy yawns on dates. As long as she's so digital and full-bodied with me in bed, who cares about these ghosts on the cold glow? Now she mentions her cyberpal "Trona" is really a great one for "tinysex," adding that the netters she tries it with usually turn out to be guys in drag.

So, I wonder, can that cathode ray cook up electronic sex like a microwave does food molecules? Is this virtual reality romance stuff automatically polyfidelitous and pansexual, or what? Is it real? Is it fake? I work in an animal shelter and love actual things like gardening and dancing. My girlfriend laughs and says I don't need "teledildonics," which I guess is a compliment, but what is "tinysex"? I can only imagine the faeries and the little folk under the stars. Is it worth it to come in from a starry night to memorize those long codes you have to pay to play?
— *Anna Logan, Lemon Cove, California*

$\mathcal{W}$ow, a cybervirgin. Way cool. "Tinysex" is cyberpatois for what I would call teenie weenie sex. Chatterbugs with a huge testosterone habit and/or easy cerebral sex arousal can actually obtain one-handed typing climaxes exchanging text sex. Thus computers extend the joys of a fling-thing. *Soooo* aphrodigital; cold boxes calculating, hot bodies coming.

Simulated sex via virtual reality's 3-D goggle helmet, data glove, sensor suit and aroma'round surely makes a wild read, a neat film, maybe even good bondage. VR however, is not a good fuck because no one in this millennium can figure out how to "do it" neuromimetically. Oh well, no one figured out how to do plain old "reality" either. My best VR tip, Sweet Cybervirgin, is to close your eyes and fantasize while dancing in the garden. You'll probably conclude that anyone who thinks disembodiment is the ultimate sexual experience must be a Holy Ghost Christian. (I had a friend who called fake orgasms "holy ghosts.") You can bet the old mind/body split Saints Paul and Augustine would sanctify VR telediddling. Virtual reality sex sounds like your typical control freak's virtual alienation. Who but someone with a death wish would want to be replaced with technology? Do let us acknowledge that VR sex may be desirable computer to computer or robot to robot, or for human beings who do not like brunch.

I myself finally did manage tinysex with a live, "interactive" Lesbian. It took so much skill, talent and time, however, I may as well have scripted an acclaimed Hollywood screenplay. The sheer attention required for the Net's mind-boggling command arcana and social protocols is certainly erotic in its intensity. Please beware of the retina burn and carpal tunnels accompanying the utter trendiness of arriving in awe at a Web 256-color panty hose ad. Color cyberspace anything, but color it "business" first.

The libidinous can also cruise the online red light district for prepackaged, high cost, hypertext. Here we have pornupixels of graphic files, photos, CD-ROMs and sound. In this swinging world, I ended up (down?) with a mild case of hardware envy, but nano-lust. (I did see great earrings. Earrings are so big and sassy on "adult" CD-ROMs, they practically need condoms.) Downloading graphics necessitates a power system which I borrowed in the interests of computer literacy, having absolutely no idea how to answer your question regarding Net nookie. I am a confirmed Leadite (that's a #2 pencil, please), living in an idyllic telecommunications backwater. We still mix our whiskey with *l'eau thèque* and have already forgotten the whole next century. The call of the modem, however, suggested pirate outposts of Lesbian polyfidelity sparkling on the Net. Here, perhaps, was the thrill of a liaison with no imperfections, burdens or responsibilities? Virtual satisfactions should mean a cheap date.

I was able, as a temp "power user," to join some of the sex bulletin board services (BBSs) for free as a bona fide, documented female of the species. Adult BBSs slaver for live women like bars in Alaska. Similarly, as they say, the odds are good, but the goods are odd. "Adult" BBSs, are, as turn-ons, the same old same old. Worse, many computer generated graphics tend to be fuzzy or, for decent resolution, well, tiny. Why someone would pay $55 every few months for the privilege of daily downloading 1.2 slow, smeary megabytes attests to the novelty of the computer as a medium, to the guys' fetish for gadgetry. Hell, maybe technoweenies are shy of adult bookstores, those other theaters where the teen male libido exists in permanent time warp. Digital stay-at-homes may also be afraid of real live bordellos. Sex workers comb the adult BBSs. Sex workers are the few interesting beings I communicated with on the adult BBSs—for a short while, however. Their meter is running for a hot chat or photo op. Otherwise I got quasi-sentient overdrive thrusters, or houseboys who lusted to do my digital laundry and lick my virtual boots. The most intelligent men came online mainly to practice English. It is easy to spot guys, who regularly introduce themselves to Lesbians as "bisexual female" or "Lesbian." You know boys by their obsession with body part size and such cheap porn flick dialog, I practically expected the omnipresent saxophone to take over.

Actual women get tough online, but virtual babes swoon while handing out measurements. At least harassment retaliation is safe on the Net. Blast 'em with flammage or splatterpunk, and yank the jack <click>. In kill-file territory, physical prowess means nothing. It is also fun to flirt and cross erotic boundaries with no fallout. Just stretching the simplistic sexual/platonic definition is interesting. I could be my wildest fantasy or dish out utter honesty. Someone told me net.sex is about self-definitions. I guess it can be one form of practice.

But let us focus on the most exotic creature online, the Lesbian console cowgirl. I was actually excited to be digitally inexperienced again; a baby dyke in the Lesbian baud parade. Did I get the girl?

Well, no . . . because the lady I found is a Tiger, topaz and lavender-eyed. I'm talking bandwidth! Even one fawn streak of her electrons stipples the entire screen. Topaz' persona—every cruising expert online has a "role" with a "handle"—is that of a magnificent seven-foot tiger with undulating, and yes, changing stripes. They can wrap me 'round in a stream of golden spice when I stroke her left whisker, enter me as blue lightning as she captures my files in her glowing paws.*

How did I ever track such a fantastic screen scroller as Topaz? With great difficulty and the feline patience of an old tomgirl, not a baby dyke. Forget the slew of Personals available online, such as America Online's gay Heart to Heart, or Usenet's alt.personals, in scores of subdivisions (alt.personals.bi, alt.personals.big.folk, even alt.personals.poly.) Cyberpersonals tend to exhaust and sadden, a universe of the desperate, wailing to be loved. Instead, I moved my concentration into the sex and romance newsgroups thicket. Of a few hundred, I hit the tantalizing fringes: alt.amazon-women.admirers, alt.magick.sex, alt.flame.cycle-sluts. Uh-Oh. Only male energy in the chat rooms. It was the month of Aries with lots of Mars action, so maybe my stars were crossed. Statistically, however, the ether is overwhelmingly young, geekey, white male—a global frat party sponsored by free university accounts. I did find assorted alt.hotstuff. Cyberpunks shoot bizarre wit, coruscating insults, surreal shock. Lots of freak show fare. Not particularly joyful, mind you. Electrons can laugh mirthlessly.

---

* Carefully guard your digidentity. The Net is populated by the good, the evil, and the indifferent, just as in real life. Change passwords often. Lovelorn E-mail is like a postcard to crackers. Private sex scenes can be posted for all to read if you connected with an exhibitionist. If you must get real, always use a p.o. box and get *their* phone number. Do not download programs or attachments except from vendors' files or well-known archives. Computer viruses can really subvert online safe sex.

Have fun before the Bit Police open trapdoors. As of this writing, there is no Net God. Wild birds still sing on the Net, but predatory economics is polluting their habitat. Any government intervention should be to protect a Net public space from raging privatization and commercialization.

So I decided to log onto cultural and political groups likely to attract "real" women, sites like WomanNet and FemNet National Lesbian Network. I visited the really fine polyamory Web site going up at http://www.wp.com/lovemore. I also aimed for general interest BBSs with a rep among the telegensia for a significant women's presence, and therefore, more salon than slam dance. I borrowed friends' accounts on PlanetOut and the WELL, on woman-owned ECHO, on MindVox. Lots of interesting women, some telecom tarts, but nothing flashed.

Then I slipped into a conference of Dharma digerati on a free BBS called Tiger Team, the Buddhist Information Network. I needed to get off the desire machine, at least in a virtual sort of way. I watched silently as a newbie, "lurking" as they say, to get the lay of the cybersanga. (System operators figure that online there are about ten lurkers to one player.) This virtual wallflower began to see a pattern of interesting reflections on women and Buddhism, then on Lesbian priests by the aforementioned Topaz. I tried to play off her forays and finally summoned the clitzzpah to invite her for a private chat. First we sang over the sweet bones of Buddha, then began straying down a seemingly lavender garden path.

By this time, I had a whole rosary of Lesbian identity beads, little queries to pose which only an actual Lesbian could finger with agility. We rolled around with the hilarious ancient Chinese "sheathed penis treatise" proving that one of the thirty-two marks of a true Buddha is a clitoris.[37] We debated the "vermilion thread" of a zen koan and discussed Dakini power amid the Lesbian Avengers. When Topaz got excited or intimate, her -er ending words became -re. The -re surely signaled heavy breathing. I wondered if Topaz was a Brit or had been a tiger cub somewhere in their lost empire. I still get excited seeing theatre, centre, even fibre-optics and spectre.

We spent late nights delightfully weaving Indra's Internet, since it is now in global gridlock during the day. I was also getting into major dollar as well as REM debt, losing my keys in cyberspace.

But I was mainlining another Lesbian's thoughts. We were jacked brain to brain in sleek, minimalist potency. Her mind was a pleasure pulse 'trode—almost mutagenic. Then it happened.

One night I followed Topaz, my dashing cybernaut, through the back door of a Net site known as a MUD for Multiple User Dungeon or Multiple User Dimensions, or Mardi Gras Until Death. A MUD is a virtual world which allows you to interact with its carefully crafted software as well as to play your own chosen role with whatever users currently occupy the MUD. As we zip around in all text-based virtual reality, expensive 3D goggles and gloves are unnecessary. MUDs underscore the mega-imagination, projection, and suggestibility our minds orchestrate. I doubt any current graphics, CD-ROM or VR could crackle like these floating fiction packets. MUDs run the gamut from theme parks (Star Trek, Tolkien, Zendo) to super intense fantasy lands (vampires, rebirthing, AIDS high mass). Program wizards usually emphasize the social or adventure aspect, with most adventures, alas, being of the slash-and-burn variety, quite devoid of romance.

Yes, people do get trapped in MUDs; they can be spellbinding.

Topaz showed me how to get into ZenMOO, one tricky Net nook. ZenMOO skewers the monkey mind of MUDs themselves, as well as spoofs typical zen encryption. It neatly shows the absurdity of our crystal-meth mind acting out on phosphorous. Topaz, it turned out, was one of the silent stars of ZenMOO. Then, her traverse dark stripes scrolling my responsive field, she beckoned a walk on the wild side, "Will you be my companion in FurryMuck?" This is the fabled electronic bestiary of MUDs, with its Truth or Dare Hot Tub, thousands of geographies and micro-climates, lacings of fabulous forests and underground caverns. In FurryMuck, all manner of silky creatures from this earth and beyond, philosophize and yes, fuck. Here, rubbing against Topaz' charged fur, I gave my cybervirginity to a Royal Bengal who could caress tiger lilies between my legs. Not everyone is that good.

Did we ever meet f2f? No. Topaz explained to me that the electronic bubble has no depth or permanence. Its sparkling, romantic foam disappears into the data sea. This is its evanescent beauty. Luckily, I had logged on as an explorer, as a player. Log on as one yearning to be loved and you'll crash. Download non-ordinary reality and it downloads you. Truth takes a backseat to a good time.

The mighty tsunami of online fantasy and projection, its "hear no evil, see no evil," can rarely be sustained in real life. All the parallel channels are missing which actually inscribe a person's love map: attraction by sight, style and gesture; facial expressions; voice intonation and inflection; touch; scent; and important behavioral cues. Most crucially, the *prana* (breath, spirit) is missing. Besides, who can French kiss a screen? Powerful as it is, cyberspace can jack you only into someone's two-dimensional passing fancy. All you have to go on is a woman's writing style in two genres—telegraphic and stream of consciousness. Lovers who shine online must type like the wind to create rich emotional detail, vivid imagery, repartee and metaphor. Real skills. Great silicon shenanigans, but hardly the designer wetware* for the golden ring of commitment. Love disappears when the modem disconnects. Afterglow is but a cold, bright, blank screen.

Online, quick-draw ingenuity supersedes reflection. Style and form count over substance. I'm afraid I sniffed a serious decline in even conversational grammatical style. Messages are bereft of the sensory vibrations of speech, while also lacking the disciplined elegance of literature. The Net is more noise than signal. Everyone is talking, few are listening. The great digital dumpster. Each user knows the answer to this riddle: "Query: If twenty million monkeys sat down at twenty million computers and started typing, what would you have? Answer: The Internet." As a librarian monkey, I can only say, look at how this Net of 50,000+ networks is organized—like a card catalog with the drawers spilled.

---

* Cyberlex for our precious packet beyond all hardware and software, organic flesh and blood, bubbly neuro-brain, and sex with silvery secretions.

Romantic old archivist that I am, however, I had saved all of Topaz' succulent scripts to print out by the fire on cold nights in the Information Age. We had, after all, more than a two-bit romance. We dwelt in perfect metaphor in our orgasmic nether world: animal blood melting into electricity, defying distance and decay, amid flowers which never fade. Two Lesbian neuro-skins, swirling in arousal past rushing blue binaries and open slipgates. Our liquid crystal libidos climbed glowing mountains and explored grottos of worlds not yet built. (Note to the S. P. C. E.: no electrons were harmed in the production of this escapade.)

Computer novice that I am, however, when I hit "Print," only one line had been saved of the megalovebytes we had shared, with all the acronyms and smileys* that Topaz had showered on me. Only the words remained which she had whispered that night, leading me from the great zendo into her golden lilied lair. Strangely, my old printer copied this one-line observation as a thread of bright vermilion on a sheet of pressed wood, one which smelled of spicy pine forests. Somehow, it was embossed with pretty stamps like bright jewels and exotic East Indian water-marks I couldn't translate. I read,

Remembre, no one has to be wired to be connected ":*)

---

* Smileys, also called emoticons, are online emotional shorthand. Turn page sideways to see Topaz' favorites:

:-)	big grin	8-O	wow! (shock or pleasure)
;-)	wink	:-P	panting
:-x	love & cyberkisses	:-*	well-kissed
>;-)	come hither	P-)	swashbuckling good
:-D	laughing	:-B	topless

Community—A Harem of Friends

Query: What do you think of the oft-repeated polyfidèle equation, "Shared bodies + shared adventures + shared values = Community?" Is community so easy? Is it wise to combine sex with close friends at all?

— *Sharon Sextet, Cottage Grove, Oregon*

Oh, the much touted jewel of community. Community is a buzz word now, its meaning as hazy as "love." People sit at screens and act like they're around a camp fire or raising a barn. Anyway, I'm afraid your three "community" ingredients also add up to "military." Each is a cohesion factor in old Greek and Mideast militarism as well as the U. S. Marines. Sane, joyous community, however, also thrives on the essential elements of shared power and shared respect. [Enter Feminism.] Set these five jewels: physical delight and caring, adventure, points of unity, equal rights and respect—all within passion's energy and attention. You form a treasure of community beyond price. Polyfidelity is one way to create such commitment and vitality. (So is hardship and imagination.)

We know that intimate sexual passion between Lesbians is often the royal road to a social melding so deep and intense we adopt certain loves as lifelong "family." We form a Body of Trust. That's loyalty, complete with authentic family values! Bondswomen via the body, we construct marvelous friendship genealogies. "Bare is the back which has no sister." For many of us, our closest community is a harem of friends, the women of whom we are privileged to hold carnal knowledge.* We come together first because of physically passionate rapport. We remain bonded if we grow in love, need, pleasure, respect—as well as in the ability to forgive lapses in all of the former.

---

* I have always preferred the term "carnival knowledge." Do Lesbians who burn every bridge to obliterate a lover live in "charnal knowledge"?

I was amazed to find virtually nothing in mental health literature on the immense value and sheer sanity of making and maintaining friendship. "Shared joy is double joy; shared sorrow is half sorrow," says a Swedish proverb, but not the U. S. therapy industry. In psychoanalytic theory, friends are not even considered a "system," like the biological family and marriage dynamic. Since a full quarter of all Americans live in single-person households, who are these people relating to? From 1974-1994, psychological studies' lone article on friendship suggests that friendship (only male being studied) is based on homoerotic volatility which causes problems. Oh. In a recent Gallup Poll, however, respondents were five times more likely to report that they were helped to make an important life change by a friend rather than by a therapist.[38]

Euro-American ethical theory has largely negated the friendship affiliation by ignoring it. There is no entry for Friendship in the *Encyclopedia of Philosophy*. Abstract individualism underlies most of our political theory too. It took feminists like Carol Gilligan to highlight the moral significance of personal relations. Anthropological literature, in contrast, holds a plethora of "friendship" cites. Non-Western societies devote elaborate rituals and explicit social contacts to celebrate, formalize and ardently maintain friendship.[39]

The discussion frequently came up among my polyfidèle interviewees why Lesbians, at least in the two decades we've been able to openly explore our sensuality, are not yet as supple as gay men in combining sex with friendship. We flirt with our friends about as blatantly as nuns do. A Lesbian's core community is likely composed of former lovers, current one(s), and a circle of eternally chaste friendships, even among women who share physical attraction. Like many gay men, however, most Lesbian polyfidèles I interviewed do welcome sexual friendships. We wondered why chastity is so typical among heart friends. Seven of the twenty-five women I interviewed do remain hesitant to embark on sexual ventures with friends on whom they admit having "crushes." Reasons most often cited for their restraining order on desire? Possible rise of jealousy and increase in faultfinding. Why are we so conditioned to spare friends these horrors, but burden "love" with them? Oh, and yes, most of us noted there is a difference between being sexually attracted to a woman and having sexual desire for her. Subtle, subtle.

Here's a round robin of stories, the "sex friendly" and the reluctant.

Caroline

Actually, two of my lovers were very old friends before we ever became sexually involved. When they finally came out—shazam! It was as though our emotional bonds could finally be ritualized, celebrated in physical form. When each of my loving friends want-ed a live-in partner—I like my space—they helped their new lovers not only to recognize, but honor, our preceding "passionate friend-ship." It came with the territory and so it continues.

Everyone knows that "affairs" which last have friendship as the primary stimulus, not lust. Friendship nourishes all fronts. Lesbian culture has focused on erotics, inspiration, pleasure and emotional support. Since old age is rolling around for many of us, I hope Lesbian culture also concerns itself with each other's material sur-vival. With the average income for the U. S. woman over sixty-five being $6,500—we'd better help each other.

Let's see, why should friends make the very best lovers? Friends have a whole reassuring history to uphold them. There are fewer false expectations or crazy projections. Friends usually have worked out some tolerances over divisive issues. You, at least, know the issues, no ghastly surprises! We've had opportunity to get practice being more objective and generous in spirit. Friendship "polishes" us. It's not that I'm always this benevolent latitudinarian or any-thing, but with old friends I'm not as apt to perceive conflict as personal injury, as neglect or lack of respect. I'll think, more like, "Isn't that just like an Aries!" and not get my knickers all twisted.

What if I propose sex to a friend and she turns me down? Well, she's usually a bit flattered. I end up having no less than before the asking. I keep it light. The sun doesn't go out if its rays fall on unresponsive space.

I think lovers tend to be clearer about each others' rights and responsibilities than friends are. Expectations can be quite vague even with old friends. Loyalty assumptions are not as explored as they are with lovers.

You know what else I like? The spark of passion which adds an electricity to friendship's smallest interactions.

One other lover I have is more like a typical friend in actual "spaciousness." We hold deep social/sexual intimacy, but distance is really built in, literally—700 miles. All her other lovers are long distance too. She says she likes her world to be full of romantic hellos and goodbyes. She's a brilliant, obsessive painter and is very clear about setting up privacy from unwanted intrusions. This love "spacing," she calls it, allows her wide discretion in how she interacts and when. She says that with a wide range of intimate friends, she can even choose one to develop her shadow side. I remember this when we have a fight.

Diana

The more naked, the more physical the relationship, as the clothes fall away, well, so does the fabric unravel we've carefully woven of our projected image. Lovers explore our deepest physicality. This is the body most women are conditioned to shame—too skinny here, too full-bodied there, the psychosomatic scars, the deep tissue pain. Fashion and baubles and makeup help conceal such vulnerabilities from even our closest friends. Naked, full of desire and longing, we are pregnable. Emotional depth charges reverberate. Of course, sexual friends can also be more freely open, pleasured, connected—able to explore.

Most of us also sense we can never control a passionate, sexual relationship the way we usually control a friendship. Friendship naturally expects "time out" separations; equilibrium reasserts itself. Friendship's cooling distance allows objectivity and tolerance to irrigate hot spots.

The more intimate, more intense the relationship, however, the closer we come to who we really are, going deeper than the egocentricity we so carefully craft. Aren't our greatest defenses to protect our fabricated image? Because egocentricity forges a little universe with us at the center, we regard "our" universe as true. We are the glorious freewheeler at the center of everything. Until other people get very close, that is! The closer another "reality" brushes our concept of self, the more confusing it can be. We usually regard as positive whatever reinforces our ego image, negative whatever threatens it. Passionate sex between friends certainly may not leave "reality" the way our egocentricity set it up. Open sensuality can make things more authentic, infinitely richer, but it may crash some cherished props. I wonder if our choice of intimates comes from a seed force in us which wants to grow?

In sexual love, we often touch the rawness of the heart. Be brave enough to discover this rawness has a sweetness all its own. If you are afraid when your friends really "know" you in physical love that they will leave . . . well, work at becoming a more loving friend to this little ball of fear you've created. Any woman, even half-awake, has accumulated a crown of thorns by the time she's ready for love. The knack is to wear it over one ear. Insecurity is not that bad, it's our fear of it. Enjoy, or at least watch, the cycle: nothing lasts forever in one form, whether sex or continency. Staying open to both is life's aphrodisiac.

Lee

I don't know, I guess I'm a great compartmentalizer: lovers here; friends there. I'm a loner in the sense of being more at ease one-to-one rather than in a group or community. Lord knows, we could use more social harmony, but when I look at a group I usually see a cage in search of a bird. My mother always said, "Don't take a fence down until you know why it was put up."

Actually, I am sexually attracted to one friend of long duration.
I think, though, that we have different bedroom tastes. Yet she's
hinted she'd like to "tousle my wishes," that she has always kept "a
special nook" waiting for me. What if I woo her one night, but the
sex turns out not so hot? She is not a movie I can walk out on. I
am so curious I'd be willing to take the chance of hurt feelings, but
what if, from her point of view, sex damages the friendship? Our
hearts are divided over religion, and we've weathered these differences, so maybe we could do the same with whatever comes up
sexually... Still, I'd rather fantasize; nothing lost, nothing gained.

Sometimes I feel becoming a lover with her could also bring up
that "we-ness" which delights and reassures, but also raises my
anxiety we'll lose our selves within us. Does that sound confused!
I mean I like our very differences, and I find them fascinating as
friends, but if we become lovers ...

I am embarrassed in mentioning this—I wonder if, as "Lover," my
obligations go up? Like seeing her more and having to call and
help out more? She's pretty demanding with lovers, I've noticed.
Lovers are supposed to be this one-stop affiliative service.

This woman is the only one of my very close friends to whom
I happen to be sexually attracted, my "type." I realize I usually
choose a different type of woman for a lover than I do for a friend.
I tend to choose lovers who are lighthearted, wild, even devil-may-
care. I am not concerned how intellectual a lover is. I prefer blaz-
ing femmes. My closest friends, however, are almost all academics,
sober, thoughtful, most of them butch of center. I love how they
process things with me, while lovers act out a storm.

Which type do I keep longer, lovers or friends? Guess.

Melinda

I love making love with friends. I already love them, so why not
celebrate our very body of connection? Why not use our touch for
all its healing power too? I must distinguish here between the sea-

soned love of old friendship and being "in" love. In love is that initial romantic rush 'n' mush where dazzling, crazy emotions burst forth, born of curiosity, newness, magnificent illusion, altered neurochemistry. In love has a shelf life of what . . . maybe three years, top? I don't think women are as realistic about this romantic evanescence as men are. During its time, romantic love's brilliant, drunken emotions have actually unhinged possessiveness and control in rational old me. The usual, cultivated boundaries all start to melt. Romantic love is, by definition, irrational. In contrast, "liking" tends to be quite rational, based on thoughtful respect.

It is rarer to feel this volatile, romantic love for an old friend. By the reckoning of years, she is no longer an exotic, surprising creature. Old friends offer few illusions of perfection; they don't tap into infantile longings of "happily ever after." My love story is quieter and deeper with a friend. My love is grounded, not lightning on the loose. With romantic love, every small issue may light a fuse of humiliation, fear of selfhood, a power struggle. It's harder to "make room" for a lover than a friend when conflict comes up.

I stare at a new lover; I look into an old friend.

The hesitation about whether to jump the fence from physically desirable old friend to lover is probably a fear of greater intimacy. Sex does have the power to awaken our deeper nature. Sex in our culture seems to be a trigger for almost every emotion, from the fabulous to the frightening. Most humans want to keep things placid, not to take risks.

In any event, sex is not the important thing. Sex doesn't matter as much as how we treat each other. The human need for emotional and physical contact matters. It's just that sexual energy can be such a luminously present mode of attention. And I don't mean bowing to the tyranny of genitality. Touch a friend, including your cat, and feel yourselves move effortlessly from ordinary, distracted consciousness into relaxation and interconnection. You can actually monitor your brain waves changing from beta to alpha via a friend's massaging strokes. By the time you become theta in her hands, with all gateways open, the self becomes larger, more spacious. We may go beyond our wondrous connection to each other; we may almost merge with the universe. Talk about Community.

Molly

Well, my grandmother said that I treated my friends better than my family—and I really loved her. Then my first lover also said I treated my friends, including my dog, better than her. I began to wake up that I had taken on some weird-ass behaviors in how to treat my most precious people.

I'd made "love" an emotional minefield, just like my childhood family. Now, before I get to feeling all rejected and freeze up or just rage real primitive, I stop. I ask myself, "Isn't this lover my friend?" Lighten up. Get some manners, like with fine friends. A soulmate is also a playmate. We're just playing house here.

Cynthia

I laugh at my hippie-chick commune days now, the loving innocence, the excesses. I also spent time at Twin Oaks, this country's longest-lived, secular intentional community. Then my Lesbian land trust wanderings (Space of Our Own!) were far more tumultuous, despite the sanctuaries we were trying to create.[40] One of the big issues was, of course, sexuality. What city girl didn't subscribe to the rural *Womenspirit Magazine* just to see naked communards, arms around one other? Cuntry writing didn't put that sexy "y" in "womyn" for nothing. *Country Women* did one issue entirely on the transformative power of sex in collective building, even between mother and daughter! Sex between friends, hey, that's tame.

For the last few years, I've been working and going to school to get a degree just to earn a "claim stake." I want to invest in women's land in a co-housing community. Like other Lezoboomers, I'm thinking about later years and want to begin creating a safe, joyous space in nature. In co-housing, we can share things hard to maintain so well alone like a food garden, a library, entertainment space, a temple, arts studio, whatever the group decides are quality of life concerns. We can share material things. It's silly for everyone to duplicate washers and dryers, cars, tools. Also buy in quantity to save. Share childcare if we want to. After all, "It takes a whole village to raise a child."

But in co-housing clusters, each of us has her separate living and dining space too. Then there's a commons, where we can go to eat and socialize as we wish. The hub of most co-housing communities seems to be its dining area. There are around two hundred U. S. co-housing communities in various stages of planning, building and living. Europe is far ahead of us. We do have a fine quarterly networking magazine here.[41] I wish it talked more about severing ties to the state, though.

For now I live in a large cooperative house of seven women. Some of us are casual (maybe I should say "calm") lovers with each other, some splash in romantic firewater. Three, like me, have girl friends who live elsewhere, too. The house keeps a really low profile on the intramural sex here because of jealous girls outside our living circle, but mainly in fear of heterosexual male violence.

The overwhelming thing I've felt to be a problem in sex with a friend is when her partner objects. Hello, I must be going. Now, for the very first time, I'm in love with a woman who is in an open relationship—and I'm very attracted to her longtime partner as well! This has happened slowly. Dorothy, my love's live-in partner, and I became friends, too, mainly through all the kids. Dorothy and Emily have this huge old barn house and lots of teens I call the "Lavender Hill Mob." Of course I'm always telling them their acreage could be perfect land for co-housing and a cooperative community.

My lover, Emily, is still afraid for me to be sexually involved with Dorothy. The best thing we did, however, was take time and talk about what was becoming sexual tension. It's like when you're getting drunk. Take a walk. After our discussion, I didn't have to feel sneaky anymore. No one has to pretend nothing is going on. Dorothy was flattered by the whole thing. Emily was reassured over and over by both of us. What seemed most vital to talk about was the material, property and family ties which Dorothy and Emily have created. The sex wasn't such a big deal to them in itself. Just that it could be disruptive if some sort of three-way claim to the estate went wild. So we made up worst-case scenarios. It was ludicrous; it was cleansing. I like what's going on now, so remaining friends, not lovers, with Dorothy, is fine. I especially like that we all just have this warm sexual charge, but not the tension.

I guess some people want to stay with a friendship, not lover, relation precisely because friendship is largely free from domestic and financial entanglements. Only in big emergencies involving shelter, health, clothing, kids, do friends get involved. But lovers do, practically on a daily basis. So do people who pledge communitas. Community has always been in my blood, so this particular friend/lover boundary is not real pronounced for me, I guess.

One thing I do know from my years of friends/lovers is that human beings can tolerate just so much relational intensity. That's why we often pick fights—to make distance. Friends tend to respect boundaries and permit distance more easily than lovers. I love the co-housing form specifically because everyone's private space is valued and acknowledged. Autonomy/connection needs are rarely static for long, so both are honored.

Something else—in my experience, sex is most likely to be dangerously naive or to end the type of friendship I call a "transactional" friendship. I distinguish transactional friends from those I call "core," or "forever" friends. Core friends' channels always seem to be open to one another, even after long times apart, and as personal cycles come and go. Core friends get together just to *be,* not necessarily to *do* something. But I also like and need to have friends "for the road," wayfarers with whom I share certain goals in life's journey. Such transactional friends come together in mutual self-interest, warm and real, to share information, to accomplish a task.

Schoolmates, work and sports mates and political activists can be great transactional friends.

If you get physical with a transactional friend, be careful because you may not merge only physically. You may open psychologically, too, and not be able to edit. We always edit some with a transactional acquaintance. Two acquaintances' psyches, however, may never have been designed to be at peace unless each keeps her self-interested distance. One valued transactional friend finally told me that in our sex, she felt she gave too much away. She has a right to keep to her own ground.

I guess I don't always understand why people make sex a stage for childish or teenage insecurities, and for old outrages. I was raped night after night, but I won't let him or the therapists or the fundamentalists stain my sex with eternal angst. My Lesbian sex makes even the air seem lighter. I mean it's certainly okay if lovers share the darker side, but why let darkness control? For me, the mystery of goodness is greater than the mystery of evil. If your love's been an intimate friend, she's already seen your shadow anyway. So it can just go out and play while you all glow in the dark.

'Course me, I don't even see anything wrong with using sex to create a bond in the first place. Nude, you've really put down your weapons! Sex as the ultimate handshake. Let each person make of this elemental gesture of peace what she wishes.

Our culture imbues sex with such tremendous deep, dark symbology, like we must always choose between the ascetic rocks of friendship and the sensual whirlpools of lovers. This is a trick! A community of "friendly sex"—they've nailed a taboo on this deeper than the grave. While the couple's power sex is vaunted, friendly sex is considered dangerous or impolite! Even domestic partnership laws limit "partners" to a queer Noah's Ark, two by two. The progressive changes in marital laws, like those occurring in Hawaii, will only protect the community based on two. Can't we re-envision, not merely reform? Make marriage a civil contract between any number of committed people of any gender!

Western society clamps us with this tight conditioning, this dualistic processing, where the reigning idea is that the friend respects space while the lover longs for fusion. Why not temper each with each, search for a new balance? Notions like this are constructed. They can be deconstructed and revitalized. I don't want to have to buy that bumper sticker: New Millennium, Same Old Crap.

Esperanza

We're just now completing negotiations on an "urban homestead" in which to create a community of eleven loving friends. I'm so excited, I can hardly talk! It's taken three years to find this space, with major redesigning yet to come. Yes, most of us are Lesbian polyfidèles, though we have no eternal promulgation on any woman's sexual preferences. We just don't intend for the community to be rent by monogamy's typical serial divorces.

All of us try to live by the Buddhist precept of non-exploitative sexuality and the neo-Pagan principle "Do As You Will. Harm No One." An observant romantic, Rousseau said, "Keeping citizens apart has become the first maxim of modern politics." Our national security state mercilessly uses this divide and conquer tactic. We refuse to bring such Us/Them fears into our own community. Since there is no one formula for sexual intimacy, diversity is our ideal. Therefore, polite and agreeable men and transexuals are welcome as guests and even lovers. It took me a year to agree with the "lover" part, and I've been married to a man, not once, but three times. I finally realized I do consider sensual love to be a diverse, abundant and renewable gift of grace. It is an energy any pioneering soul should be able to use however it comes and works for her. Men, however, are not allowed to be homestead owners or policy makers until that time when all the women title holders unanimously agree that Earth is being stewarded by women and men in parity.

They say co-housing is a "meeting way of life." True, and we try to make meetings convivial too. We also use silence in meetings.

Quakers and Buddhists call in silence to "open the spirit." When we sit together silently to deal with brokenness or conflict or problems, we seem to soften, issues become clearer. I used to think group speaking was hard, well, silence and real listening are much harder!

I don't mind saying that we are classic utopian dreamers. In our blood, we're gamblers. People shake their heads, but I'm proud not to be a cynic. Cynicism is too easy. I admit the utopian way is long odds, and a long time journey. But who cares since I'm in such good company! What else is more fun than to invest in quality of life issues once shared survival needs are done for the day? Creating a woman's intentional community is a quest of hope, far beyond optimism. Hope is a moral quality. To struggle for something not widely accepted, like a loving non-dyadic community, means to underwrite it with our lives. Like moths attracted to a flame, some of us just can't bear to live the conventional way, mindlessly repeating the pattern of the age. Meanwhile, our means are our ends, every struggle is a victory. A great deal of lateral, in contrast to linear, thinking is a good plan too.

Yes, yes, we've already made many mistakes! Don't pioneers always have a little dirt under their fingernails?

Deephaven

Of all the topics I proposed to interviewees, none was greeted with the relish of "community," not even sex. When we combined both—ah! There was also realistic fear, considering a history of terrorism unleashed on unorthodox sexual communities. The reason why even white, devout Christians had to flee the Midwest to Utah was these Mormons were being massacred specifically for their polygamous sexual behavior. As a former Oregonian, I am no apologist for the ill-fated Rajneesh community there. The initial flame to stir up Oregon hatred, however, was the Rajneesh advocacy of communal free love. Or, take Camp Sister Spirit, a truly peace-loving, cultural and educational community in

Mississippi. Unlike Rajneeshpuram, it is not territorially expansionist, nor cultic, nor the purveyor of "suspicious" religious ritual. Camp Sister Spirit is being terrorized for its sexual/love practices alone. So, in buying land and building a community of lovers, let's do as we damn please, but do it slowly, carefully, and in a good neighborhood.

May we judge any community we build by the safety it guarantees its members to hold unorthodox, totally unpopular views. Here's mine: view sex as a hilarious sacred act. What can this old Buddhist do but suggest our coda be the poem of a great mystery-writing Catholic:

> *As I grow older and older*
> *And totter to the tomb*
> *I find that I care less and less*
> *Who goes to bed with whom.*
>
> — *Dorothy Sayers*

May you find the libidinal community best for you, knowing there are myriads of erotic ecologies. I suppose the polyfidelitious ecology includes soft, stable boundaries, diversity, adaptability, novelty, and interrelation. Make a new tryst with life. Who knows what we will discover in this universe as
we glimpse...

Chapter Notes

1
(page 14)
The incomparable Natalie Barney (1876-1972) is, with Sappho, the most famous polyfidèle of yore. "A woman, take her or leave her, but do not take her and leave her." Do take Anna Livia's brilliant translation of Barney's selected works from the French, *A Perilous Advantage: The Best of Natalie Clifford Barney* (New Victoria, 1992.) Barney's charming vignette, *"The Climbing Rose,"* describes a rambler with roots in one garden and blossoms in another. See also Natalie Barney's *Adventures of the Mind* (1929), translated by John Gatton in 1992 (NYU Press) and Karla Jay's *The Amazon and the Page* (Indiana University Press, 1988.)

2
(page 22)
A third edition of Nearing's excellent guide now titled *Loving More: The Polyfidelity Primer* is available for $14 from PEP Publications, Box 6306, Ocean View, HI 96737. (808) 929-9691. E-mail RyamPEP@aol.com.

3
(page 22)
Anapol's *Love Without Limits: Responsible Nonmonogamy* is available for $19 from IntiNet Resource Center, Box 4322, San Rafael, CA 94913. Workshop information: (415) 507-1739.

4
(page 28)
Loulan, JoAnn, *Lesbian Passion,* Spinsters, 1987, p. 194; Blumstein, P. and P. Schwartz, *American Couples,* Morrow, 1983, p. 307; "Lesbian Polyfidelity Survey, 1995," p. 319 this book.

5
(page 28)
Fisher, Helen. *Anatomy of Love: The Natural History of Monogamy, Adultery, and Divorce.* Norton, 1992. pp. 109-12.

6
(page 50)
The five-pound *DSM* pharmaceutical cookbook is often dubbed *The Malleus Maleficarum* by feminists, comparing the *DSM* to the medieval inquisitors' diagnostic guide for witch persecution. See Paula Caplan's *They Say You're Crazy* (Addison-Wesley, 1995) on how the world's richest psychiatrists decide who's "normal" or who's inside the *DSM*.

7
(page 58)

Spretnak, Charlene. *States of Grace: Recovery of Meaning in the Postmodern Age.* Harper, 1991. p. 79.

8
(page 58)

Termites, some birds, muskrats, some bats, the Asiatic clawless otter, deer mice, dwarf mongeese, the Klipspringer, reedbucks, dik-diks and a few other antelopes, some seals, a few South American monkeys, and wild dogs. (Fisher, Helen, *op. cit.*, p. 150.)

9 (59)

Fisher, Helen. *op. cit.*, p. 66.

10
(page 59)

Wright, Robert. *The Moral Animal: The New Science of Evolutionary Psychology.* Pantheon, 1994. p. 70.

11
(page 61)

Eisler, Riane. *The Chalice & The Blade.* Harper, 1987. p. 66.

12
(page 61)

Gimbutas, Marija. *The Early Civilization of Europe.* UCLA,1960. pp. 22-25.

13
(page 62)

Batten, Mary. *Sexual Strategies: How Females Choose Their Mates.* Tarcher/Putnam, 1992. p. 115.

14
(page 65)

Pagels, Elaine. *The Gnostic Gospels.* Vintage, 1979. p. 64. See also Haskins, Susan, *Mary Magdalene: Myth and Metaphor.* Harcourt, 1994.

15
(page 68)

Small, Meredith. *What's Love Got To Do With It? The Evolution of Human Mating.* Anchor, 1995. p. 211.

16
(page 110)

Ford, C.S. and F.A. Beach. *Patterns of Sexual Behavior.* Harper, 1959.

17
(page 203)

Lorde, Audre. *Uses of the Erotic, The Erotic as Power.* Crossing, 1978.

18
(page 205)

Wolff, Edward. *Top Heavy: A Study of the Increasing Inequality of Wealth in America.* Twentieth Century Fund, 1995. p. 7.

19
(page 205)

Zeitlin, Maurice. *The Large Corporation and Contemporary Classes.* Rutgers University Press, 1989.

20   Schor, Juliet. *The Overworked American: The Unexpected*
(page 206) *Decline of Leisure.* Harper, 1992.

21   Ehrlich, Paul *et al. Ecoscience: Population, Resources,*
(page 206) *Environment.* W. H. Freeman, 1977. p. 142-3.

22   Steinberg, David. *Erotic Impulse: Honering the Sensual Self.*
(pg. 232) Tarcher, 1992. pp. 24-29.

23   Bufe, Charles. *Alcoholics Anonymous: Cult or Cure?* See
(page 234) Sharp Press, 1991.

          Christopher, James. *How To Stay Sober: Recovery Without*
          Religion. Prometheus,1988.

          Kaminer, Wendy. *I'm Dysfunctional, You're Dysfunctional:*
          The Recovery Movement and Other Self-Help Fashions.
          Vintage, 1993.

          Kasl, Charlotte. *Many Roads, One Journey: Moving Beyond*
          the 12 Steps. Harper,1992.

24 (236) *Sojourner,* January 1993, p. 9; *Denver Post* 9/6/92 C1:1.

25   A wonderful organization to help HIV+ women is
(page 248) *WORLD, Inc.,* Box 11535, Oakland, CA 94611. 510/568-
          6930.

26   Padian, Nancy, *et al.* "Female-to-Male Transmission of
(page 249) HIV," *JAMA,* 9/25/91:664.

27   Weller, Susan. "A Meta-Analysis of Condom Effectiveness
(page 250) in Reducing Sexually Transmitted HIV." *Social Science*
          Medicine, 36:1635-44.

28   See also the famous Turin, Italy study on Lesbian couples,
(page 250) one member of each couple being HIV+. During six
          months of no-barrier sex, all HIV negative partners
          remained negative. *Genitoruin Med 1994,* 70:200-205.

29   San Francisco Department of Public Health. *HIV*
(page 251) *Seroprevalence and Risk Behaviors Among Lesbian and Bisexual*
          Women and Health Behaviors Among Lesbian and Bisexual
          Women. 1993.

30 (251) *San Francisco Sentinel*, 10/20/93:20.

31 Cohen, Judith. "Assessing Risk in the Absence of
(page 251) Information: HIV Risk Among Women Injection-Drug
Users Who Have Sex With Women," *AIDS and Public
Policy Journal*, Fall 1992; and Rice, Louise, "Lesbians &
AIDS, Rethinking Dental Dams," *Sojourner*, August
1991:13-4.

32 Dean, Shea. "Slut Team Uses Eroticism To Raise HIV
(page 253) Awareness in Women." *S.F. Weekly*, 3/2/94:7.

33 O'Sullivan, Sue and Parmar, Pratibha. *Lesbians Talk (Safer)
(page 253) Sex*. Scarlet Press, 1992. p. 17.

34 Ridgway, Mindy. "Research Finds Lesbians, Bi Women
(page 254) Twice as Orgasmic as Straights." *Bay Times*, 11/3/94:13.

35 Elliott, Beth. "Does Lesbian Sex Transmit AIDS?—G.E.T.
(page 255) R.E.A.L.!" *Lesbian Contradiction*, Spring 1992. pp. 1-2.

Gorna, Robin. "Sticky Moments: Do We Need Latex
Sex?" *Diva, The Lesbian Lifestyle Magazine*. August 1994:
11-13.

Louise, Barbara. "An Alternative to Latex." *Lesbian
Contradiction*, Summer 1992. p. 21.

McDaniel, Judith and Judith Mazzo. "Safe Sex for
Lesbians: What's It All About?" *Sojourner*, June 1994,
p. 4P and "Letters," August 1994, p. 6.

Munson, Marcia ♥ very special thanks to a brilliant sex
educator for reviewing this chapter.

36 Breggin, Peter. *Toxic Psychiatry*. St. Martin's, 1991.

(page 276) Chernin, Kim. *A Different Kind of Listening: My Psychoanalysis and Its Shadow*. Harper, 1995.

Hillman, James with Michael Ventura. *We've Had a
Hundred Years of Psychotherapy and We're Getting Worse*.
Harper, 1992.

Kitzinger, Celia and Rachel Perkins. *Changing Our Minds: Lesbian Feminism & Psychology.* New York Univ. Press, 1993.

Malcolm, Janet. *Psychoanalysis: The Impossible Profession.* Knopf, 1981.

McCullough, Christopher. *Nobody's Victim: Freedom from Therapy & Recovery.* Clarkson Potter, 1995.

37
(page 295)
Gross, Rita. *Buddhism After Patriarchy: A Feminist History, Analysis, and Reconstruction of Buddhism.* SUNY, 1993, p. 62. Great Lesbian—and age—screening devices on the Net: books, music, films. Buddhist dykes know and love this book.

38
(page 300)
Family Therapy Networker, July/August 1995:35. Happily, the *Networker* just devoted an issue to friendship.

39 (300) Brain, Robert. *Friends and Lovers.* Basic Books, 1976.

40
(page 306)
Country Lesbians by Womanshare Collective (Womanshare Books, 1976) and *Lesbian Land* edited by Joyce Cheney (Word Weavers, 1985) are great accounts of our history. To tap into the Lesbian Land Movement with 50+ self-publicized projects (others are private), see the listing for women's land groups in bimonthly *Lesbian Connection,* Box 811, East Lansing, MI 48823. The national voice for dykeland is *Maize: A Lesbian Country Magazine,* Box 130, Serafina, NM 87569.

41
(page 307)
Co-Housing: Contemporary Approaches to Housing Ourselves. Quarterly, Box 2584, Berkeley, CA 9470. See also the seasoned *Communities* journal for provocative issues and profiles of the intentional community movement, anarchistic to theocratic: Route 1, Box 155, Rutledge, MO 63563.

Lesbian Polyfidelity Survey

© Celeste West Associates, 1995

Herein, we define "polyfidelity" as an ongoing relationship by a Lesbian or by a bisexual woman who is sensually, romantically intimate with more than one woman concurrently, while not lying about it, *i.e.,* women who are in honest multiple sensualove partnerships. In polyfidelity, the women may or may not live together. Polyfidelity is not serial monogamy (sequential polygamy) nor a secret affair. It may include, but is usually more emotionally involving than a recreational one-night stand or casual group sex.

Please comment freely in the spaces provided or add sheets of paper. If you dislike any conceptual framing or words used, please say so, and advise how you would handle the difficulty. If you feel we have not asked questions on important aspects of polyfidelity, we would be grateful if you would enclose your ideas.

Note to *après* survey readers: We have, where possible, entered percentages, average and median figures from the total 500 respondents. Polyfidèles represent 105 women of this 500 (21%). Polyfidèle answers are highlighted in questions #10, 20-24, 48-54. These are the answers of significant difference from the non—or not yet—polyfidelitious women. Each respondent did not always answer every question. Some women answered in a deliciously non-quantifiable manner, so percentages do not always equal 100%. The survey fill-in blanks ("other") often became text and interviews for *Lesbian Polyfidelity*. Again, to our 500 adventurers and 25 interviewees, A Thousand Blossoms of Gratitude!

Name/Address/Phone(optional):

1. **Please note your current sexual/affectional preference:**
   "Lesbian"   75% for 12 years (average)
   "Bisexual"   20% for 7 years   (average)
   "Other," "ambisexual," "pansexual," "sense-u-all," etc.   5% for 5 years (average)

2. **Are you out as any of the above to**
	Yes	No
Close friends	❏	❏
Biological family	❏	❏
Deserving public	❏	❏

   Approximately 3 in 5 women surveyed are totally out. Almost one-third signed the survey with contact information.

3. **What is your age?**
   Median age, 36 years, within a 16-to-88 year-old range.

4. **Please give your highest level of formal education.**
   Median level, 15 years.

5. **What is your ethnic heritage?**
   Color: 28%   White: 70%

6. **Residence now:**
   U.S. Area: West 26% Central 18%   NE 24%   SE 16%
   Canada 6%   Europe 5%   Australia/New Zealand 3%   Asia 1%

7. **What is your economic class background** _____ **Presently** _____
   Background: "Middle Class" 62%   "Working Class" 25%   "Rich" 8%   "Other" 5%.
   Median income $23,000 year

8.   **Are you currently employed? Occupation** _____
     No 20% (retired 6%) Yes, full time, 59%; part-time 25%

9.   **If you have a spiritual practice, how would you name it?**
     Judeo-Christian 55% Neo-pagan 20% Buddhist, Sufi, agnostic, atheist, etc. 16%

10. **Astrological sign of polyfidèles? Enneagram?**
     Gemini leads with 19%; Sagittarius 11%
     Enneagram number #7, "The Adventurer," leads with 22%

11. **Do you consider yourself a feminist?**
     Yes 85%   No 4%. Question provoked "feminist" definition controversy.

12. **Do you identify as femme or as butch or in any sexual role?**
     Femme 21%   Butch 9%   Other 70%
     Another definition controversy, with several observations in the sense of,
     "Why identify when you can play?"

13. **Please list your substance drug(s) of choice, if any:**

Sugar	90%	Nicotine	29%	Cocaine	2%
Caffeine	46%	Marijuana	23%	Ecstasy, Smart Drugs,	
Alcohol	39%	Psychedelics	10%	GHB, etc.	7%

14. **Would you say you spend a significant part of your time in activist politics?**
     Yes 26%

15. **Would you say you spend a significant part of your time creating in
     the arts?** Yes 32%

16. **Does your pre-adult personal history include any incidence of
     sexual abuse?**
     Yes 32% Unsure 12%

17. **Currently, how are you satisfied with you sex life?**
     (a) Not at all 10%   (b) Somewhat 26%   (c) Quite well 51%
     (d) Completely 13%

18. **During a typical month, how often do you have sex with another woman?**
     (a) never 29%   (b) once 31%   (c) 2-5 times 21%   (d) 6-10 times 10%
     (e) 10-20 times 7%   (f) 20+ times 2%
     Provoked "sex" definition controversy (see text pp. 230-232.)

19. **What is your average sensualove relationship length?**
     3 year average

20. **Please circle how independently minded you would consider yourself to be
     on a scale of 1-5, with #1 being a preference for convention, #5 being quite
     the renegade:** 1   2   3   ❹   5.   Cluster median for polyfidèles 3.7

21. **Please circle how much sexual energy you have on a scale of 1-5, with
     #1 being a taste for abstinence, #5 being hotter than a pepper sprout:**
     1   2   ❸   4   5.   Cluster median for polyfidèles 3.1

22. **Please circle how much you enjoy juggling many variables on a scale of 1-5,
     #1 with having a preference for as few distractions as possible, #5 being a high-
     variety seeker:** 1   2   3   ❹   5.   Cluster median for polyfidèles 4

23. Please circle where you are in the jealousy spectrum on a scale of 1-5, with #1 being jealousy-proof and #5 being extremely jealous: 1 2 ❸ 4 5. Cluster median for polyfidèles 3

24. Please circle your intimacy threshold on a 1-5 scale, #1 prefers infrequent high-intensity relating, #5 revels in long, frequent intimacy exchanges: 1 2 3 ❹ 5. Cluster median for polyfidèles 4

25. Present relationship status
single, not looking   9%   If involved, 67% live together
single and looking   40%   Average live-in 3.3 years
involved   40%

26. About how many women lovers have you had sex with? Median number: 14

27. How many significant sensualove relationships have you had? Median number: 4

28. How many loves have you lived with? Median number: 5

29. Are you a mother or co-parent living with your children? Yes 28%

30. Count up the good women you have truly loved, and multiply by πr^2 __
Add to this figure enjoyable crushes over which you have blushed. __
Subtract any celebrity with whom you've ever been infatuated. __
Add the number of times you've cried this year because of the pain of some creature besides yourself.
Add the number of changes you've made this year which have had the effect of making you more loveable to yourself. __
This final number is your "Poly Preparedness Quotient." ═

31. Do you believe women are socially conditioned to be monogamous? Yes 97%   No 2%   Not sure 1%

32. Do you believe women are instinctually programmed by genetics to be monogamous? Yes 39%   No 50%   Not sure 11%

33. Do you believe the human sexual strategies of monogamy and polygamy continuously evolve or are fixed? Evolve 75%   Are fixed 9%   Not Sure 15%

34. In a non-judgmental world (gasp!), please rate the following six sexualove forms in your order of preference, with #1 being your <u>most</u> ideal, <u>most</u> of the time (please note the query # 35 alternative):
(a) life-long monogamy (monogyny)   11%
(b) serial monogamy over a lifetime (sequential polygamy)   36%
(c) primary partner with all sensualoves in secret   1%
(d) honest, responsible polyfidelity, *i.e*, 2+ sensualovers, none hidden   34%
(e) recreational, uncommitted sex   4%
(f) solo sensualove by choice (intentional celibacy)   4%

35. If none of the forms listed above describes your ideal sensualove form, please describe your ideal vision here: Goddess spousal; extraterrestrial; art; athletics; etc.

36. Check the one <u>most</u> usual type of sensualove relationships you've been in so far:
(a) life-long monogamy   5%
(b) serial monogamy   30%
(c) primary partner with any additional sensualovers in secret   26%
(d) honest, responsible polyfidelity, *i.e*, 2+ sensualovers, none hidden   21%
(e) recreational, uncommitted sex   5%
(f) solo sensualove by choice (intentional celibacy)   4%
(g) other _____   9%

37. Have you ever fantasized being in sensualove relationships with more than one woman at a time? Yes 92%

38. If you have, or would you like to have, more than one lover concurrently, please give reasons why. If not, skip to #39.

(a) autonomy, individuality	51%	(h) being loved	86%
(b) sexual fulfillment	41%	(i) friendship	78%
(c) attention	80%	(j) fun	95%
(d) understanding	91%	(k) economic, lifestyle benefits	52%
(e) drama, adventure	49%	(f) risk, danger	10%
(l) revenge	3%	(m) other _____	7%
(g) intellectual stimulation	95%		

39. If you are not presently in a polyfidelitous relationship, please give reasons why not:

(a) opposed because of religious doctrine — 3%
(b) never considered polyfidelity as an option (lack of role models, experience) 71%
(c) have energy for only one woman lover — 65%
(d) enjoy keeping affairs secret from my partner as excitement — 5%
(e) cannot find polyfidelitous partners to try polyfidelity — 81%
(f) my own jealousy — 41%
(g) my partner's jealousy — 88%
(h) other intense emotions being with more than one woman may engender — 43%
(i) fear polyfidelious lovers are more likely to leave me — 49%
(j) feel the form may be too complex (scheduling, processing, etc.) — 68%
(k) my community's negative opinion of polyfidelity — 86%
(l) believe I am more likely to pick up sexually transmitted diseases — 25%
(m) other reasons _____ — 3%

40. If your partner becomes deeply committed to honest, responsible polyfidelity will you (select one):

(a) whole-heartedly experiment with polyfidelity as a relationship form — 31%
(b) feel initially ambiguous, but try it — 38%
(c) decline to try polyfidelity yourself, but tolerate hers — 6%
(d) grin & bear it, hoping she will change — 11%
(e) tell her poly is not your style and end things if necessary — 12%
(f) other _____ — 2%

41. Check if you think a commitment to monogamy has been violated if you or your partner:

(a) has a romantic meal or "date" with another woman, but with no physical caressing — yes, 80%
(b) enjoys a one night stand without lingering emotional attachment — yes, 90%
(c) participates in phone sex — yes, 87%
(d) exchanges "aphrodigital" text sex on the Net — yes, 80%
(e) watches woman stripping or having sex in sex clubs — yes, 31%

42. Did you ever, while ostensibly monogamous, have another lover on the side? Yes 78%

43. Did you ever, using deception, try to hide your romantic/sexual liaison with one intimate from another? Yes 72%

44. If yes, please note reasons for deception:
    (a) fear of lover's strong emotional reactions   91%
    (b) fear you would lose a lover   72%
    (c) other _____   4%

45. Do you think deception is the most functional way for you to have more than one lover?
    Yes 33%   No 65%

46. Rate from 1 to 4 the <u>most</u> likely avenue, in your experience, for an affair to be discovered:
    actual evidence   4%   told by acquaintance   3%
    intuition   91%   rambler volunteers information   2%

47. Do you have any jokes about polyfidelity that you could send me?

48. If you have ever practiced polyfidelity, for how long? If not, skip the rest of the survey except for the BIG thanks.
    Median number of years polyfidèle: 5 years

49. Besides your lovers, are you out as a polyfidèle to your community?
    Yes 15%   No 71%

50. When you come out as "poly" in a new mutual attraction situation, what are the approximate odds the woman will remain interested in you–or cool out?
    Average odds: 1 in 3 still interested

51. If you are, or ever were polyfidelitous, would you try it again?
    Yes 80%   No 10%   Undecided 10%

52. Overall, would you say that honest, multiple sexual liaisons bring you
    (a) much happiness   88%   (c) only a little happiness   4%
    (b) some happiness   7%   (d) no happiness   1%

53. Overall, were your multiple liaisons worth any difficulties involved?
    Yes 80%   No 2%   Not sure 13%

54. If you are, or have been in polyfidelitous relationships, are you willing to be interviewed in person or by phone for my book on this topic? If yes, please make sure your name and address are on the first page.

Polyfidelity
Select Bibliography & Films

Titles preceeded by ▼ embrace Lesbianism

I. Filmography

Few great role models or enlightened vision yet, but these films are a cut above mere adultery in exploring multi-partnered sensuality.

▼ "Bar Girls" (1995) Nancy Allison Wolfe, Liza D'Angostino

   "Brief Encounter" (1945) Celia Johnson, Trevor Howard

   "Caesar & Rosalie" (1972) Romy Schneider, Yves Montand, Sami Frey

   "Dangerous Liaisons" (1988) Glenn Close: best version of three "Liaisons" made.

   "Earrings of Mme. de…" (1953; new print 1994) Danielle Darrieux, Charles Boyer, Vittorio De Sica

▼ "Entre Nous" (1983) Isabelle Huppert, Miou Miou

▼ "French Twist" (1995) Josiane Balasko, Victoria Abril.

   "Jules and Jim" (1962) Jeanne Moreau, Oskar Werner, Henri Serre

   "Love After Love" (1992) Isabelle Huppert

   "Micki & Maude" (1984) Dudley Moore, Amy Irving, Ann Reinking

   "My Other Husband" (1985) Miou Miou

   "Paint Your Wagon" (1969) Lee Marvin, Jean Seberg, Clint Eastwood

   "She's Gotta Have It" (1986) Spike Lee, Tracy Camila Johns

   "Summer Lovers" (1982) Daryl Hannah, Valerie Quennessen

II. Fiction

Bradley, Marion Zimmer. All the "Darkover" novels, especially *The Forbidden Tower* (Daw, 1977), relate to multi-partner loves. *Mists of Avalon* (Knopf, 1982) is the Camelot triad.

▼ Durrell, Lawrence. *Alexandria Quartet.* Faber & Faber, 1962.

▼ Gearhart, Sally. *The Wanderground.* Alyson, 1972.

Godwin, Gail. *The Odd Woman.* Knopf, 1974.

LeGuin, Ursula. *The Dispossesed.* Avon, 1974.

McMurtry, Larry. *Leaving Cheyenne.* Viking Penguin, 1979.

Mackey, Mary. *The Year the Horses Came.* Harper, 1990.

▼ Meigs, Mary. *The Medusa Head.* Talonbooks, 1983.

▼ Piercy, Marge. *Woman on the Edge of Time.* Fawcett, 1976.

Moore, Imga. *Six-Dinner Sid.* Simon & Schuster, 1993.

Rimmer, Robert. All his novels map inclusive relationships; try *The Harrad Experiment* and *Proposition 31.*

▼ Stein, Gertrude. *Fernhurst, Q. E. D. & Other Early Writings.* Liveright, 1971; (1904-5).

Walker, Alice. *Temple of My Familiar.* Harcourt, 1989.

▼ Winterson, Jeanette. *The Passion.* Vintage, 1987. *Written on the Body.* Knopf, 1993.

▼ Woolf, Virginia. *Orlando.* Harcourt, 1960; (1928).

III. Nonfiction & Periodicals—Polyamory Advocacy

▼ Anapol, Deborah. *Love Without Limits:Responsible Nonmonogamy.* IntiNet Resource Center, 1992.

Carpenter, Edward. *Love's Coming of Age.* Methuen, 1896.

Fourier, Charles. *The Utopian Vision of Charles Fourier: Selected Texts on Work, Love, and Passionate Attraction.* Beacon, 1971.

Goldman, Emma. *Anarchism and Other Essays.* Dover, 1970. *Living My Life, Volumes I and II.* Dover, 1930.

Heyn, Dalma. *The Erotic Silence of the American Wife: On Affairs.* Signet, 1992. Banned in K-Mart for truth telling.

▼ Johnson, Sonia. *The Ship That Sailed Into the Living Room: Sex & Intimacy Reconsidered.* Wildfire Books, 1991.

▼ Kassoff, Elizabeth. *The Diverse Nature of Nonmonogamy for Lesbians: A Phenomenological Investigation.* UMI, 1985.

Lano, Kevin and Clair Parry. *Breaking the Barriers to Desire.* Fire Leaves, 1995.

▼ *Loving More Magazine*, quarterly of the feminist/ polyamorous community. For sample issue, send $6 to PEP Publications, Box 6306, Ocean View, HI 96737. (808) 929-9691.

Meade, Marion. *Free Woman: The Life & Times of Victoria Woodhull.* Knopf, 1976. Excellent for young adults.

▼ Nearing, Ryam. *Loving More: The Polyfidelity Primer.* PEP Productions, 1992.

▼ Ogden, Gina. *Women Who Love Sex.* Pocket Books, 1994.

O'Neill, Nena and George. *Open Marriage.* Avon, 1972.

▼ Tessina, Tina. *Gay Relationships.* Tarcher, 1989.

Underhill, Lois. *The WomanWho Ran For President: The Many Lives of Victoria Woodhull.* National Book, 1995.

▼ West, Celeste. *A Lesbian Love Advisor: The Sweet & Savory Arts of Lesbian Courtship.* Cleis, 1989.

Whitney, Catherine. *Uncommon Lives: Gay Men & Straight Women.* NAL, 1991.

Adultery/Betrayal

The modern scarlet "A" genre is aimed to soothe wives (forgive, forget) while rousing them to fight, no holds barred, for their kids and man. Though as gripping as soap opera and cheatin' heart music, I include only one of the best of the myriad "self-help" books, Vaughan's "Monogamy Myth." Mass-market adultery books are usually self-blame, rather than self-help, and hopelessly mired in old fashioned, double-standard heterosexism. Titles below are sociological studies on humankind's rambling ways.

Brown, Emily. *Patterns of Infidelity.* Brunner/Mazel, 1991.

Family Therapy Networker Magazine, May/June 1993. Special issue on infidelity with psychotherapy focus.

Lawson, Annette. *Adultery: An Analysis of Love & Betrayal.* Harper, 1988.

Reibstein, Janet and Martin Richards. *Sexual Arrangements: Marriage & the Temptation of Adultery.* Scribner, 1993.

Vaughan, Peggy. *The Monogamy Myth.* Newmarket, 1989.

Weiner, Marcella and Bernard Starr. *Stalemates: The Truth About Extra-marital Affairs.* New Horizon Press, 1989.

Community & Friendship

Brain, Robert. *Friends and Lovers.* Basic Books, 1976.

Cheney, Joyce. *Lesbian Land.* Word Weavers, 1985.

CoHousing: The Journal of the CoHousing Network. CoHousing Network, Box 8524, Berkeley, CA 94702. $5 per issue.

Communities: Journal of Cooperative Living. Route 1, Box 155, Rutledge, MO 63563. $4.50 per issue.

Family Therapy Networker Magazine, July/August 1995. Special issue on friendship with psychotherapy focus. A first! $4.

Klaw, Spencer. *Without Sin: The Life & Death of the Oneida Community.* Penguin, 1993.

Maize: A Lesbian Country Magazine. Box 130, Sarafina, NM 87569. Quarterly, $10 year.

McCamant, Kathryn and Charles Durrett. *Cohousing.* Ten Speed, 1988.

Porcino, Jane. *Living Better, Living Longer: Adventures in Community Housing for Those in the Second Half of Life.* Continuum, 1991.

Ramy, James. *Intimate Friendships.* Prentice Hall, 1976.

▼ Raymond, Janice. *A Passion for Friends: Toward a Philosophy of Female Affection.* Beacon, 1986.

▼ Rubin, Lillian. *Just Friends: The Role of Friendship in Our Lives.* Harper, 1985.

Famous Lesbian Philanderers

▼ Gidlow, Elsa. *ELSA: I Come With My Songs.* Booklegger, 1987. *"Where Eros Laughs & Weeps,"* audio tape, Booklegger, 1987.

▼ Leaska, Mitchell and John Phillips. *Violet to Vita: The Letters of Violet Trefusis to Vita Sackville-West.* Viking, 1990.

▼ Livia, Anna. *A Perilous Advantage: The Best of Natalie Clifford Barney.* New Victoria, 1992.

▼ Meigs, Mary. *Lily Brisco: A Self-Portrait, an Autobiography.* Talonbooks, 1981.

▼ Nicolson, Nigel. *Portrait of a Marriage: Vita Sackville-West & Harold Nicolson.* Atheneum, 1973.

History of Polygamy and Monogamy

Ackerman, Diane. *A Natural History of Love.* Random, 1994.

Batten, Mary. *Sexual Strategies: How Females Choose Their Mates.* Tarcher, 1992.

Eisler, Riane. *The Chalice & The Blade.* Harper, 1987.

Engels, Friedrich. *Origins of the Family, Private Property & the State.* Pathfinder Press, 1972; (1884).

Fisher, Helen. *Anatomy of Love: The Natural History of Monogamy, Adultery, and Divorce.* Norton, 1992. *The Sex Contract: The Evolution of Human Behavior.* Morrow, 1982.

Ford, C. S. and F. A. Bach. *Patterns of Sexual Behavior.* Harper, 1959.

Gimbutas, Marija. *Civilization & The Goddess.* Harper, 1991. *The Early Civilization of Europe.* UCLA, 1960. *Goddesses & Gods of Old Europe.* University of California, 1982. *Language of the Goddess.* Harper, 1991.

Haule, John. *Pilgrimage of the Heart: The Path of Romantic Love.* Shambhala, 1992.

Hunt, Morton. *The Natural History of Love.* Anchor, 1994.

Margulis, Lynn and Sagan, Dorion. *Mystery Dance: On the Evolution of Human Sexuality.* Simon & Schuster, 1991.

Meade, Marion. *Eleanor of Aquitaine.* Hawthorne, 1977.

Mellaart, James. *Catal Huyuk.* McGraw, 1967.

"Monogamy on Trial," by Robert Pickett in *Alternative Lifestyles,* May 1978 August 1978.

Platon, Nicolaas. *Crete.* Nagel, 1966.

Small, Meredith. *What's Love Got To Do With It? The Evolution of Human Mating.* Anchor, 1995.

Tannahill, Reay. *Sex In History.* Stein & Day, 1980.

Wright, Robert. *The Moral Animal: The New Science of Evolutionary Psychology.* Pantheon, 1994.

Philosophy & Psychology

Baumgart, Hildegard. *Jealousy: Experiences & Solutions.* University of Chicago, 1990.

Clanton, Gordon and Lynn Smith. *Jealousy.* University Press of America, 1986.

Dinesen, Isak. *On Modern Marriage & Other Observations.* St. Martin, 1977; (1923-24).

Gilligan, Carol. *In A Diferent Voice.* Harvard, 1982.

Hamburger, Lottee and Joseph. *Contemplating Adultery: The Secret Life of a Victorian Woman.* Fawcett, 1991.

▼ Hoagland, Sarah. *Lesbian Ethics: Toward New Value.* Institute of Lesbian Studies, 1988.

Katherine, Anne. *Boundaries: Where You End and I Begin.* Parkside, 1991.

▼ Kitzinger, Celia and Rachel Perkins. *Changing Our Minds: Lesbian Feminism & Psychology.* New York University Press, 1993.

Mill, John Stuart. *The Subjection of Women.* MIT Press, 1970.

Pines, Ayala. *Jealousy.* St. Martin, 1992.

Russell, Bertrand. *Marriage & Morals.* Liveright, 1929.

Salovey, Peter. *The Psychology of Jealousy & Envy.* Guilford Press, 1991.

Shaw, George Bernard. *Bernard Shaw: Selections of His Wit and Wisdom.* Follett, 1965.

Suzuki, Shunryu. *Zen Mind, Beginner's Mind.* Weatherhill, 1970.

White, Gregory and Paul Mullen. *Jealousy: Theory, Research & Clinical Strategies.* Guilford Press, 1990.

Truth Telling

Bok, Sissela. *Lying: Moral Choice in Public & Private Life.* Viking, 1978.

▼ Lerner, Harriet. *Dance of Deception.* Harper, 1993.

Pittman, Frank. *Private Lies: Infidelity & the Betrayal of Intimacy.* Norton, 1989.

▼ Rich, Adrienne. *On Lies, Secrets & Silence: Selected Prose 1966-1978.* Norton, 1980.

"May you sleep on the breasts of tender companions"—*ones who also read in bed.*

Polyfidelity Index

abortion 4, 39-40, 64, 268

addiction 233-243, 277
definition 237, 239, 242
love 235
relationship 241
romance 237-240
sex 236-237
substance 182, 243, 275

Adulterer's Bible 65

adultery 3, 4, 16, 26, 35, 52, 57, 58, 64, 65, 73, 76, 86, 133, 146, 170-172, 174, 178, 183, 286, 326

affairs 31, 162-164, 301. *See also* liaisons.

AIDS 158, 248-255, 316-317

Al-Anon 233-234

Alcoholics Anonymous 234-235, 242, 316

amor puris 172

Anapol, Deborah 22-23, 314, 325

animal promiscuity/monogamy 13, 58-59, 119, 315. *See also* individual species.

applause response 238

argument *see* conflict management

attention *see* presence

Barney, Natalie 11, 14, 53, 127, 223, 227, 314

battering *see* violence

Bechdel, Alison 28

behavioral psychology 117, 135-148

Berry, Wendell 188

betrayal 35, 75, 80, 112, 153, 161, 164, 183, 239, 282, 322, 326

Bible 63, 65

Bibliography 324-329

bigamy 23, 197

bisexual 15, 18, 22, 27, 38, 42, 53, 124, 152, 167, 179, 192, 210, 221, 248, 249, 251, 274

Blake, William 90

Bloomsbury Group 11. *See also* individual names.

body language 89, 92, 127, 154, 214, 220-221

Boston marriages 48-56, 227-228, 247

boundary development 84, 114, 164, 166, 176-180, 184-190, 213, 214, 226, 238, 241, 245, 274, 278, 308
temporal 96, 186, 196-218
territorial 186, 191-195

Bowen, Murray 30

brain neurochemistry 67-69, 70, 305

breakups 8, 29, 45-46, 54, 105, 146, 152, 163, 167, 216, 227, 233

breathing 138, 189, 195, 220, 242, 289

Buddhism 9-10, 46-48, 79-80, 136, 195, 209, 239, 264, 283, 290, 295, 296, 310, 311, 312, 318

Burkett, Elinor 253

Burning Times 64

*C*amp Sister Spirit 311-312

cancer 135, 157, 158, 255

capitalism 4, 5, 128, 135, 198, 204-205

Capote, Truman 262

Carpenter, Edward 11, 34, 325

Catharism 171

cats 16, 30, 137, 189-190, 238, 305

celestial marriage 1, 311

celibacy 8, 227, 242, 245, 246, 278

censorship 82, 313

chase, wild goose see wild goose

children 28-29, 30, 37, 59, 61, 62, 72-73, 122, 124, 134, 261, 266-274

chimpanzees 58-59

Chodorow, Nancy 68

Christianity see Judeo-Christianity

Christie, Agatha 85

Christina, Greta 232

Chu, Susan 253

Churchill, Jenny Jerome 263

circles 29, 34

civil and human rights 39-40, 62-66, 72, 76, 272, 274

classic dangle 168-169

Clinton, Hillary Rodham 111

Clinton, Bill 205

clitzzpah 219-223

Code of Hammurabi 63

Code of Urukagina 63

co-housing 22, 191, 306-307, 308, 310-311, 318

Colette 56

commitment 162, 212, 297. *See also* loyalty.

communication *see* Right Speech

community 37-38, 156-158, 160, 226, 271, 299-312, 327

compassion 87, 218, 239, 281, 285, 289-290

conditioning, social & cultural 70, 117, 118, 127, 127-128, 321

conflict management 75, 143-144, 151-156, 163-164, 169, 185-186, 211, 214-215, 245, 267 (children), 278, 301, 305, 308, 311. *See also* boundaries, jealousy, loyalty, territory, time.

Connolly, Cyril 79

computers 207, 283. *See also* cybersex.

consumerism 204-207, 261-262

corpus callosum 68

couple cracker 113, 146

courtly love 169-180

Courts of Love 173

courtship strategies *see* clitzzpah

crime of passion: none. There are only crimes of possession.

crypto-poly 27

Cuckholdry Clues 92-93

cuckoo 123

cuddle chemical (oxytocin) 28

Cult of Idleness 202-203, 208

cybersex 27, 222, 283, 291-298

"Dangerous Liaisons" 123, 324
deadlines 201
death 135, 158, 170, 200-201, 216, 230
* deconstructivism 78-79
DeLaria, Lea 211
desire discrepancy 244-247, 278
DeVore, Irven 57
Diagnostic & Statistical Manual of Mental Disorders (DSM) 50, 133, 314
Dickinson, Emily 53, 264
difference feminsm 68
digamy 23
Dinesen, Isak 11, 90, 329
discipline 173, 181, 197, 211
domestic partnership 39, 84, 309
diseases, sexual 248-255
drugs 20, 25, 49, 50, 51, 120, 138, 182, 199, 235, 249, 277, 320. *See also* addiction, substance.
"Earrings of Madame de ... " 123, 324
Earth 58, 59, 61, 62, 78, 111, 125, 182, 206
economics *see* wealth
eggs 66, 259. *See also* wild goose.
Eleanor of Aquitaine 169
Elizabeth I, Queen 206
ELSA: I Come With My Songs 201, 327, 352

endorphins 67
Engels, Friedrich 11, 328
"Entre Nous" 230-231, 324
Epicurus 73
Erasmus 88
erotica and pornography 225, 226, 292-293
eroticism 25, 202, 203-204, 224-232, 246-247, 302. *See also* romance, courtly love.
equality feminism 68
evolution of sexuality, 57-72. *See also* sex (biology).
evolutionary psychology *see* sociobiology
exclusive, the 168, 211
Fame 203
family 3, 22, 39, 61-62, 65-66, 120, 151, 299
family values 2, 66, 299
fatigue 168, 257
fear 26, 73, 75, 77, 242, 253, 280, 303, 310, 311
fear-zone relationship 26
feedback loop 76, 128-130
feminism 1, 64, 68, 69, 82, 124, 181, 234, 245, 277, 289, 299, 300
fidelity *see* loyalty
fighting, fair *see* conflict management
films, Lesbian 230-231, 250, 324
Fisher, Helen 58, 204, 328

---

* Q: What do you get when you cross a deconstructionist with a mafioso?

A: An offer you can't understand.

five families of mental energy 140

flirting *see* clitzzpah

"Flowers of Cherry" 240

food 25, 257-260

forgiveness 287, 299

Foucault, Michael 203

Fourier, Charles 11, 325

Fox, Robin 57

Freud, Sigmund 132-133, 134, 178, 224, 277

friendship 37-38, 56, 72, 160, 172, 200, 232, 247, 265, 269, 299-312, 327

frivolity 87

Gable, Cate 284

Garbo, Greta 142

Gary, Romaine 139

general systems theory 76, 78, 117, 125-131

genes/genetic determinism 71-72, 118-124, 125, 321

genital mutilation 63-64

gibbons 58

Gidlow, Elsa 8, 53, 201, 327, 352

Gilligan, Carol 68, 300, 329

"Go Fish" 28, 250

Goddess culture & worship 9, 20, 22, 61-62, 72, 135, 169, 170-172, 227, 310

Godwin, Gail 42, 325

Goldman, Emma 5, 11, 203, 325

Gomez, Marga 7

gorillas 60

Great Lesbian Adulterers' Hall of Fame 53

group marriage 22, 24, 168

guilt 189, 272, 273, 282-290

Hawthorne, Nathaniel 166

health care 168, 207, 228-229, 243, 248-255 (STDs), 257-260 (nutrition)

hetaera 178-179, 279

Heyward, Carter 176-177, 179

hominids 58

Homo erectus 58, 59-60

honesty, spontaneous 87, 90. *See also* Right Speech, truth telling.

hotels 191, 262-263

hot stuff 352

housework 209

humor 94, 116, 139, 183, 199, 201, 289. *See also* jokes.

human rights *see* civil & human rights

Hunt, Morton 2, 328

hypergamy 24

I Ching 108-109 (parody), 211

impermanence 9, 28, 66-67, 94, 131, 160, 165, 170, 173, 182, 203, 216, 223, 229, 239, 240, 241, 296-297, 303, 305

infatuation *see* romantic infatuation

intimacy 25-26, 48, 54, 75, 121, 157, 160, 164, 165, 176, 205, 227, 232, 241, 269, 279, 281, 305

intuition *see* "laydar"

Islam 63, 72, 128

James, Alice 55

Jay, Karla 314

jealousy 7, 20, 28, 39, 54, 110-159, 272, 283, 300, 307, 329
  behaviorial therapy 117, 135-148
  fair fighting 94, 143-144
  gene "driven" 110, 117, 119-124
  loyalty 3, 24, 52, 150, 156-159, 168, 187, 218, 266, 302
  melodrama 117, 132-134
  systems theory 117, 118, 122, 125-131
  target 130, 149-159
  useful 111, 112, 114-116

Jesus 64-65, 78

Johannseniella nitida 64

Johnson, Sonia 2, 4, 325

jokes, *see* Von Kluck

Jong, Erica 285

Jordan, June 76

Judeo-Christianity 63-65, 171, 173. *See also* monotheism, sky god.

Jung, Carl 132, 178

Juvenal 77

Karma 140-141

Kasl, Charlotte 235, 316

Kassoff, Elizabeth 22, 325

Katherine, Anne 187, 329

Kerista Commune 22, 24

Krishnamurdi 281

labor 5, 62, 65, 198, 203, 205, 207, 209

Ladies of Langollen 55, 202

Laing, R.D. 276

Lawrence, D.H. 11

laydar 20, 74, 80, 92 126, 185, 323

leisure 202-209

Lesbian bed death 49, 69-70

Lesbian land trusts 306, 318

Lesbian Love Advisor 7, 219, 326, 352

Lesbian philanderers, famous 53, 327

Lesbian Polyfidelity Survey 1995 319-323

Lewis, C.S. 169

liaisons 161-169. *See also* affairs.

lies *see* truth telling

listening 94, 155, 214, 283, 311

Livia, Anna 314, 327

Lorde, Audre 203, 228

Loulan, JoAnn 17, 252

love 223, 235, 247, 287, 305

Loving More Magazine 22, 326

loyalty 3, 24, 52, 150, 156-159, 168, 187, 218, 266, 302

Lucretius 86

Machado, Antonio 287

Magdalene, Mary 65

Machiavelli 76

Madonna, The 64, 170, 171-172

Manicheanism 171

mantra 137-138

Marie, Countess of Champagne 169

marriage 5, 22, 24, 52, 59, 61, 65, 168, 171, 173-174, 309

Mary *see* Madonna, The

Mead, Margaret 53, 61, 67

meditation 137, 141-142, 203

Meigs, Mary 53, 325, 327

melodrama 117, 132-134, 163, 168-169, 176, 183, 274

midwifery 59-60

misogamy 24

money *see* wealth

monogamy (monogyny) 2, 4, 7-11, 23, 27, 35-36, 38, 39-40, 52, 57, 63, 64, 65-66, 72, 73, 76, 95, 110, 112, 119, 144, 146, 150, 152, 182, 183, 192, 216, 218, 227, 229, 231, 241, 242, 246, 253, 259, 266, 268, 276, 278, 279-280, 286, 288, 310, 314, 328...monotony...

Monogamy Myth, The 73, 326

monotheism 20, 135, 234, 285

Moore, Marianne 286

Mormons 1, 311

Morris, Desmond 57

mothers and motherhood 28-29, 59-60, 61, 62, 66, 72, 121, 124, 205, 208, 225, 266-274

mutual deception 83-85, 95-107

mystery 71, 229, 309

Myth of Romantic Marriage, The 276

Nature/nurture debate 71-72. *See also* conditioning, sociobiology.

Nearing, Ryam 22-23, 314, 326

Neolithic era 61, 110

Neural Darwinism 70

neurochemistry 67-69, 70, 305

Net of Indra 125

Nin, Anaïs 53, 228

noble lie 80-83

normality 14

Norwood, Robin 235

Noyes, John Humphrey 11

nuclear family 3, 61-62

Odd woman 29, 42-46, 114, 126-127, 145-146, 161-180, 276

Ogden, Gina 230, 326

L'Omlette Ardennaise 259-260

Oneida Community 2, 24

open marriage 22, 24, 326

open zone relationship 26

opiates 67

orgasms 16, 47, 180, 225, 227, 228, 230, 292

Orlando 60, 75, 203, 228

other woman *see* odd woman

Overworked American 204, 316

oxytocin 28

Paganism *see* Goddess culture and worship

pair bonding 7, 28-29, 51, 58, 120. *See also* monogamy.

Paleolithic era 61, 204

parallel play 161

Pascal, Blaise 288

passion *see* eroticism

paternity 59, 61

paternal insecurity 2, 36, 123-124

PEA (phenylethylamine) 67, 69, 238

personal ads 27, 56, 222, 294

pheromones 69, 92, 176

Piercy, Marge 204, 325

Pilate 78

Pines, Ayala 129, 329

Platonism 171

polyamory 22, 23

polyandry 23

polyfidèle
  freelance 27. *See also* odd
    woman.
  profile 19-20, 320-321
  social persecution of 19, 39-40,
    77, 280. *See also* fear, secrecy.

polyfidelity
  benefits 35-56, 116
    boundary development
      184-190, 191-195 (terri-
      torial), 196-218 (tempo-
      ral), 312
    child care 37, 72, 266-274
    civil and human right 39-
      40, 62-66, 72, 76, 272,
      274
    creativity 37, 56
    diversity 37, 38, 41, 49,
      83, 144, 147, 163, 312
    economic *see* "wealth" entry
    ethical development 36,
      73-107, 272
    feminist *see* "feminism" entry
    independence 41, 166, 185
    novelty 38, 194, 312
    romance *see* "romance" entry
    self-discovery 36, 46, 48,
      73-74, 144, 165, 241
    sex *see* "sex" entry
    spirituality 72, 81, 139-
      141, 169-174, 226-227

polyfidelity benefits *(continued)*
    stability 38-39
    support system 37-38,
      156-158,160, 226, 271,
      299-312, 327

polyfidelity definitions 3, 21, 25,
  73, 150, 230, 232, 241, 247,
  278, 312, 319

polyfidelity films 324

polyfidelity novels 324-325

polyfidelity survey 17-20, 230,
  319-323

polygamy 1, 2, 23, 28, 57, 59,
  65-66, 71, 119, 120, 311

polygyandry 24

polygyny 23

population control 66, 71-72, 122

pornography and erotica 225,
  226, 292-293

privacy 1, 41, 42, 86-90, 150,
  165, 191, 209, 262, 284, 302

presence 43, 47-48, 216, 217, 239

Principle of Least Obtrusiveness
  160

promiscuity 28, 37, 43, 66-67,
  71, 119, 124. *See also* animal,
  plant, Earth, Cosmos.

prostitution *see* sex workers

psychiatry 277

psychotherapy & psychotherapists
  38, 49-51, 97, 98-99, 100, 104-
  105, 112, 117, 126, 132- 136,
  174-180, 184, 234, 237, 244,
  245-246, 252, 270, 275-281,
  283, 300, 317-318, 329

Quadrangles 29, 33-34, 166

Rajneeshpuram 311-312

rape *see* violence

rapture 47 have some today

recipes 257-260

recovery movement 133, 233-243, 283, 316. *See also* Twelve Step Program.

relationships 23-24, 68-69, 81, 150-151, 170, 174-180, 183, 184, 185, 230, 237, 240, 241, 244-247, 262, 284

religion 227, 234. *See also* Buddhism, Goddess, Islam, Judeo-Christianity, monotheism, sky god, spirituality, Zen.

reproductive strategies 28-29, 57-58, 60, 66-67, 122

residential monogamy 192

Right Speech 85-91, 115-116, 127, 129, 282-284, 290

Rich, Adrienne 74, 91, 329

romance 173, 180, 227, 237-241, 246, 261-265 (economics), 291-298. *See also* clitzzpah, eroticism.

romantic infatuation 25, 54, 67-69, 96, 98, 187, 305, 307

Roosevelt, Eleanor 53, 111

Rougemont, Denis de 170

Rule, Jane 71

Russell, Bertrand 11

Sackville-West, Vita 53, 100, 106, 228, 246, 327

Sayers, Dorothy 312

Schaef, Anne Wilson 235-236

schedules 160, 197, 200, 210-218, 268

Schor, Juliet 204, 316

Schulman, Sarah 253

secrecy 86, 96, 168, 253, 266, 278, 280, 289, 323

sensuality *see* eroticism

setting sun vision 290

Sex & Love Addicts Anonymous (SLAA) 233, 242

sex (biology)
 arousal ("drive") 55, 224-225, 227, 247
 diseases 16, 20, 248-255
 hormones 67, 69, 92, 176, 224-225, 238, 305
 human evolution of 57-60, 66-72
 reproductive strategy 28-29, 57, 58, 60, 66-67, 122

Sex in America: A Definitive (*sic*) *Study* 15-16

sex workers 26, 33, 46-47, 73, 177, 179, 224, 249, 279, 293

sexuality & sex acts 224-232. *See also* clitzzpah, courtly love, eroticism, friendship, intimacy, love, marriage, monogamy, polygamy, romance, romantic infatuation, spirituality.
 addiction 236-237
 age 15, 16, 19, 36, 257
 anal sex & rimming 249, 251, 252, 255
 Christian 140-143
 cozmic 313
 cybersex 185, 246-251, 246-251
 danger 39, 74, 168, 227, 247, 248-255
 definitions 25, 147, 224-232

sexuality & sex acts (*continued*)
  desire discrepancy 244-247, 278
  ecstasy 140, 172, 180, 199, 240
  fisting 255
  friendly 299-312
  Freudian 133, 134
  infantile 30, 188, 260
  intensity 43, 44, 170, 174, 241, 292, 299, 308. *See also* intimacy.
  kissing 229
  mystery 71, 229
  "normal" 14
  orgasms 16, 47, 140, 180, 225, 227, 228, 230, 292
  power 6, 203-204, 229, 240, 262, 270
  promiscuity 28, 37, 43, 66-67, 71, 119, 124
  satori, la petite 230
  spontaneous 210-211
  surveys & studies 3, 13-20, 119, 230, 319-323
  tantric 81, 139-140, 171, 226-227, 237
  tongue 229
  virtual 27, 291-298
sexually transmitted diseases (STDs) 16, 20, 248-255
shame 75, 86, 134, 136, 152, 168, 175, 182, 189, 226, 227, 234, 246, 282-290, 302
Shaw, George Bernard 5, 11, 236, 261, 329
Shakespeare, William 83, 243, 289

significant udder theory 36, 81
silence 89, 94, 154, 155, 214, 220, 283, 310-311
simplicity 202-203, 206, 209
sky god 62-66, 135, 170, 234
s/m 27, 181-182, 254
Small, Meredith 2-3, 328
Smith, Stevie 64
socialism 264
sociobiology 69, 117, 119-124, 125
space 83, 157-160
spirituality 30-31, 71, 72, 76, 81, 134, 170, 173, 199, 226-227, 230, 234, 240, 280-281
spontaneous sex 210-211
Staël, Madam de 282
STDs 16, 20, 248-255
* Stein, Gertrude 9, 12, 247, 264, 325
Stud Muffin Supreme Mix 258
Sufism 171
surveys, sex 3, 13-20, 119, 230, 319-323
Suzuki-roshi, Shunryu 264, 329
swinging 24, 147
systems theory 76, 78, 117, 125-131
Szasz, Thomas 276
𝔍annen, Deborah 68
Tantra 81, 139-141, 171, 226-227

---

* "Everyone gets so much information all day long that they lose their common sense." —G.S.

Taoism 78, 171, 201, 202-203, 206
telephone 27, 93, 193-194, 221
television 202, 204, 283, 288
Teresa, Mother 203
Teresa, Saint 272
termites 58, 315
territory 83, 157-160
therapy *see* psychotherapy, psychiatrists
three way 45, 167-168
three year itch 66-67
Tiger, Lionel 57
Tillich, Paul 281
time 36, 165, 196-218
time management systems *see* schedules
Tomlin, Lily 206
transactional analysis (TA) 30
transference 132, 177-178, 179
Trefusis, Violet 53, 100, 106, 327
triangles 9, 29-32, 134
triangulation 30
troubadour, trobairitz 54, 169, 177, 202, 222
truth telling 7, 20, 45, 52, 73-107, 163, 236, 286, 297, 323, 329. *See also* "Right Speech."
Twelve Step Program 233-235, 242, 283, 316
Unconscious, the 132, 277
underground economy 264-265
unions, labor 207
Vaughan, Peggy 73, 326

Vidal, Gore 5
violence 4, 39-40, 61, 62, 63, 66, 76, 111-112, 124, 133, 147, 152, 182, 225, 245, 277, 307, 309
virtual reality 27, 121, 207, 226, 279, 290-291
Von Kluck *see* eggs
Warnings for Wantons 160
wealth & economic considerations 38, 62-63, 72, 73, 93, 111, 128, 171, 197, 198, 202, 205, 206, 238, 261-265, 273, 301, 307, 308
Wells, H.G. 11
white lie 85-86
wild goose chase *see* Von Kluck
Wilde, Oscar 52
Wilson, Bill 235
Winterson, Jeannette 81, 325
Woodhull, Victoria 5, 11, 326
Woolf, Virginia 53, 75, 203, 228, 290, 325
workaholics 196, 208
WORLD, Inc. 316
writing 61, 63, 142-143, 156, 178, 201, 297
XXX *see* as Lesbian, possible
Yin/yang dynamic 162, 220
yoga 137, 229
Zen 195, 209, 264, 295, 296. *See also* Buddhism.

AND tHAT'S NOT ALL...

Order Booklegger ◈ *We pay U.S. parcel post & sales tax!*

	Quantity	Amount

Lesbian Polyfidelity by Celeste West. Signed.
    ISBN 0-912932-15-5 ❐ $15 paperback   _____ $_____
    ISBN 0-912932-16-3 ❐ $25 hardback   _____ $_____

Lesbian Love Advisor: The Sweet & Savory Arts of Lesbian Courtship by Celeste West, Signed by author. Illustrated by Ferentz. ❐ $12   _____ $_____

Words In Our Pockets: The Feminist Writers Guild Handbook On How To Gain Power, Get Published & Get Paid. Celeste West, editor. Signed. 386 pages
    ISBN 0-912932-10-4 ❐ $14 paperback   _____ $_____
    ISBN 0-912932-09-0 ❐ $20 hardback   _____ $_____

Zen In A Nutshell, compiled by Celeste West.
    Zen grits, zen gravy booklet. ❐ $5   _____ $_____

ELSA, I Come With My Songs: Autobiography of Elsa Gidlow. Photos.
    ISBN 0-912932-12-0 ❐ $15 paperback   _____ $_____
    ISBN 0-912932-13-9 ❐ $25 hardback   _____ $_____

Sapphic Songs: The Love Poetry of Elsa Gidlow. Includes photos. ❐ $8 paperback   _____ $_____

Where Eros Laughs & Weeps. Audio tape interview with Elsa Gidlow. ❐ $10.   _____ $_____

Book and audio tape **TOTAL**   _____ $_____

Subtract bookstore/library discount: see "Terms" below. $_____

Allow 3 weeks for Booklegger's free parcel post service.   Free Shipping
First Class & UPS: $4 one item; $1.50 each additional item. $_____
Canada/International: $5 one item; $1.50 each additional. $_____

U.S. currency **TOTAL ENCLOSED** $———

❐ Check if gift; we'll enclose card in the name you print here.

Name _____

Ship to: _____

Address _____

City/State _____ zip_____

Phone ( ) _____

TRADE TERMS TO BOOKSELLERS & LIBRARIES

Order via quality wholesale distributors or direct from Booklegger. Booklegger discounts 1-4 titles at 20%, 5-9 at 30%, 10+ at 40%. Assorted titles okay. Carton quantities of same title, 50% discount. We pay shipping to stores and libraries. Terms: *prepaid* orders only! No returns. No credit cards. No unfinished business. Make inquiries and payments to:
Booklegger Publishing, P. O. Box 460654-B, San Francisco, CA 94146 (415) 642-7569